The
MAVERICK CAREGIVER

Carolyn Connelly

PublishAmerica
Baltimore

First printing

Hardcover 978-1-4512-2566-2
Softcover 978-1-4512-2567-9
PUBLISHED BY PUBLISHAMERICA, LLLP
www.publishamerica.com
Baltimore

Printed in the United States of America

Presented to:

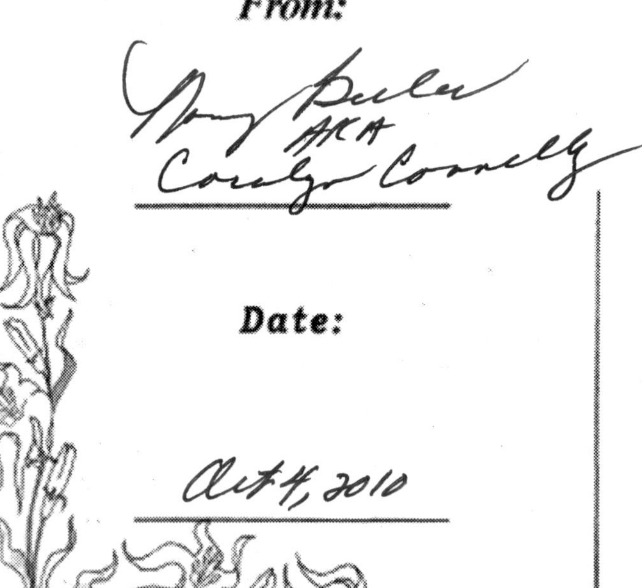
From:

AKA

Date:

More praise for Carolyn Connelly and *The Maverick Caregiver*

"Very well written and the subject is GREAT. People will be very impressed to see through your eyes. I think the main strength of your writing is your direct, straightforward style. It seems to immerse the reader into the action."
—Kent Marcuson, MD, USAF

"Excellent work! Your manuscript is very readable and engaging. Your topic is an important and difficult one that you approach with knowledge and compassion."
—Space Coast Writers Guild, Inc.

Dedication

There are countless typists to thank and all of the wonderful people at the Gulf Coast Writers Association who critiqued my writing. They guided me from the manuscript phase to the published book.

After the failure of the first edition, two more people stepped into my life: Jeany Pontrelli—once again—and Kim Carpenter. These two friends guided me through this renewed book.

How can I truly thank these wonderful people?

Thank you, Herb, for being patient and helping me through the rough times.

Thank you all from the bottom of my heart for guiding me in the right direction.

Table of Contents

Introduction

For twenty years I kept notes on little scraps of paper about the elderly who lived in several Assisted Living Facilities (ALFs) that I owned. At times I would pull them out and daydream about the book I would someday write. Prior to owning ALFs, I was director of several nursing homes but finally left, disillusioned by the substandard care residents were receiving and the frequent failures of my efforts to improve it. The battle to improve elderly care was a long and arduous one for me, but I felt that future caregivers could at least learn from my mistakes and successes if they were documented. Writing the book from those scraps took several years, hundreds of hours, a lot of help from friends, and sheer determination never to give up.

In *The Maverick Caregiver* you will read about the atrocities suffered by aging people who did not have the mental capacity to help themselves. Herein are some of the worst cases of dementia and elder abuse that I confronted. If family members, caregivers, or legal guardians weren't looking out for their welfare, the elderly often ended up in the hands of hardhearted, professional caregivers who placed their own interests before that of the aging charges. In many homes residents existed like zombies waiting to die.

The events described in these pages took place from the 1970s to the early 1990s, during a time when Alzheimer's was still considered a mysterious illness and when other forms of dementia were considered a natural evolution in the aging process. Today, through research and public awareness, caregivers better understand the aging mind and are better equipped to cope with those afflicted with mental deficiencies. We may be better educated today and there may be more and better choices for elder care, but abuse is still rampant because of society's belief that the elderly have little value. Until our society respects and honors the elderly instead of viewing them as burdens, their lives will continue to deteriorate to a bitter end.

Thankfully, because of the methods my staff and I used in caring for over 300 residents in about twenty years, the vast majority knew respect, dignity, and peace during their latter years. I strove to provide our residents with clean, pleasant surroundings, good food, and compassion. My methods made a difference in my residents' lives. Making a difference requires caring people determined to make that difference, and I like to think I was one of those people. Sometimes, I didn't quite measure up to my own standards, but all I can say is, I did my best.

I lost the battle in the end, coming full circle to where I started—penniless, exhausted, and discouraged. For the past few years, my health has been failing, making the last push to publication urgent but also difficult. Heart disease, a visual handicap, and diabetes have all taken their toll, but I felt compelled to continue writing. Now in my sixties, I relate all too well to those whose lives are described in this book. Their fates may too soon be my husband's and mine. Our four children live in other states and have families of their own to care for. Retirement pay barely covers necessities. Medical expenses have threatened to overwhelm us, and we have only recently found affordable housing. We simply don't know what the future holds.

I appeal to readers who are in the sandwich years between growing teenagers and aging parents. As you watch the wrinkles of your parents multiply—as you watch their shoulders slump and the minds go to frustrating places—be home for your parents. Fight for their rights and treat them with the dignity they deserve. Remember…one day you will be there, too.

Chapter One
Genesis

In the beginning, there was a man, a woman, a house full of kids, two dogs, a bird that whistled Yankee Doodle Dandy, and cats—I never knew how many because the kids hid them—and an empty bank account. Woman begot an idea, and then there were May, Mary, James, Ilga, Naomi, Laverne, Roma, Minnie, and 300 more…and no, these weren't cats.

I was that woman, and, before these people entered my life, I had run the back roads of Florida as a home health nurse, feeling frustrated, going broke, and wondering what to do with the rest of my life. The majority of my patients were poor, elderly and unable to take care of themselves. My heart broke over and over again each time I encountered helpless geriatric patients covered in lice, living in filth, left alone by family and by a system that considered them expendable. There was so much that needed to be done for them, and living alone with a part-time nurse was not the answer. Nursing homes didn't seem to be either. All nursing homes were bad, no matter how nice they seemed to be. They all cared for the indigent, but the care reflected the lower-than-average Medicaid payments. The best of them had a fancy lobby for guests to see, but what lurked behind the door down the hall were elderly people purposely hidden from view because of their poor condition, appearance, or behavior. Some were even drugged into pleasant submission. The eyes of the world were not on these poor souls.

During traveling time, I had often dreamed of opening a small home for the elderly, ideally a home large enough to accommodate my family and a few elderly residents. Our family could use additional income, considering our increasing finances. At the same time, I believed I could charge according to the amount residents could afford and still provide excellent living conditions for them.

With only a few elderly people to take care of, I could treat them with the respect and dignity they deserved. The home was real in my daydreams. It had comfortable beds with sheets and spreads that matched, a table set with matching plates and glasses, and a homey-looking living room with a TV set, a stereo system, and a bowl of fruit sitting there for the residents' pleasure.

The clothing my dream residents wore was always fresh, neatly pressed and wrinkle-free. Residents would look especially good when going out to church, or the store, or for a leisurely stroll around the neighborhood…then I would pull up to another trailer and the reality of my financial limitations would hit like a brick.

I would probably still be running the roads were it not for a phone call I received from my social worker Bonnie. She and I frequently shared our dreams over coffee.

"Carolyn, two elderly ladies are in danger where they live. They're being abused by the husband of the woman who takes care of them. He has locked them in their rooms and made them suffer for hours without food, clean clothing, or even a toilet. They have to get out of there!"

"My God, why haven't you called protective services or the law?"

"I did, but they won't intervene unless they have proof. One of the ladies has complained to me and others, but she is too afraid to tell HRS."

"Where are they now?" I asked

"They still live with the abusive husband and his wife, but it's only a matter of time before something terrible happens. Carolyn, this could be your chance. You've been talking about opening a home for years. These two ladies are God's way of telling you to get off your home-health ass and do it! They desperately need help, and you desperately need to change professions. How can you possibly say no? And you know Ron and I will help you any way we can." Ron was a physician specializing in geriatrics, and his and her support would help a great deal.

"Bonnie, you know my heart goes out to these women, but I'm just not ready. Mike and I have toyed with the idea; we've even driven around and looked at properties…but that's a far cry from being in a position to accept two elderly women into our home! You know the industry and how much I would have to do to get started…

I promised to try and hung up with a heavy heart. I knew Bonnie was right. If ever there was a time to act, it was now. But I thought I would need a lot of start-up money. And how could I find an affordable large home to house us all? I knew the two ladies Bonnie told me about would welcome better living conditions, but what about other potential patrons. How would I find them? Would they want to leave their present living conditions? Could I handle the responsibilities? My mind reeled on and on with the doubts, but my heart grew more excited by the minute. I began to believe my dream would come true.

After many fast and furious debates with my family and me, the decision was made. I called Bonnie and told her that to make this workable, I would have to have three months rent in advance from each of the ladies, plus a security deposit. I thought I was asking for the moon, charging $500 a month and the same for deposit. Little did I know that other Assisted Living Facility (ALF) owners were charging $1000 and more for dumps? But Bonnie was thrilled and quickly collected the money for me. I made arrangements to pick up the ladies in two weeks. Yes, two weeks to quit my job, find a home, take care of the necessary licensing, etc. This superwoman façade would dominate my future career as a director of a home for the elderly and get me into all kinds of jams.

The search for just the right home was tough. Some of the houses we saw were too small to comfortably accommodate my family and a few residents. Others were large enough but had unwanted features such as bedrooms located only on the second floor. My residents would need bedrooms on the ground floor.

In some large homes, the owners refused to sell to me because of their fear of lawsuits involving the elderly. They mentioned accidents the elderly might have like falling down the stairs, drowning in the pool, dying in a room. The excuses seemed endless and revealed despicable discrimination that made me angrier every time I met up with it.

As a home health nurse, I had to purchase my own liability insurance, so I took care of that. City codes allowed me to rent any two rooms to any two persons in my home without a license. And I did not need a license from HRS unless I rented to four people. These facts did little to allay the fears of these landlords.

I was about to give up the search when I stumbled upon a gorgeous home right on the bay. Shaped like a *U* to conform to the line of the bay, the house had a swimming pool and over 5000 square feet. It had two stories, two bedrooms downstairs and five up. It would work if I rented the downstairs rooms to residents. My husband and I loved the house but debated the wisdom of our plan because of our limited finances.

Then Bonnie came up with the idea of asking the owner if we could rent to own at first. Surprisingly, the owner was very enthusiastic about the idea. The neighborhood, Southern Breezes, was built for exclusivity, but property values were dropping because some of the homes were not maintained as they should have been. He was most anxious to cooperate with us. We agreed on the purchase plan, and I wired him three months' rent in advance.

My family was ecstatic. I could tell they were apprehensive about living with the elderly, but they had played a major role in the decision making from the beginning. They really loved the home and the neighborhood. Furthermore, we would now have room for one of my married daughters with her two children Marty and Timothy. Her husband was scheduled for six months of military duty out at sea, and she didn't want to live alone.

Moving day arrived, and we woke up to the roar of the moving truck. Luckily, the ringing of the phone was somehow heard over the roar of the truck because a crisis had already occurred.

The abusive husband finally snapped. He threw the ladies and their belongings out onto the front lawn. Bonnie had called the police, who were protecting them, but the ladies had to be moved—and soon. Bonnie begged me to come to get them right away. So much for having two weeks to prepare! Only a few days had passed since I agreed to take the ladies.

I had purchased new furniture, but it wasn't due until the next day. I phoned the company, and they could deliver early. With that taken care of, I sent my son and daughter after the two ladies, and sneaked outside by the pool for a few minutes to collect my wits. Even though I had met the ladies before, the only thing I could remember was Mary's finger-waved, short hair. As I tried to enjoy a break from the chaos, my mind reeled with questions and concerns.

Suddenly, I realized it was late afternoon. My new residents would be hungry when they got here. What would they sit on? I noticed several patio chairs. The ladies might not be very comfortable, but these chairs were better than nothing. One problem solved. Then I ran to the corner convenience store and ended up with peanut butter, jelly, a loaf of bread and a package of vanilla ice cream. So much for lace tablecloths, matching silverware, and a healthy meal on this moving day. What I could offer them would have to do.

My son John drove up with the two ladies. I went out to greet them and to help them in but stopped dead in my tracks, not because of the ladies who looked surprisingly calm after what they'd gone through. It was John. The look on his face would stop a freight train. Oh God, something else was wrong. He didn't say a word while he helped the ladies into the house, and neither did I. He would tell me soon enough, and the ladies came first.

We walked into the kitchen and dining room first, and then I showed them the room they would share. They looked pleased except for Mary, who thought she was going to get a private room. I explained that there would be no private rooms because I would have to charge double the price and they would get lonely in a room by themselves. She didn't have much to say after that.

I heard a truck roar into the driveway. The movers and the furniture had finally arrived. After May and Mary sat down in the lawn chairs, I excused myself to give the movers instructions. On my way outside, I heard John calling me from the garage. He was livid.

"Ma, do you know who had those women?" he said.

"No, I don't."

"It was that SOB I had to throw out of the restaurant every morning for spitting in his and other people's food."

Apparently, this guy spent his spare time doing this in restaurants, which sent restaurant food prices skyrocketing to replace the meals he ruined.

"Ma, we had to call the police to throw him out over and over again. We tried to catch him when he came in the door but didn't always see him. I should have known it was someone like him who would abuse defenseless old ladies! It was all I could do to keep from decking him."

We both went to help the movers and, after giving instructions on where the furniture should go, I returned to the ladies, shaking my head in disbelief at the news Tim had given me.

"Are peanut butter and jelly sandwiches, okay?" I asked. "I'm so sorry, but with the confusion, that's all we have."

"Don't you worry," Mary said quickly. "I would like them everyday for lunch. I don't want anything else, ever. I'll take a glass of milk and a bit of vanilla ice cream, too."

I looked at May for her approval. She just sort of shrugged. I started to sit down with them to rest a minute when I heard my daughter screaming at one of the dogs. The dog was in the pool already! I asked my daughter, a teenager, to get him out, but she ran off to pick out her bedroom. I'd have no help from that quarter. I screamed at the dog in the pool and then remembered my poor cats were shut up in a room with no food or water. When I mentioned them, May and Mary emphatically informed me that their walking sticks were for dealing with cats. With that statement, I knew we had to establish some ground rules right away. They had already been told that I owned cats and dogs, and neither had objected.

"The cats are mine," I told them. "And I will not tolerate any abuse. If they bother you, please let me know, and I will get them out of your way." I could see that caring for Frick and Frack (my nicknames for May and Mary) was not going to be a piece of cake.

When their beds were set up and their furniture was in place, I went in to put the bedding on, hang up their clothing, and place other items in their chests. They both sat down to supervise the operation. This day would prove to be the best experience I would have in caring for the elderly and, I realized, the one that could make or break me. I lay Mary's suitcase on her bed and suggested that she put things where she wanted them.

"I can't stand up long enough to do that," she said quickly. "You can put them wherever you want things to go."

I was stressed out, so tired I could hardly stand up, and I desperately needed a break.

"Ladies, there's the bathroom. I'll leave you to settle in. Good night." As I left the room, I thought, what have I gotten myself into???

Chapter Two
Frick and Frack

May, or Frick as we referred to her, was small and cute, with an extremely humped back. Her hair was light brown with a smidgen of gray, which she kept short and softly curled. Because of her familial tremors, she walked with a cane. I was to learn that she had a difficult time eating and could not cut or prepare her own food. I gave her a straw to sip her liquids, thus avoiding the shakes when she tried to hold a cup or glass. She choked easily. I made sure that her meals were taken with us or with an employee when she ate. Most of the time, she was okay.

May was not one to feel sorry for herself. She liked to go downtown two or three times a week to have lunch at her favorite place. She also went to the library once a week to exchange her books. I even found her a book exchange where she could get the latest publications without spending any money. When my husband Mike was not busy or at work, May would ask him to take her to town instead of calling a taxi.

We soon grew to love May and consider her part of the family. Even the children, who usually only tolerated their new living situation, liked being around her. She was clean, pleasant, intelligent, educated, and fully aware of what was happening in the world. She respected our privacy as we did hers.

May and I developed a warm relationship. I felt a real and genuine love for her and enjoyed our daily conversations. She had had a fascinating life of travel with her now estranged husband, Tad, and loved reminiscing about her adventures. She also had a quick and biting sense of humor.

One day we laughed together about the cat-and-cane incident that happened just after she moved in. We were eating lunch and everything was going along fine until one of the cats jumped into May's lap, obviously anticipating a tasty morsel of her macaroni and cheese casserole.

"Get this damn cat off my lap!" I heard Frick scream as she vigorously swung her cane. Quickly, I tried to move the macaroni and cheese casserole I was holding to the table but burnt my hands instead. It dropped to the floor. The bowl and yellow goop scattered all over the floor and all over our feet. In the heat of the moment, I swept the cat off May's lap to the floor.

Almost in unison Frick and Frack said, "Are we going to eat or not?" The poor cat was not in their thoughts; they just wanted to eat.

"That darn cat used up half his lives that day, Carolyn," laughed May as we enjoyed a glass of ice tea by the pool.

I wish I could have become friends with Mary, but we never seemed to enjoy each other. In fact, I honestly had a hard time liking her. She was a tall and lean Bostonian with a haughty and smug personality. She wasn't quite as sharp as May, and she was manipulative and complaining.

Her right arm had been injured and had nerve damage, so I had to apply a very tight stocking every day for relief. I came to dread this daily task because it hurt her when I applied the stocking. She blamed me for the pain and for not doing it correctly.

Her hair had to be done in finger waves, which I did not know how to do. I sent her to the beauty shop once a week at her own expense. She didn't want to pay and wouldn't ever let me forget how much she had to spend because I wouldn't do her hair.

A member of the Audubon Society, Mary never tired of watching the sea birds over Tampa Bay. It was the one thing that brought her pleasure. She resembled one of the egrets that came calling everyday for food. John fed him chicken parts and hot dogs. We named him Bill. We were proud to have tamed a wild bird, at least to a degree, and it was fun watching the wobbly, skinny legs of Frack and the egret.

John said to me once, "I don't know whether to throw the food to her or the bird!"

On one afternoon, it became apparent that we might have more than a few Bills since there were about fifty egrets hanging around in the yard and on the sea wall. It was then that we realized that most likely we had been feeding a different bird every day. They all resembled Bill. Mary was thrilled at seeing so many birds at once and knew for sure that they had come because of her. We let her think it.

The elderly need healthy food, just as all of us do, but they rarely get it when they're on their own. Fatigue, lack of money, and sickness frequently get in the way of shopping, preparing, and cooking healthy meals. After many years of visiting their homes as a home health nurse, I'd seen the devastating effects of diets of canned meat and cinnamon rolls on their minds and bodies. It was important to me to provide a healthy diet for residents. In fact, it was one of the first rules I set in place. I spent a lot of time educating the cooks I had hired about low fat and low sodium cooking and found it hard to believe how new a concept this was to most of them. What came off the bakery shelf or out of a can seemed to be the mainstay of their cooking. Sugar and fat dominated most of their recipes.

I liked to use wheat germ on top of baked custard made with egg substitutes. It made a very crunchy crust. Real eggs were served for breakfast; otherwise, we cooked or baked with egg substitutes. Nothing was fried. We baked or broiled. Biscuits were made with non-fat buttermilk and low-fat margarine. Everyone raved about them. Almost all foods were cooked from scratch and prepared in our own kitchen, and fresh fruit and vegetables were served at almost every meal.

Since we were just starting out, thankfully I didn't yet have to teach the cooks specialty diets such as those for heart disease or diabetes—or so I thought…

There was one thing Mary never complained about, and that was lunch. On a lace tablecloth, with matching china, glasses, and silverware, Frick and Frack ate peanut butter and jelly sandwiches every day for two months. My family and I simply couldn't understand why they requested them. They wouldn't eat anything else. I asked them numerous times to please eat a healthier lunch, but always got the same response, "We are quite pleased with the meal." I realized later it was Mary who responded and May who was covering up for Mary. Then, finally, the secret was revealed. One day May blew a gasket and I was astonished. I had never seen her lose her cool. Her tremors grew so bad it was difficult for her to drink.

"Get this damn fancy-ass glass out of here and give me a plastic one I won't break when I shake it to death. And, while I'm at it, I want to ask, 'Are we ever going to eat anything else??' I am so damn sick and tired of peanut butter and jelly sandwiches I could scream. Please, Carolyn, you're a good cook. Why do I have to eat this crap? Mary's the one who always wants it, and you want to know why? I don't care if I promised you, Mary. You're a diabetic, and I'm not going to be responsible when you keel over from eating all that jelly! So there you go." She glared at Mary and took the fancy-ass glass into the kitchen.

"A diabetic. Mary? Please tell me it isn't true." She said nothing and just ate the jelly with her eyes focused on the floor.

I went to my desk and read her paperwork. There was nothing about her being a diabetic. While I began to question her, John went to the kitchen and fixed May a ham and cheese sandwich with some potato chips. She grinned from ear to ear.

Before discussing anything more with Mary, I called her doctor. The nurse confirmed my worst fears and said Mary was supposed to be on Micronase. Terrific! The doctor didn't write this on her transfer papers! Doctors didn't usually make such a devastating error. I asked her if she would have him call me. She said she would. Now it was Mary's turn. Wide-eyed with fear, she cringed when I approached the table.

"Why on earth didn't you tell me you were diabetic, and where is your medication?"

Flustered, she got up from the table, went into the bedroom and brought back her purse. She pulled the Micronase out and handed it to me.

"Mary, how could you keep this from me?"

"They wouldn't give me dessert at the last home, and I knew you wouldn't either if you knew."

I left her standing in the doorway, afraid of what I might do or say. This could have been a very serious problem. Why didn't Bonnie or Mary's doctor tell me? I was the one responsible to Mary and her son.

The next morning I called Bonnie and just blurted out: "Did you know that Mary was a diabetic?" There was a silence for a few seconds.

"Mary threatened not to go to your place if I told you, and I didn't have anyplace else to send her," she said.

"Do you realize that you put her life in danger by keeping this information from me?"

"Yes, but I thought her diabetes was under control with diet," said Bonnie.

"I've been feeding her peanut butter and jelly sandwiches for over two months. Do you think that's going to lower her sugar?!" Getting angry, I knew I had better not say anything else. As soon as I hung up, the phone rang. It was Mary's doctor. He was very puzzled about what had happened. He stated to me that he had enclosed a medication sheet with the Micronase on it as well as some other meds. I never received it. He also told me the diagnosis was on the cover letter. I didn't receive that either. I wanted to blame it on the social worker, but instead I asked him when he could see Mary and if he would call the pharmacy to order her medications. The doctor was very agreeable and put me through to the front desk to make an appointment.

Because Mary's memory was poor, she kept forgetting why I wouldn't serve her ice cream and jelly anymore and complained that I was mistreating her because she didn't like the taste of sugar-free jelly and sugar-free ice cream. I, too, was not enjoying the taste in my mouth—the sour taste I was beginning to have about my new venture. Oh well! I was committed now.

May's visits to her favorite restaurant downtown became more and more frequent. She stayed longer each time she went and was quiet and reserved when she returned. One day she brought the restaurant owner home with her. The woman barely acknowledged me. Then she and May went into May's room and closed the door. Instinctively I distrusted the woman but didn't want to pry into May's private life, but I suspected the visit had something to do with money because I knew her husband Tad was dying of lung cancer. Although May and Tad had been estranged for years, they had never divorced. When he died, she would inherit the estate. Tad lived near by, and Mike frequently had taken May to see him. After one of these trips, May called Mike and me into her room. With a chuckle, she asked me to please give Mary a piece of cake so she would leave the room. I fixed her a dish of sugar-free Jell-O and told her May had something private to discuss with us.

The discussion we had would later prove to be a work of art. May pulled out a will and gave it to me. She had Mike open it and read it aloud. Everything went to All Children's Hospital except for a certain amount she willed to Mike for driving her around. Gas money she called it. How thoughtful of her!

She then gave me Tad's will and asked me to read it aloud. This one left all to May but requested that he be buried in Falmouth, Massachusetts, in the family plot. May made us promise to make sure these wills were adhered to. The next day I called her lawyer to make sure he had copies. He assured me he did and would keep in touch with me.

With the money left to Mike, I began to think we could add a third resident to our home. I didn't need to get a license for three residents, and, besides, our family needed the financial cushion another resident would provide. I made a call to my favorite social worker Mandy and let her know I would take another one. She was thrilled and hinted that she would like to see the house, so I invited her over for lunch.

Several days later, she and her assistant arrived. I gave them a grand tour, and they were awestruck at how well these ladies lived. The residents enjoyed lace curtains, expensive bedspreads, new furniture, and, of course, a set table at every meal. As we ate salmon and salad by the pool, we talked about how nice it would be if more of the elderly could live this way. Mandy encouraged me to license the home and take in more patrons.

I told her, "I'd love to! But this is a residential neighborhood, and, even with a license, I can only have four tenants. The money I would have to spend to license can't be justified by having only four people. And because there's a second story, whether lived in or not, I would have to install full sprinklers and fire alarm systems. It's just not worth it."

They didn't know about this requirement and were just plain angry at the system. I explained that I would look for a similar home, all on one floor if and when I decided to expand.

After their visit, I'm sure they went away with mixed feelings, extremely pleased to see such wonderful care but disappointed to know that there could only be one more person to receive it.

My disappointment increased, too. I recognized the need for strict requirements but felt frustrated that I didn't have the money to expand. Nevertheless, a few days later I began a serious search for a new place. May was not happy about the possibility of moving. She loved being where she was. One day she asked me to promise her I would never put her in a nursing home. I did.

"If that time comes, and you cannot keep me, just bring me out to the sea wall and I'll jump in." We frequently brought this up in a joking manner.

Tad died. We all knew it was going to happen but not quite so soon. I remembered his will and offered to make the arrangements for May. May and Tad had different accounts, and, even though she was still legally married to him, Tad's assets would have to go through probate before she could acquire them. Knowing probate law concerning spouses had been part of my duties some years back when I was a home health nurse. Back then, even if a married couple had a joint account and the husband died first, the wife had to wait until after probate to acquire the estate. I had already told her that I could help her arrange her finances now that Tad was gone. She asked me to wait before I did anything. It was early in the morning when the call came about his death, and by noon, May and Mike left in the car. They came home several hours later. Mike told me they had been running around to banks and stock market exchanges. May had cleaned out all of the bank accounts Tad had, sold his stocks and bonds, cashed in his CDs, and bought new ones in her own name. Mike told me that there had been over $1,000,000 change hands in one afternoon. I wondered if she knew what she was doing. I had no idea what her worth was before all this transpired.

The next morning, I overheard May on the phone talking to a crematory. When she hung up, she told me emphatically that she was going to have him cremated.

"May, do you mean you aren't going to grant Tad's dying wish? You know perfectly well his will states that he wanted to be buried in the family plot in Falmouth."

"I will not spend that kind of money to ship his dead body up north. He will be cremated, Carolyn, whether you like it or not," she said as she stormed out of the room.

I felt that I couldn't stand by and let this happen. I called her lawyer and told him of May's intentions to cremate Tad remains. He was extremely upset and said he would be right over. When he arrived, he talked to May for a long time about the cremation. Afterwards I asked him about the conversation, and he said that, as far as he was concerned, she could do whatever she damned well pleased.

I wanted to cry. This was not fair to Tad. All he wanted was to be buried with his family. I approached May again, but she was determined she was not going to spend the money on him. Seeing this new, selfish side of someone I thought I knew was a horrible shock. Why hadn't I seen it before?

I tried to talk her out of it. "May, please do what Tad wants. This is all he asked for. Look at what you have gained by his death," I begged her.

"Carolyn, just leave me alone. It is my decision and I'll do what I want," she angrily responded. There was nothing more for me to say. I was upset with Mike for his part in her actions, but she had relied on him to drive her around and trusted him as her confidante. I knew he had only wanted to help May. I would ask questions later when I wasn't so upset about the ashes I was spooked over.

One morning the mailman knocked on the door with a package from the crematory. She had dared to mail those ashes to this house. Damn her! I was not going to have those ashes in my house and told her so. She paid me no mind as she picked up the box and put it on her dresser. We argued and argued to no avail. She informed me that she paid rent on her half of the room, and she was entitled to have the ashes in there.

I was so upset I started to cry, not only because of Tad, but because I hated the thought of human ashes in my home. I guess you could call me superstitious, but they gave me the creeps. I left her room and after a while she called Mike in. They left with the box and came back an hour or so later without it. I didn't ask where they had been, but I'm sure Mike knew I would ask questions later. May just looked defiant.

I tried to lose myself in the normal routine of dinner, cleaning the kitchen, and getting everyone ready for bed, but my anger would not subside. Earlier than usual I told Mary it was time for her bath. When she said it wasn't bath time yet, I told her she could have her bath now or not at all. Tonight was going to be an early night for me. After the ordeal of pulling the stocking off her arm, I told her to get her gown and wait for me in the bathroom. Everything had to be done for Mary, and it had to be done her way, a place for everything and everything in its place. It took over an hour to complete the routine. By then I was ready to scream. I felt I would lose control at any minute.

May informed me she wanted a bath at 9:30 p.m. It was only 7:00, and I had planned to be in bed asleep by 9:00. I told her she could have her bath now or wait until another night, her choice. She chose to wait. I knew she would have a hard time undressing, but this was one time she would have to do it by herself. John told me a few days later that my daughter, Alyssa, had undressed May and helped her to bed.

I left the room, took a shower, and sat down to watch TV. I was emotionally and physically exhausted, too tired to question Mike. I simply couldn't get over May's refusal to spend money to send Tad's body to his requested burial site

After that day the relationship between May and me was strained.

She was quiet and didn't say much. I guessed she was either ashamed of what she had done or just didn't give a damn. In any event, we just muddled along, sharing the same space but no longer communicating.

Several weeks later, I answered the phone to a very irate man. He tore into me like a duck on a June bug.

"How dare you have so little respect as to throw a box of a person's ashes into the bay?"

"Sir," I said, "Whom do you wish to speak to?"

"Mrs. May Norris," he screamed at me.

"Well sir, may I have a moment to get her for you?"

I called May to the phone without telling her who it was. She answered and apparently listened to him, for she said, "I will be there as soon as I can." She looked pathetic, but I was too stubborn to be sympathetic. She asked me when Mike would be home.

I told her, "Soon." She went to her room.

When Mike came home, I told him I thought May wanted to see him. He grumbled, but went to her room.

I heard him say, "Oh no! What did he say?" I couldn't hear May's response, but Mike was definitely angry. They came out of the room and stated they would be back in a few minutes. The day we fought over her decision to cremate Tad I told her he would haunt her until her dying day if she did not respect his wishes. She didn't care! They came back with the box in hand. Now, we had soggy ashes. I could read the heavy black printing on the box from the crematorium. Her name and address were on there as well as the return address. Mike told me the box had washed up in a man's yard down the road on another finger of land surrounded by water. He had called the crematory to get her phone number.

I told May to make arrangements to have his ashes poured in the gulf. She quietly asked me if I would make the arrangements. I did. I also sent May and Mike to take the ashes to the boat. I didn't want that box in my house another moment.

Ever since I had taken in residents, I had begun a waiting list of potential ones. I wasn't making much money so far, and, because I couldn't take in anymore people into my home, I decided to lease a second place that would be an Adult Living Facility (ALF) because my family wouldn't be living there. That would mean I could bring in more residents, but I would also need to hire help. Luckily, I found a home only a block away. Frick and Frack were moved there while my family stayed put. May hated the new place, and after only a couple of weeks, announced that she would be moving out the first of the month. I tried to talk her out of it, but she just didn't want anything to do with me anymore.

"May, will you please tell me where you are going?" I asked her.

"Carolyn, we were getting along fine until you decided the money you were getting was not enough. Now, I don't even like you anymore."

"But…." I couldn't finish. Her reasoning was unbelievable to me. I was the greedy one? The situation would have been funny if it weren't so sad.

"May, how can you say that after what you've done to Tad?"

"Never you mind. Where I'm going I'll be the only one, and they will take care of me."

"Where are you going?" I begged.

"None of your concern, but they want me, and they love me."

"May, nobody loves you more than we do. Just remember that." I walked away. I didn't want her gloating over upsetting me. I knew what would happen to her. She wouldn't be gone a month before ending up in a nursing home.

May left and went to live with the waitress who worked in the coffee shop she frequented. Sure enough, a friend of mine called me a few weeks later and told me that May was in a nursing home and she was dying. I went to see her as soon as I could, and she was indeed in bad shape. From what I was able to find out, she had been at the waitress's home for less than two weeks when May was put in a nursing home. She was too emotionally beaten to fight. I talked to her and told her I wanted to take her home with me.

She cried and said, "Carolyn, I love you. I will think about it and have the nurse call you tomorrow."

I stayed with her, holding her hand until she went to sleep. Back at home, I called her attorney and asked him if there was anything he could do to the waitress who had taken her in. He said he would look into it.

May's nurse called me the next morning to tell me May had expired. I was heartbroken and so was Mike. I gave him the will to take down to the attorney. I called the nursing home to arrange for her belongings to be given to anyone who needed them. There would be no funeral or service. She was to be cremated and her ashes thrown into the bay by a professional person.

Her lawyer called me the next day. He was very quiet. He said that Mike had inherited a small amount, but then the lawyer estimated that after all of May's bills were paid, over a half a million dollars would go to a lady named Lana Esop.

"Who the hell is she and what happened to All Children's Hospital?" I yelled.

"Ms. Esop is the waitress who took May in."

"Oh, my God!"

"May and Ms. Esop came to see me two days before she was placed in the nursing home, showed me her new notarized will, and asked me to tear up the previous one. There was nothing I could do, Carolyn, but follow her wishes. I asked her several times if she was certain about her decision to change her will. She just looked over at Ms. Esop and nodded her head. I too am saddened by her actions, but the will is perfectly legal."

I told him I was very concerned because All Children's Hospital would not receive the inheritance. I also told him I felt like running a car over her. There was so much abuse in this state of people stealing everything the elderly had, and I was trying to protect them. He just smiled and said he would look further into the matter to see if anything could be done. As it turned out he wasn't able to do much other than to keep her from getting her hands on the money anytime soon. He put it in probate and assigned the case to a junior partner, telling him not to rush.

After I hung up, I went in to lie down before I realized it was time for Mary to eat. I fixed her a peanut butter sandwich with real jelly and a dish of real vanilla ice cream.

Chapter Three
They Came

A few weeks after May's death, a doctor called to see if I had a room. He had a lady who could not be cared for at home any longer. She was ambulatory, fairly alert and coherent, and had few medical problems. I asked him why the family could not care for her and he hesitated. Uh oh…, I thought.

"Frankly, the daughter will be more trouble than the patient. But if you appease her, she'll be fine."

"Well, I'm good of that. I've had a lot of experience taking care of the families. I'll come by the hospital and see her," I said, deciding this would be my policy from then on.

When I walked into her room, I knew there would be trouble with Nell. My introduction was met with a glare and a look that could kill. She was one angry lady. When I tried to introduce myself to the daughter, she quickly took me outside the room.

"I wish you hadn't come up here. We weren't going to tell her until she got to your house."

"I don't take anyone in until I see whether they're compatible with me and whether I can provide the care she needs," I said. She was quiet and hesitant.

"Would you like to go in and tell her what the plans are?" She did not, so I thanked her for the conversation and left.

When I arrived home, I called Dr. Manning. He asked me if I would take the lady. I hesitated but said I would if the daughter at least met me half way. I agreed not to rent the bed until I heard from her.

The next day the daughter came over. This time she introduced herself to me and was almost civil. I showed her the room, gave her the contract and required papers to sign, and explained what few rules we lived by. She wanted a private room for the same price I had quoted her—$700 per month. I said that there would be no private rooms. I also explained that there would be a $700 deposit.

Her eyebrows went up. "What could a little old lady possibly do that would require a security deposit?" I started to rattle off all the possible damages, but since I needed the money and needed to make friends with her, I stopped and simply told her it was my policy.

I asked her to tell me a little about her mother, but she clammed up. I knew this was her first experience with placing her mother in a home for the elderly because her brother had been in charge of Nell until now. Doing this was hard on the daughter. She was obviously a very private person, so I didn't push. I told her that I would need the completed paperwork upon admission. At least the demographic forms would tell me a lot about Nell.

She called me that night and said she would be bringing mother in the next day. I could feel my blood starting to boil at her audacity. The decision as to if and when to bring in a patient was mine to make, not hers. Relax, Carolyn, I told myself.

"Yes, we will accept her," I said.

I prepared half the room, much to Mary's chagrin. She thought she was finally going to get her private room.

Dr. Manning had told me that Nell's son-in-law was an ex-marine colonel, a real stickler for details. He had berated the staff at Nell's previous nursing home for every slight infraction. He was also the publisher of a very large newspaper, and didn't miss a chance to criticize geriatric care. I felt intimidated at first but was proud of my operation and knew he would only find positive things to write about.

When they arrived the next day, I immediately sensed much hostility. The daughter and son-in-law were angry with each other. Nell seemed to be short of breath and sort of shuffled along instead of walking. Her daughter handed me the contract and the mandatory medical records but said she was still working on the demographic form, which she never did turn in. I read over the papers she had brought as she and Nell started putting Nell's belongings into the dresser and hanging up the clothes. I volunteered to help, but it was a mother/daughter thing. One was going to see how much she could annoy the other.

Nell was short and overweight and not a happy camper. Her hair was white and very pretty, though my compliments about it were ignored. In fact about everything I said to her was either ignored or answered with a look that could kill. She was going to be a pistol, but I was determined to break through the ice. The daughter was just as bad. She left with a curt goodbye and thank you. Breaking through or melting the ice was not going to be easy.

I had baked chicken, corn bread muffins, apple pie and cooked mashed potatoes and fresh green beans for dinner. We all ate together as a family when everyone was home; I didn't set separate tables.

Because of Mary's diabetes, dinner was at 5:00 p.m. to fit her schedule. I fixed Mary's plate first, much to Nell's agitation, and cut up the meat into bite size for both women. After fixing Nell's plate I started to hand it to her, but she snatched it out of my hand. Then, she stood up and yelled in a loud voice, "Gimme some chicken!"

"There's a whole breast on your plate," I said. She gave me a dirty look and yelled it again, only louder this time. She reached for the platter, but I moved it out of her reach. She was not going to manhandle everyone's food.

The third time she yelled out, I said to her, "You may eat at the table or you may eat outside. It is your decision." Her face turned so red I was afraid her blood pressure would rise.

"Nell, what can I do to make you understand that there is chicken on your plate and the rest of your food is getting cold?"

She stood up again and walked to where the chicken was.

John moved the plate and said, "If you put your hand in that plate, I will break it."

"John, that's a terrible thing to say. Now you apologize!" John looked rebellious and didn't say anything. Certainly, he needed to work on his people and management skills, but I had to hide a grin. This lady was infuriating!

Hoping to salvage dinnertime, I picked up a chicken leg and put it in her plate. After she wolfed that one down, I gave her another. She ate four.

Of course, mealtimes would have to be more pleasant. I would have to set up another table in an alcove of the living room for Nell and Mary. Separating the residents from my family wasn't fair to Mary, but my family came first, and I didn't want them to be subject to Nell's barbaric table manners.

After dinner I prepared Mary for bed and offered to help Nell. All I got was another of her dirty looks, so I left. I tried to settle down for the evening but didn't trust her and had to make sure she was in bed. I went to check on her about an hour later, and, thankfully, she was in bed. I had set up a TV for her but didn't offer it tonight. With a sigh of relief, I retired to the family room to plop in front of my TV with my family.

No sooner was I settled in my chair when something caught my eye. I realized I could see everything going on in the dining room and kitchen by simply looking at the reflection in the sliding glass door that led to the patio, and there was Nell. We all stared at her reflection; she was obviously up to no good.

John looked up and said, "Ma, watch her." I did. She was making her way to the kitchen. I got up as she opened the refrigerator door and caught her by surprise. She jumped when I asked her if I could get her something. Of course, I got a dirty look.

"Nell, do you remember I told you not to roam around the house at night? That was for safety reasons. That's why I gave you a banana and some milk before bedtime."

Grunt. Grumble. Dirty look. Shuffle down the hall…

A little later I was lying on the family room floor just about asleep when a sound caught my attention. When I looked up, I could barely detect a form moving toward the kitchen. Nell was slinking closer to the walls so no one would see her, but her humming gave her away. John and I watched as she opened the refrigerator, stuck her hands into the containers, and shoved food in her mouth as fast as she could. We were struck dumb. Next she took a carton of ice cream out of the freezer, stuck her hands in and shoved her mouth full, handful after handful. Surely this woman had not been deprived of food! She had to be stopped. All of the food she had put her dirty hands in had to be thrown out.

She hadn't seen us enter the kitchen. I touched her arm so as not to startle her. She threw a handful of ice cream at me, gave me a dirty look, and shuffled off to her room. We both followed her and tried to make her understand that we couldn't tolerate her behavior. John left the room shaking his head. I might as well have left her, for she was totally ignoring me, humming her monotonous song of defiance.

We dumped all the leftovers and the carton of ice cream Nell had ruined and all agreed that throwing out food was a luxury we could not afford. Hence, a lock was put on the refrigerator door. Mike put a small chain through the handles of the double door and secured it with a pad lock. Then he hung the key on a part of the wall where she would never find it.

The first complaint from the daughter came after I told her about the midnight raids. I felt that Nell knew exactly what she was doing, and I told her daughter that she needed to do something about her mother's spiteful behavior. However, she always had reason upon reason why her mom did the things she did, and mostly she placed the fault with me. She said her mom was bored, that she needed to get out more, or that I didn't feed her enough. The complaints never ended. One day she suggested I take her to the park downtown where they were holding a carnival. I agreed.

Mary, Nell, Mike, and I headed for the park the next day. Driving there was a nightmare, and I thought my kids were rowdy in the car when they were growing up. Nell was yelling at Mary, "Scoot over and gimme some room!" She was overweight and needed her full half of the seat, but Mary wanted to take her half in the middle.

In Mary's pristine voice, she said, "I am entitled to part of the seat, and I will take just that." Nell would not shut up about her half of the seat. I finally turned around and spoke to them as I would to two year olds to get them to calm down.

When we arrived at the park, I honestly fantasized about losing them. We walked around a bit until I noticed Nell was chewing on a hot dog. I asked her where she got it. All I got in response was a squinty-eyed dirty look, so I don't know why I ever asked her anything.

A man standing nearby said, "She took it out of my hand." How embarrassing! I offered to pay him for it, but he mumbled something about some people not belonging in public. I agreed.

A few feet further down the path she grabbed a stick of cotton candy from a child. The poor kid screamed and cried, but it was too late. Nell had already mauled the pink swirl and gone on shuffling down the path with a vicious gleam in her eye. I handed the family some money with profuse apologies and hurried on, embarrassed, upset, and incredulous.

When I finally caught up, I turned Nell around to face me. "If you touch one more thing I'll...." She snarled and pulled her arm lose and shuffled away. I turned to Mike to beg him to do something when I heard a scream. Nell had slapped a little boy in the face.

Before I could intervene, I heard a male voice say, "Mom, stop that." When I looked up, I saw her son-in-law standing there with her arm in his. Nell's daughter was standing next to him.

He looked at me and said, "If you would feed her, she wouldn't do these things." Then he just walked away. They had seen everything and hadn't stopped her. Damn, these people were not stupid! I couldn't believe what was happening. I asked Mike to watch Nell and Mary while I ran after them.

When I caught up with them, I said, "You asked me to take her out. I did. So far, she has stolen a hot dog, a big cone of cotton candy, and slapped a little boy. She is a glutton, has no manners, and is obnoxious in public. What do you seriously expect from me?"

"You are not feeding her; she must be starving."

"If you honestly believe that, then take your mother with you, and move her out of my home!"

Just like Nell, they gave no response. "That's what I thought. Look…I will have to take care of Nell MY way as it is obvious that the two of you are not going to help me. You are too proud to admit that "Mom" has a serious problem. She needs professional help. She is a typical little old lady who is angry at the world and especially at her children. She doesn't care that you cannot take care of her. You have put her out to pasture, and she is resentful. She will continue this behavior if something isn't done. I will call Dr. Manning in the morning for a therapist recommendation."

"You will do no such thing," the son said, "Just do your job, Carolyn, and Mother will be fine." With that said, they turned on their heels and walked away, leaving me in total shock.

By the time I got back to the table, Mike was having a fit. Nell had taken off and he hadn't been able to find her. I looked where the food was and, of course, found her by the cakes that were to be raffled off. She had stuck her hands in all of them. I apologized and explained that she didn't know what she was doing. What a lie! I promptly pointed out her daughter and son-in-law walking toward us, who perhaps would reimburse them for the cakes. I took her and put her in the car and went back for Mary and Mike. We went home where I put Mary and Nell down for a nap.

The son-in-law phoned around 9:00 p.m. It took a lot for him to apologize. He was a very proud man who wasn't used to airing his dirty laundry in public. He was also a man of few words, but he did say that his wife could not take care of Nell. Nell's daughter seemed to me to be a strong woman who, for whatever reason, had weakened and was unable to cope with her mother's uncivilized behavior. As a matter of fact she didn't look healthy, and to take on the responsibility of her mother's welfare from her brother was probably overwhelming to her. The son-in-law also told me that he now understood a lot more about Nell after seeing her in the park. I assured him I would continue to care for her as long as I had cooperation from him and his wife.

"Carolyn, do the best you can," he said, and then hung up.

The nightmare continued. I constantly begged Nell's family to hire a therapist, to no avail. Nell tore up two ceiling fans by climbing up in a chair and sticking a broom in the turning blades. She blew out the electricity so badly that an electrician couldn't get the outside lights to work. She stuck something in her bedroom outlet—we never found out what—and fried the house wires again. Three electricians, a few hundred bucks, and two blackout days later, we had electricity again. Through all the catastrophes, she never said a word. She just kept glaring at me and humming, sometimes inaudibly, sometimes obnoxiously loud.

Also, her raids in the kitchen continued. She couldn't open the refrigerator, but she could open the cabinets. We even woke one night to smoke in the kitchen. She had eaten half a loaf of bread by toasting it. She was standing there eating a stick of margarine and holding the button down on the toaster. Rat-a-tat-tat-tat.....it sounded like a machine gun going off. Smoke was pouring all over the house. We opened up all the doors and windows, and turned on the ceiling fans. But that wasn't all. Bread and margarine were spread all over the floor. And Nell! Grease from head to toe, and the margarine still in her hand. I took it away and told her to go wash up in the bathroom. Another dirty look. If only she would talk to me, I might be able to help her. She obviously still had her mental faculties, and it seemed that she had complete control over her behavior. She also spoke clearly to her family, reserving the humming and "Gimme some chicken!" for me. I think she just had an unpleasant personality to begin with and age had turned a mole hill into a mountain! I left her and returned to the kitchen to clean up the mess.

I was met by two of my kids. "Ma, you have to get rid of her!"

Alyssa was crying hysterically. "She could have burned the house down!"

"You cannot control her unless you hire someone to watch her every move. Can't you get another home to agree to take her?" asked Mike. I could do that, but it wasn't simple for me to put a person out. I had a soft spot for everyone and knew what the families of the elderly were up against. I asked Mike to check on Nell and told the kids to go to bed and sleep on it. I knew no one would sleep unless Nell was watched all night, so I volunteered to stay on the couch the rest of the night. I positioned myself so I could see Nell if she came out of her room.

I was a dreamer to think I would get any sleep. That woman was obsessed with getting to the food. I ran her back to her room three more times and literally threatened her with her life if she came out again. Poor Mary didn't sleep either. Soft spot or not, I realized that Nell was more than I—or my family—could handle. I would have to start the ball rolling for another lady and request Nell's removal.

Before I had the chance to act, one of my favorite doctors called me about a lady who was 95 years old. She had been living alone but could no longer take care of herself or stay in her trailer. The owners of the park gave her a 30-day notice.

Her granddaughter, who was in town to make sure she was taken care of, called me after speaking to the doctor. I suggested she come to the house. I fell in love with her instantly. Karla was sincere and apparently loved her grandmother. It was not a chore for her to help out. She hadn't the vaguest idea of what she had to do, having left details of her placement up to the doctor. She didn't even know the right questions to ask. I started by telling her what choices she had: placing her into a nursing home, private home, retirement home, moving her into her own place and hiring 24-hour-a-day help, or taking her back to New York with her. She preferred the latter but worked full time, and her husband traveled a great deal. I armed her with papers to look over and told her what she could expect from me.

Because Karla hadn't been with her grandmother for a while, she didn't know that her grandmother had changed, but, unfortunately, I was soon to find out what Karla didn't know. I invited Karla over for dinner, and she accepted. Then she left for her motel to think things over and to call her husband.

When I got home, I sneaked outside to sit on the patio before facing whatever might have transpired in my absence. The sun felt good, warming my weary body. It was the end of spring, so I knew I'd better enjoy the cooler days here in the South while they remained. From where I sat I could see for miles out over the sea. I watched the ships on the horizon. They were the prettiest at night with all the lights twinkling. I used to play a private game, trying to figure out which cruise ships were out there. I knew every ship and its schedule. One of these days, I thought, I would be on one of them, viewing my home from the deck.

I knew the peace wouldn't last long, but I was unprepared for the overwhelming smell of bleach as I opened the sliding glass doors. The kitchen barricade was still in place, and I never kept bleach anywhere but in the laundry room on the other side of the kitchen. Baffled, I followed the smell into the living room where I saw a coffee cup and piece of bread on the floor. Venturing further, I found the horrible source: a hole in the carpet about two feet in diameter. The pile on the carpet was literally gone! Oh my God! How in the hell had she done this? Coffee had obviously spilled, but how did she get the bleach? And why was the front door open?

First I looked in the bedroom. Mary was asleep and Nell was sitting on her bed, smiling at me…no, not a dirty look, just a smile. I went to close the front door and saw the bottle of bleach in the walkway. I picked it up. It was empty. As I looked around, I realized how she had done it. She had walked out the front door, down the walk to the garage, through the laundry room, into the kitchen, where she fixed herself a cup of coffee. Then she proceeded to drink it in the living room. After spilling it, she followed her first route back to the laundry room, picked up the gallon of bleach, and went back to the living room to dump it on the coffee stain on the carpet. I started to give her the benefit of the doubt. After all, she did try to clean up the mess, didn't she? Then I stopped. This woman was clever like a fox and as vicious as a wolf. I knew the bleach spill was intentional.

The smell of bleach permeated the house. I opened all the windows and doors and sopped up the bleach, but the damage was done. I called my carpet man and asked if he could cut out the spill. He said he would be right over. He was he only one I would allow to clean my white carpets because he knew what he was doing.

When he got there, he had a funny look on his face. I quickly explained that I had not done it and told him what happened. We found carpet pieces large enough to work with in one of the closets. He did an amazing job but the large patch showed anyway. At least some of the smell was gone.

Enough was enough. I typed up a thirty-day eviction notice for Nell and sent it by certified mail, for which a receipt is required.

Emma's granddaughter arrived for dinner. I had already fed Mary and Nell. This meal would be in peace! Mike, John, and Alyssa came in, and I made the introductions. We went into the family room for a drink and chatted. Karla told us that she and her husband had given considerable thought about where to place her mother and had decided to place her with us. She had completed all of the papers and had given me power of attorney to make all the medical decisions in her absence. She explained that she would not be of any help living in New York, and they both felt that I should be able to make the decisions since I was the one taking care of her. I knew that Karla had obtained legal guardianship of her grandmother, and I was confident she was making the right decision.

Since I had not met Emma, I went with Karla after dinner to the hospital to see her. Tall and stately, she had black hair streaked with white and tied back in a bun. Her golden tan showed off her ruddy complexion. Obviously an outdoors type, she seemed lively and kind. She responded to me in a friendly manner and engaged in polite conversation rather than voicing the tirade of complaints I had come to expect. I knew Karla had told her that I would be coming after her in the morning. She seemed pleased.

She hugged me when we were ready to leave but made no effort to hug her granddaughter. Karla was in tears outside the room.

"Carolyn, why do they turn on us?" she asked.

I knew the answer was easy, but she would never understand it. Karla had done what she thought was right, but, in Emma's mind, she had been dumped on a stranger, and everything she had in this world was gone. It was a no-win situation.

Karla gave me the signed admission papers and a check for $2000 for the first month's rent and a security deposit. She left and I never saw her again, though she called frequently and wrote to Emma regularly, sending pictures every time.

Thank goodness, Nell had cooled her jets. She was very quiet and, as far as I knew, she had not damaged anything else. However, her daughter hadn't responded to my thirty-day eviction notice. I really didn't expect the daughter to leave her the full thirty days. The daughter and her husband were a proud pair, and it was probably very difficult for them to come to terms with having to move her. The rent would be due the next day. I sat down to figure up what she was going to lose from her deposit. The two fans cost $59.95 each, the electricity repair bill, $248.00, and the carpet bill, $148.00. All together the total was $515.90. I wrote out a check for $184.00, the amount left of the deposit, and placed copies of all the bills in an envelope. I was ready whenever they made the mad run in to get her. I made sure all of her clothes were clean and her belongings placed within easy reach. Believe me, I watched her like a hawk now. There would be no more damage and no more kitchen raids.

When John came home, I left to go to the hospital to pick up Emma. I met her doctor in the hall. He asked me if I was sure I wanted to take her. I was puzzled but thought he was just being cautious. What could he have meant? She smiled as I entered her room, again friendly and talkative. I bent over to pick up her suitcase and…WHACK! Something hit me on the head. My knees buckled, I saw stars, hit the floor like a rock, and screamed "HELP!"

"Oh, my God, not again….get her up….she's bleeding….call the doctor…" What the hell happened to me? I couldn't see or stand up! A nurse lay me down on the other bed and another woman brought in a doctor. He examined my throbbing head, and I guess it was fine because he told the nurse to apply a pressure bandage and left. A brusque, all-business administrator came in and stuck papers under my nose. Everything was so fuzzy. I had no idea what was going on.

After a few minutes, I slowly came to my senses and asked what had happened. Instead of answers, I was taken to another room. Emma was left behind. Someone was asking me to fill out an incident report and the doctor returned. The person shoving that paper at me was beginning to annoy me, and I told her so.

"Please tell me what happened, and I will do your damn paperwork!"

It seemed that dear, sweet Emma had hit me over the head with the IV pole. Okay, now that I knew the score, all I wanted to do was leave as fast as I could.

Another nurse came in to tell me that my son was on the phone. I hobbled out to the desk and took the call. Wouldn't you know it? Nell's daughter and son-in-law had come to take Nell and wanted me there. I quickly filled out the incident report and started to leave before I realized that I was too weak to drive. The doctor took me home and then informed me that Emma would be a risk to take care of and had suggested to the granddaughter that she put her in a full-security home where she could be watched more closely. I agreed wholeheartedly. I didn't want her. That was certain.

I thanked him and hobbled up the front steps. The daughter met me at the door as though she was my only concern. She was furious but remained calm.

"What do you mean charging mom with all of those expenses?" I had told her about incidents and the repair costs as they happened, but apparently she chose to shrug them off. I tried to explain the damages again, but she would not listen. I walked off for I didn't want to have a war. She was not physically well. I had learned this a while ago and far be it from me to add to her misery. When her husband came in to start loading Nell's belongings, she stopped him and handed him the bill.

He looked at it and motioned for me to come into the family room. "There is no way Mom did any of this. What are you trying to pull?"

I had long since lost any fears I might have had about people, so he was not in the least intimidating to me. I quickly stated what she had done and how she had done it and that I had informed his wife each time, reminding her that the security deposit was insurance against just such damage that her mother was incurring. If looks could kill, his certainly would have. I didn't know whether his anger was directed toward me or his wife!

Then John came in and entered into the conversation, telling the son-in-law about all the things she had broken and the fact that we had to hire extra help just to keep her from burning down the house.

He honestly didn't believe what he was hearing.

Instead, he struck out by saying, "Isn't that your job? To take care of these people and keep them from tearing things up?"

I was beginning to get a headache. Arguing was futile. He asked me if I would reconsider, and I told him, "No." He turned around and left in a huff with his wife and Nell.

It was then that John first noticed the bandage on my head. "What the hell happened to you?"

"You just noticed? It was nothing much. The new patient just bopped me on the head with an IV pole," I said.

"That does it. You are not going to take her!"

I went in to clean Nell's bed and her part of the room. Once again Mary thought she have a private room. Of course, I told her she would be sharing her room with someone new. Her face showed her disappointment, but she said nothing. I knew she felt the tension with Nell because she had been unusually quiet lately. To compensate I had spent extra time with her to talk, observe the birds, and just relax whenever it was possible. I asked her if she would like to join me for a cup of tea. She was truly delighted. She knew that there would be cookies or cakes with the tea. When we got to the dining room, I sat her down and went to the laundry room to start washing Nell's sheets.

John asked me, "Will Mary be the only one for lunch?"

I said, "Yes."

"Good, I will fix her a peanut butter and jelly sandwich and a dish of vanilla ice cream." I had to laugh in spite of my headache. Thank God we all had a sense of humor. It was the only thing that kept us sane. We sat down for a few minutes, and I took some aspirin. As I rested, I realized how seldom I sat still…never had time!

Later I called Emma's granddaughter and told her what had happened. She was upset, but years before she had heard from her mother…before she died…that Nana was mean. No kidding. I asked her if she could pay for another pair of hands to help me watch her, and, if so, I would take her until I could find suitable placement. She agreed and asked me what sort of placement I would look for. I explained that there were only a few places where patients were allowed to be locked up, and if Emma continued to behave abnormally, she would have to go to one of these facilities. She sighed and I could tell she was not pleased, but she had to realize that a locked facility was the only way I could see to go, short of a mental institution, which I certainly would not recommend. My deal was going to cost her $2000 a month unless I could find a worker who would work at a lower salary. The granddaughter said the money was on the way. I thought of a previous coworker Maxcine who would be a good pair of hands. I wondered if she would like some extra work.

First I called Mandy, a social worker, told her what I had arranged with Emma's granddaughter, and asked if she would help me place Emma if I couldn't handle her. She was so thrilled that I would take Emma, at least for a trial period, she could hardly talk. I told her to keep Emma until the next morning, and I would try again to hire an employee.

Next I called my former coworker Maxcine and asked how work was going. She said she was sick of her job. Her employer wasn't giving her enough work time to meet her financial needs. My first employee! I offered her a ten-hour shift at night and explained why I had to have someone. She wasn't afraid of anyone and readily agreed to start the next night. I was pleased as punch.

When I awoke the next morning, I wondered why I had agreed to take Emma. As I lay in bed thinking about it, I realized I still had this dream of making life good for the elderly. I still believed that a good environment, loving caregivers, and good food would work miracles for them. Well, so be it. I knew I would be picking up Emma. First I fed Mary and got her off and running for the day.

I arrived at the hospital and went directly to Emma's room, careful not to turn my back to her. She was sweet as pie. Her apology seemed genuine, but I was afraid to let my guard down. Deciding to be pleasant, I made small talk, though I watched her, never letting my guard down. The nurses watched her closely, too, while we finished the paperwork.

One of the nurses asked me to come to the nurses' station for the copies of the rest of the papers. As we stood discussing the papers, I heard something behind us. Quickly I spun around, but it was not fast enough. "WHACK!" I hit the floor. The blows continued for what seemed an eternity. Where was everyone?

I heard male voices screaming for someone to pull her off.

"This is a hospital! Get that woman restrained!" said a voice that sounded like Dr. Manning. He was leaning over me, and again a nurse was cleaning up the blood. God! What happened this time? I was coming back to the world, but it was really unclear. Dr. Manning was asking me something, but I couldn't reply. I heard him tell someone to take me down to ER for treatment and x-rays. I was too weak to argue with him. I heard the ER personnel talking about the patient who had beaten me two times. Oh! So it was Emma again. Well, this old girl was headed for Chattahoochee, a town with a mental institution. I was not taking her to my home!

I asked someone to call Mike to come for me. He was furious when he saw me. I guess I looked a wreck. Those medical charts were made of a heavy metal. They had done a number on my head and face. I required sutures in several places.

Sadly, it took a quiet hospital bed to give me time to think. I knew I couldn't take care of Emma, but I also knew I was committed to give Maxcine the full-time job I promised her. Besides, I had already spent some of Emma's advance rent money. Also, I didn't have anyone else lined up to come in. I was crying when Dr. Manning came in to let me know nothing was fractured. He told me he would do whatever I needed him to do. I poured my heart out to him, telling him I felt stuck, that I had to take in Emma.

I called Mike in, and by then John was there, too. They left the decision of taking in Emma or not to me. I asked Dr. Manning if he could prescribe Valium or Thorazine to keep her calm. He agreed to do this but only for one month and until the hospital could make arrangements for her to go to a mental facility. I wanted her drugged before I would even attempt to take her home. I called Mandy and told her to get me another lady soon, for Emma was going to be short-lived.

Dr. Manning came back in to say that he had a better solution. He was going to *Baker Act* her to the mental institution in town and see that she be medicated. According to the Baker Act, a medical doctor had the power to commit a patient to a mental institution for evaluation during a period of twenty-four hours. Then I could take her back. This sounded good to me. After I was discharged, I took my headache and went home.

I tried to rest up before what I was sure would be a living hell came about. Mary and I sat outside and watched the birds. As I watched Mary's frail body, it occurred to me that I was placing her at risk as well as my entire family. Maybe I should be the one drugged in a mental facility.

The next day Emma was ready for discharge after being mentally evaluated, and I was told me what medications she was on. Wow! That mental facility surely hadn't wasted any time! The more I thought about it, the less I wanted to go get her, and I certainly didn't want to go alone. Someone would have to run interference for me while I drove, or I would have to control her while someone else drove. Because John was out of school, he could drive me.

Surely, the least they could have done was to give her a bath, I thought to myself when we arrived. She looked as if she hadn't been bathed in months. I would have to be the one to get beaten up while she got a bath.

I saw her sitting on a couch outside the social worker's office. The SW was afraid to let her in her office, and yet they expected me to drive her home!

I approached her and said, "Good morning Emma. Are you ready to go home with me?"

She smiled and politely said, "Yes." I definitely did not like the expression on her face. I knew she had been a school teacher and probably a strong disciplinarian, but I was not one of her students. I kept my eyes on her hands. I didn't want to see a ruler, or worse, come out of her pocket. She was statuesque and quite beautiful in spite of the mean streak in her. Her manner commanded respect, and she damn well was going to get it from me.

We escorted her to the car, John on one side of her, I on the other. I put her in the back seat and climbed in beside her. I could protect John this way. I don't know what I was expecting, but not what happened. She was a perfect angel all the way home. She carried on a conversation with me, talked incessantly about her past and her family. She had lost both her children years ago. She cried when she spoke of it, trying hard to hold on.

"We are not supposed to lose our children. We should go first. God didn't mean it to be this way," she said to me.

At that moment I saw a woman who was bitter because of those deaths. After all, she was ninety-nine years old and didn't see any purpose for outliving her family. I wondered if anyone had ever let her voice her thoughts or if she had been drugged out of fear for her violent behavior. First, after home health care didn't work, she had been thrown out of her home in the trailer park. Then she had gone through several social workers with her granddaughter trying to care of her. Now all she had was me.

"Do you know why all of this has happened to me?" she asked in her soft voice. I couldn't answer her right then.

As we pulled into the driveway, I glanced over nervously. She looked calm but did not appear to be medicated. I'd have to review the papers when I had a chance. Whatever she was on didn't seem strong enough. But her bath HAD to come first.

Into the house and straight to the bathroom we went. I asked John to put on a pot of coffee because I would need it when I got through. I didn't even introduce her to Mary, although Mary was right there trying to get into the bathroom.

"I have to use the commode," she said.

"I'm sorry, Mary, but you will have to wait." She was prepared to put up a fight until I raised my voice with her. "Why did you wait until we got home? Why didn't you go before now?"

I let her go first, but it took her forever to pull down and pull up. Then, as usual, nothing came…she just had the urge. She wobbled out and sat down in her chair.

The big event was at hand. I had linens ready, clean clothes, a foot brush, nail clippers, and shampoo. I discovered that Emma's hair was very long when I took the bobby pins out, and her scalp was encrusted with dirt. I reached into the medicine cabinet for the bottle of Kwell lice medication, just in case. She was cooperative. I wondered what she was scheming and what would be her next weapon.

When the water was the right temperature, I eased her down to soak. I had hooked up a shower hose and had a shower stool for her to sit on, but this gal needed deep water. This bath was going to take a while. I started with her hair, using a brush. Her scalp would take two or three washings, but I had time. Emma had picked up the washcloth and unbelievably began washing her body. She wanted to help me. When I was sure her hair was clean enough, I put a conditioner on and pinned it up until we finished the rest of the bath.

Her feet were next. The brush went to work. It would take another bath to scrape all the crud off her feet, but I was pleased that I got them as clean as I did. I helped her to sit on the stool now that she had soaked enough so I could cut her nails and wash her back and privates. Her long pendulous breasts were caked underneath, but the crud finally came off. She would need a lot of good lotion after all this.

With her toe nails cut and her fingernails clean, I let her hair down for a final rinse. Her long black hair, mixed with only a little gray, glistened. I dried her off and applied the Kwell lotion. It was wonderful for the skin. I dried her feet especially well and put some foot powder on them. She surely smelled better. There was a smile on her face when she looked into the mirror, and I noticed that her eyes were almost pure black. I could see the years of anguish in those eyes and the delight in the simple pleasure of being clean. How sad that something so basic had been denied her for so long.

I dried her hair, putting it in a pony tail, and she almost went to sleep while I combed. Her clothes were cleaned and washed the minute her granddaughter brought them over. I turned down her bed and we walked across the room and I introduced her to Mary. I told Emma I would come and get her when lunch was ready.

With my mess cleaned up, I headed for the coffee. That Mary! She made no effort to get to the bathroom now that we were finished.

I went outside for a few minutes with my coffee. The sun felt so good on my face. Emma was unblemished now. Her disposition was docile and mellow. Oh! I had forgotten all about the transfer papers. I yelled to John to bring them to me. He had already read them.

"Ma, I thought she went there to be evaluated and placed on medication."

"That was my understanding."

"Well, think again. There is nothing here about medication. They have written about a nice, pleasant lady who was brought in to them for evaluation," he said.

"Give me that!" As I read, I saw that he was right. Nothing had been done. The papers read like a damn psych exam. If the psychiatrist wasn't present when she pitched her fits, he would believe they never happened. I called Dr. Manning and read him what had been written. He called in some Thorazine to be given orally and some more to be injected if needed.

I never had to medicate her. In fact, she was a joy to have around. She was very active. She liked to play games, work in the garden, and walk around the neighborhood. I was pleasantly surprised to learn that Emma was intelligent and even kind and loving! She had been married to an attorney and shared delightful stories of their life together. She seemed content and happy, and Mary and my family enjoyed her thoroughly.

She stayed with me for an entire month with never another incident. Then her granddaughter's husband came for her and took her back up North because Karla was grieving for her, and he felt he had to make this sacrifice of letting Emma live with them.

Before she left, Emma called her lawyer and changed her will, leaving everything to charity. When the lawyer told me that she had left nothing to her family, I questioned her about it. She said she would never leave a cent to her family because they had put her in homes instead of letting her live with them. The bitterness and anger toward her family that she had evidently bottled up while staying with me finally came out. For all the time she had lived with me I thought she had mellowed out. She had truly been a pleasure to have around. Leaving all to charity was unquestionably a good deed, but I didn't like the motivation behind it.

She had millions, yet she had lived like a pauper. When Karla's husband arrived, I told him that he should see the lawyer before he and Emma left town because Emma had made changes to her will. I don't think the fact she changed her will to exclude her family would bother him because Karla and he were fairly wealthy, but I thought they should know. She died several months later from complications of pneumonia. The family called me to thank me for everything. I grieved for Emma for a long time. She had been angry yet had so much to give. She had lived through many wars and a big depression. She had been married to a good man and had raised their children. If only she could have let me into her private hell, perhaps, just perhaps, I could have helped her cope, but it was never to be.

As a child envisions sugar plums, so I envisioned creampuffs. In geriatrics creampuffs are residents who are sweet and need little care, but it didn't look as though I would ever have one. So far, all I had attracted were the people no one else wanted. It was hard for me to come to terms with this. I charged the least of all other elderly care facilities; did the most for the social workers, taking those people they couldn't otherwise place; and I certainly had the best contacts. I knew care givers who were getting a fortune taking care of frail persons and not providing them with a fraction of the care I gave them. I decided to be a little more particular with the next patient. I could still have two more before having to license, and I vowed to make them as *puffy* as possible.

Famous last words. Why I agreed to accept a total bed patient, I may never know, except perhaps for thinking I must be a glutton for punishment. I was beginning to understand myself in dealing with the elderly. My basic instinct was to help others, not to live life easy, though living life easy was what I thought I wanted. But, happily, agreeing to take this new person turned out to be a good decision. Nancy and her laughing face entered my life like a cool, gentle breeze on a warm day. She came from a loving, caring family that was heart broken about having to place her in a home. After the initial consultation, the family felt comfortable about placing her with me and was relieved to discover the kind of care she would receive.

Nancy was without a doubt the sweetest person I had ever met. She didn't talk but had a way of communicating with us. Her smile could make a gloomy day shine, and her saintly look lit up every corner of the room. She couldn't walk or even sit up without assistance, but she could smile, and she did whenever someone entered the room.

Nancy ate what I fed her and never showed any disappointment. Of course, I had consulted the family about her likes and dislikes and made sure her food was to her liking. We bathed her and washed her hair in bed, and rubbed down her small body several times a day with lotion, but doing so was a pleasure because Nancy smiled and cooperated the entire time. She was truly a creampuff, being easy to care for and never complaining. She was loved by all.

I got her up after breakfast and morning care and put her into a large recliner until after lunch. She took a nap for the afternoon and was up again for her supper. I talked to her as though she talked back and relayed the events of the world on a daily basis. Most of all, I liked to sit and brush her beautiful, thick, glistening hair. It was white as snow. No one has ever touched me as much as she and her family did. They were the kind of people who made one want to change their life for the better. They didn't have much in riches, just each other and the endearment they held for one another.

I would later learn that Nancy had played saxophone in a ballroom-style band with three of the residents I would have later at The Grand, a home yet to be opened. They played together for twenty years but didn't recognize each other in my home. I only knew about the band from relatives asking questions when they recognized a resident's name.

At about this time I began worrying about Mary, for sometimes she slept too long and no longer asked me for food she wasn't supposed to have. Although I took her to her doctor regularly, I knew she wasn't her normal self. Depression almost always is a key diagnosis for those who have lost the ability to care for themselves. Their lives are winding down with little to hope for in the future. Mary was no exception. She had had a full life with her husband and son, and now that they were both gone, she had nothing to live for. I could do a lot, but I couldn't replace her son or his love for her.

Now that May was gone, Mary spent her time looking for birds.

Before this period she was excited when she saw a gull or an egret, but now she barely reacted when one appeared on the seawall.

One day she developed a bad cough and a fever some time later. I called her doctor, and he sent out an antibiotic. He wanted me to call him the next day.

She was worse the next morning. Her lungs were full and she was extremely weak. When I called the doctor, he wanted her to go to the hospital right away.

She was in the hospital for two weeks before she died. She just didn't have the will power to live. I cleaned her room and packed all of her belongings for her son to pick up. Instead of coming, he called me and sent certified letters wanting her deposit back. I refunded it to him and called Good Will to pick up all of her worldly possessions. I packed up three hair nets, a package of bobby pins, a comb, some Pond's face cream, one book, a few pieces of clothing. What a pitiful way to end a life, with so few possessions and children who didn't care.

May and Mary—Frick and Frack—my first patients, now both gone. The problems I faced with them now seem so minimal compared to those of the two who replaced them. If only I could have turned back the clock…

Chapter Four
What Have I Done?

Before Mary died, Margot entered our lives, providing us with another harrowing experience.

When I got the call from the Home Health Agency, some particulars about a potential new resident named Margot sounded strangely familiar. I had worked part time for this agency and thought I recognized the name Margot, but I had cared for so many people that I wasn't sure. I told the supervisor I would come to see Margot and then call her back. When she gave me the address, it hit me. I didn't need to go to her home; I knew her well already. But I thought it best to see her again (with mixed feelings), so she would know whom she would be dealing with. I wondered if she would remember me.

When I walked into her place, I could tell by the look on her face that she was trying to place me. It was better if she didn't recall, for after I realized who she was, I felt betrayed by her. She had nearly cost me my job when we last met, but I doubted if she would remember me or the situation.

Months earlier while nursing for the Home Health Agency, I received a call from my supervisor about a complaint from a patient. Margot had complained to another nurse that I had insisted she be placed in a nursing home. This conversation never took place, nor did

I say anything remotely similar to this. In order to save my job and reputation, I demanded that the supervisor accompany me to Margot's home. When the supervisor asked Margot to repeat the complaint, she admitted making up the story. She said she had no problem with me. The particular nurse she initially spoke to was always looking for a fight with me for some unknown reason. Why they picked on me, I'll never know.

It could have been disastrous, but I landed on my feet. So, the question now was, did I want her? Margot was a clinical psychologist who had just quit practicing only three years before. She lived in a small, filthy trailer with only a few meager furnishings. She slept in her chair and did nothing until the Home Health Aide came to bathe her.

Her long, thick hair was golden and absolutely beautiful. I knew she had to be tall, but I had never seen her out of that chair. Her body was thin and well cared for, and her skin was soft to the touch.

As far as I knew, she had never married and had no children. I reintroduced myself to her and told her why I was there. She seemed pleased to hear where she would be living and about the other people there. We had a lovely, lucid conversation as if I were a total stranger. I was pleased to see that she still maintained a bright, clear mind.

Margot agreed to pay $900 month and said her nephew would bring her to my house the next day.

I bid her farewell and left for home, thankful, yet disappointed, that she didn't recognize me. I still wondered why she had tried to hurt my reputation.

They showed up the next day around noon. We chatted and I gave her nephew the rental agreement and the other papers to sign. He balked at the deposit, but I stood firm. He wrote the check, signed the papers, and deposited Margo, never to be seen again.

The papers he signed are the ones required by HRS for a licensed home. He was not required to sign them since I wasn't licensed, but I realized they would protect me and the resident if there was ever a cause. Besides, my dream was to have one large home that the entire city would be proud of, and everything I did now was practice for that dream.

Margot walked in with a cane. I had no way of knowing this would be her last trip across the floor. It was only a short time before she found out I fed Nancy in her chair or bed, and this was what she wanted for herself. I fought her for a while over it, but she became so nasty that we didn't want her in the dining room with Mary. It was easier to take her food to her.

We had placed a beautiful antique chair in the room for Margot. It had a high back which she needed with her height. When bedtime came, she asked me if she could sleep in the chair. I knew that was what she had been doing in her apartment, perhaps because she had no assistance. However, here she had someone to help her.

"No," I said. "I am here to help you get ready for bed, and I know you can walk to the bathroom." She had a look of horror on her face. "Margot, I leave a light on in the bathroom and you can call out if you need help. There's a lady named Maxcine who works the night shift, and her job is to help you." Thankfully, she let us help her to bed, and help during the nighttime bathroom runs, but this cooperation was very short lived. We soon found out she would get out of bed and walk to her chair to sleep after she thought we would no longer come to her bedroom.

A few days later, I opened the door to Margot and Nancy's room to feed them breakfast. The room smelled so bad, I almost dropped the trays. I called John to take the trays away so I could clean up the cause of the ungodly stench.

Oh, I didn't want to clean this up. I told Margot to walk to the bathroom and get into the tub. She ignored me. I told her again. This time she flatly refused. I reached for her to help her get out of the chair. When she stood, a pile of feces fell to the floor, and I was able to see what had been left behind in that beautiful chair. Why did I put that chair in this room? I wondered in dismay. I must have been totally nuts, but making a good impression was important to me. I wanted her to have the best.

I had placed large blue pads all over the chair, but they had been wallowed on so much that they didn't provide much protection. Anger started to rise, but I pushed it back and tried to look at the situation professionally. Margot was not senile; her mind was clear. Why was she doing this? Perhaps she had a control problem. It would be typical of the agency not to tell me if this were true. Or was she mentally ill or depressed? If the latter were true, soiling oneself is a sign of severe depression and despondency. What would Margot do as a professional if she had had a patient like herself? Oh, the irony of old age.

I led Margot to the bathroom, sat her down on the toilet, and told her to wait while I fetched the cleaning supplies from the kitchen. Thank God Flossie arrived at that moment. I had hired her to clean the house on the recommendation of some of my neighbors. She was truly all they had said and much, much more. She said she smelled feces as soon as she came in. No kidding…we would both need a beer after this cleanup. We went into the room armed with Lysol and trash bags. Flossie said she would clean the carpet and the chair if I would bathe Margot. That was fine with me. I went to the bathroom and there she sat. She had not even made an attempt to clean herself.

I set up the stool in the tub and got her in. At first, I just ran water over her with the spray hose. After putting on my gloves, I started soaping her up.

Margot said nothing. When I asked her what just happened, she shrugged. "Why couldn't you go to the bathroom, Margot? Or at least call one of us? I told you to call Maxcine for help; she's usually here…." Then it hit me—Maxcine didn't work last night. Guilt overwhelmed me as I pictured Margot calling out and no one around to help her.

Flossie yelled out to me that she didn't think she could save the chair. It was permanently stained and no amount of scrubbing would help. I had John take it to the garage. Thank God it was trash day. Flossie worked most of the morning on the carpet, but it still smelled. I called a carpet cleaner to come out and see if he could do any better. For $200 he tried to save what once was a clean, white carpet, but the stains never disappeared, and the smell took a couple of days to dissipate.

I decided to put a diaper on Margot in case she had an accident. Then we piled large waterproof pads on another chair John brought to her room. I asked Margot if she understood about the diapers. Most elderly balk at wearing them. She just hung her head.

"I cannot afford to have another chair ruined. And the diaper will protect you as well as the chair." She only asked if she could sleep in the chair again.

Too exhausted to argue, I said, "Yes."

Although I couldn't stomach the thought of food, the women needed to be fed, so I made up new trays and brought them into the room. Margot didn't seem a bit disturbed by the occurrences. I was glad that all was clean again and the smell almost gone. After leaving, I reflected on my part in creating this mess and forgave Margot from the heart. After all, I had forgotten that Maxcine didn't work the night before, and I was the one in charge. I promised myself I would be more careful about scheduling. At the same time I couldn't help wondering what I had gotten myself into. It turned out to be the deepest hole possible.

I really thought that this was a one-time incident. Or perhaps I was just being too optimistic. It didn't take me long to realize that this unsavory episode was only the first in a long line of nasty ones. It became obvious that Margot would simply shit and piss wherever she sat. She had neither the will nor the inclination to do otherwise, and, furthermore, she didn't seem to mind being covered in filth. I became less and less sympathetic and more and more frustrated with every cleanup because this woman still had her mental faculties. I came to realize she was perfectly capable of caring for herself, but she wouldn't. I knew that to a psychiatrist the loss of waste control was an indication of the deepest level of despair. When I was knee deep in her crap, however, I was hardly able to remain objective.

At first I tried to reach this woman, who, in one breath, appeared to me to be crying out for help and in another seemed steeped in negative feelings of worthlessness and guilt. She was clearly suffering from severe depression, serious enough to need help, but she refused all efforts to help her. Rather than talking about her feelings, she held everything inside, never explaining her behavior.

As her episodes increased, so did my frustration. I made numerous doctor and therapy appointments for her. She passed all physical exams, proving her problem wasn't physical. However, when it came time to visit one of her professional peers, Margot absolutely refused to go. In refusing she would grab onto her chair with a death hold we didn't even attempt to break. Instead, I tried scheduling home visits but couldn't get a psychiatrist or psychologist to come. The elderly are not a priority for mental care because of their age. Doctor's wouldn't prescribe anti-depressants because of conflicts with her other medications. As a last resort, I decided to call her nephew to remove her from my care, but his phone was disconnected, and he had left no forwarding information.

This was not the first time—nor would it be the last—that the medical profession and families abandoned the elderly, leaving them in the most pitiable state imaginable. Every time it occurred, I was strengthened in my resolve to somehow make a difference. People deserved better.

One psychologist did spend a few minutes on the phone, reminding me about Eric Ericson's ego analyst theory of psychological life states.

Ericson was one of the first to equate elderly dysfunction with childlike behavior. He divides human life into eight distinct stages of development. The first stage, oral sensory, describes an infant's sense of trust and how this trust manifests itself in peaceful sleep, eating well, and easy waste elimination. Distrust is reflected by sleeping fitfully, fussiness in feeding, and constipation.

The second stage deals with control of the physical waste functions. Control over these functions equates to independence. Loss of control or too much control can cause self blame and doubts. Margot had obviously lost control, whether on purpose or not.

The similarities to Margot's condition were evident through all eight stages of development, including conflicts of guilt in stage three, feelings of inferiority in stage four, and identity crisis in stage five. The strongest correlation involved numbers six through eight, from young adulthood to full maturity. During this time normal people develop intimacies and concern themselves with nurturing and caring for others. Adults who fail to develop a giving or nurturing side to their personalities drift into stagnation. During the final maturation stage, while looking back at life, an elderly individual who feels that life was a disappointment falls ever deeper into despair. It's too late to go back and do anything over and very difficult to live with the choices made. I reasoned that Margot had sunk into the greatest depths of despair, for who in their right mind could hate themselves enough to behave as she was doing? Without the help of a psychiatrist, I tried my best to sort out and understand Margot's inner motivations.

Flossie and I tried desperately to reach through to her one day. We brought a tray of tea and goodies, treats she usually liked.

"Ms. Margot," said Flossy opening up the conversation. "Can you help me understand why you do these things?" Margot's reply was simple—she shrugged.

"Margot," I said. "We only want to help you. You're making it impossible. What can we do to help you use the bedside commode and to keep you clean?" She cried but would not open up to us.

"Because of your messes," said Flossy, "we have been through three chairs and countless carpet shampoos. And the walls smell so bad that my husband is going to have to build new walls. I guess you don't care enough about yourself to stop doing this, but just think how much it affects other people." Margot sipped her tea but made no comments.

"I would like to do more for you if you would just let me. Please tell me what I can do to make your life easier," I said. It was useless. We would just have to provide comfort measures to protect her and the room.

The next morning Flossie and I covered the new chair with plastic, and put thick plastic on the carpet on her side of the room. We changed Margot's diapers more often, and I called Maxcine to hire her for more nights and asked her to check the room frequently.

Exhausted after safeguarding the room, Flossie sat down with her coffee. She was like a bolt of lightning with her work. She could clean all 13 rooms and five baths including changing all of the beds and doing the laundry and be finished in three hours. And she even did windows. She deserved the rest.

She spoke to me with a gentle, but quivering voice, "Miss Carolyn, surely you are not going to keep her here. She will ruin this whole house in no time." No truer words were ever spoken. But it would be impossible to evict Margot without replacing her, as I needed her rent money if I was to continue making payments on the house and paying the help.

At this time I was caring for only two residents, Margot and Nancy. I could take one more without a license. When Mandy, my favorite social worker, called soon after Mary died, offering a lady named Peggy who could pay only $700 per month, I put her on the back burner, hoping I could get someone I could afford to keep. I did. And, again, I was to severely regret taking in this man named Walter, for I lost a lot of respect in the community with my Jewish friends. His story will come later.

I called Mandy. Because she always treated me fairly and honestly, I would usually take the people who could not afford the high rates and others she had trouble placing. I told her I would take the low-rent lady and a man she was mentioning if she would place Margot elsewhere. Because other nursing home owners and managers were bugging her for admissions constantly, she thought she would be able to place Margot easily. She promised me she would do her best.

I went to the hospital to see the lady whom Mandy had asked me to consider taking in, the one who could pay only $700 a month. Only 49 years old, Peggy was disabled with Parkinson's disease, though she could walk with a walker and talk. She had closely cropped hair and was on the stout side. She had no teeth and her dress was loose fitting and made of cheap cotton fabric.

I was drawn to her because she was friendly and liked to chat. Before she moved in, her brother called to tell me a sad but interesting story about her. It seems he had bought her an apartment up north where she lived alone, though she had daytime help. Suddenly and without warning, her mental capacity was reduced severely from the disease and the L-DOPA she took.

When she was at home alone at night, she hallucinated so badly that she became involved with the federal, state, county, and city officials by calling them on the phone to claim she was an official herself. She claimed to be the dispatcher for the Emergency Medical System as well as an FBI and CIA agent, a police officer, and a sheriff. She also claimed to have authority over animal control. Evidently, she wreaked havoc with her numerous phone calls and was finally arrested and put into jail.

While there, it was discovered that she was simply a poor, deranged soul rather than an FBI or CIA agent, police officer, or sheriff.

Her brother, a celebrity owner of a major baseball team, told me she was in deep trouble when they finally located him. The authorities ordered him to handle the situation because they were too busy with real emergencies to waste time on false ones four or five times a day or night. It was strange that no one had gone far enough to find motives for her actions. Even after she was hospitalized for her behavior, no psychiatric evaluation was done.

I asked the hospital to keep Peggy for another day or two. They were so grateful that I was considering taking both Peggy and the man Walter that they would have given me the moon.

Walter was ready to leave the hospital before Peggy was. Through a misunderstanding, he was brought to the house before I had an opportunity to visit with him. I held my temper but inwardly screamed at the hospital's stupidity. I would be over my limit with Walter there so soon, but I knew Margot was leaving, and I was willing to take a chance. God knows why! Maybe it was because Walter seemed to be a creampuff, even though he was totally bedridden and was fed a liquid diet through a feeding tube.

He was distinguished in appearance—tall and thin with white hair, what was left of it. I thought to myself that he must have a caring family. His wife lived about three hundred miles away and his three sons even farther. I wondered why they hadn't wanted him closer to them. They wired me his money, which included a $1200 deposit, and offered me more.

Walter was semi-comatose, which meant he could do nothing. He had to have position changes every two hours, and he needed meticulous skin care as well. I bought artificial sheep skin rugs to wrap his feet and legs in and to lie on. I would not let his skin develop bed sores. Nancy required similar care and her skin was in perfect condition.

I decided not to catheterize him in order to reduce the possibility of an infection. The adult diapers were so good now he would never be wet. They pulled the urine away from the body.

When I was assured of Walter's security and comfort, I went in to check on Nancy. She was doing fine. Then I looked in on Margot and asked her if she would like to go to the bathroom. She didn't, but I warned her not to go in the chair.

I went in to check the menu to see what I had to cook. Nancy's food had to be pureed, and Walter drank his through a tube. That left Margot and my family. I tried to follow predetermined menus calculated to provide good taste plus the right nutritional balance.

Today was seafood pie, which everyone loved. I fixed a small salad and put the rice on to cook. The filling was made from eggs, cheese, shrimp, and crab and lobster meat. The rice formed the crust. Nancy was supposed to be allergic to shrimp, but she devoured her portion of the seafood pie the last time I fixed it and had no reaction. Also, this was one dish she could eat without its being pureed.

I didn't hear from Walter's family for a few weeks. When they did call, it was to ask if they could visit.

Three sons and his wife arrived the next day. After a pleasant greeting, I led them to Walter's Room. His wife seemed a little nervous. Well, a lot nervous. As a matter of fact, she was shaking. I left the family to prepare the usual tray of coffee and tea cakes and took them in. His wife ignored me and sat by the bed and cried.

Two of the sons went outside to smoke cigarettes. I needed one, too, so I joined them on the patio by the pool. One was talkative, though the other was far away in thought.

"Carolyn, may I call you by your first name?" After I nodded, he continued. "We will not be back until father dies. His funeral arrangements have already been made. You'll find everything in order." At least they were efficient.

The quiet son looked up and said, "Do you know what my father did for a living?"

"Nuclear physicist was listed on the paperwork," I said.

He smiled and looked at me, waiting for my undivided attention. "That was during the last 20 years. Prior to that time, he supervised the slaying and torturing of people."

I was not enjoying this conversation. Some families would stop at nothing to erase their guilt for not taking care of their parents. But the fury in his eyes and the look of devastation on his face made me listen. His brother had moved away from the table. Something here was too painful for him to be a part of this conversation.

Before I could comment, the talkative one asked me what my religious affiliation was. I told him I was Catholic. "Carolyn, my father was a Nazi war criminal. I doubt if they are still looking for him, but if they do find him, go along with whatever they say. He brutally murdered those people because he was under orders to do so."

We were not born yet, so we do not feel responsible. Our mother feels that he did what he had to do. I feel that I should have killed him as soon as I was old enough to realize what had happened. All of our lives we have been hiding what he did. We're not sure if his business partners knew what he had done. If they did know, they must have needed him so desperately that they also hid his true identity. In any event, feel free to send him out of your home, if necessary."

I got up, went into the house, and came back with a bottle of Christian Brothers' brandy and three glasses. Each of us had a drink while sitting in disturbed silence. When we went inside, the family stayed a few minutes longer then left without another word. I was alone and felt as though I had been hit by a Mack truck.

I called Mandy and asked if she was aware of anything about Walter's past. Of course she wasn't, and I did not want to tell her. She was Jewish, and besides hurting her deeply, it would just feed the gossip line at the hospital. I looked at Walter again. All I saw was a tired, sick old man who needed care, and care for him I did. Somehow, at least some of his story got out. I don't know how. But my standing in the Jewish community was adversely affected.

Peggy arrived the next day. I placed her in the room with Nancy and Margot, and she had no objections. The room really was huge. Even with three beds, three chests, three chairs, three tables and lamps, there was still enough room for as many more pieces of furniture with room left over. I did worry about Margot subjecting the other two to her smells, not realizing I would soon have two stinking humans to worry about.

Peggy turned out to be as smelly and messy as Margot. The next morning after she came in, I found a mess like I had never seen before. Peggy was drenched in urine as was the bed and the floor around the bed. She had asked me for a commode chair before going to sleep, but there was not a drop in it. I tried to get her into the bathroom to clean up, but she wouldn't walk right and kept trying to hold something between her legs. It was a large gob of toilet paper, soaked with urine. After it fell to the carpet, we turned to go into the bathroom. It was then that I saw the bigger mess: water flooded the foyer to the bedroom and the bathroom.

Something snapped inside. I started crying and ran out calling for help. John came running in to see what the matter was. He unplugged the toilet, which was filled with nearly a whole roll of toilet paper. Again we were left with a nasty cleanup and unacceptable behavior. Right then I needed some answers. How could she walk to the toilet to deposit the toilet paper she had urinated into and not urinate in the toilet itself? What possessed her to take such action? I would find no answers.

This behavior was the pattern for the remainder of Peggy's short stay with us. Maxcine prevented some of the problem when she was there at night, but mostly, I faced the same kind of mess most mornings. I placed a commode and her walker by her bed, thinking that if she had a walker, she could get to the commode or to the bathroom in time to urinate on the toilet. Why she would not use the commode baffled me completely. Finally, I eliminated some of the problem by inserting a Foley catheter, though she fought me as hard as she could and tried to pull out the catheter. Her attempts met with resistance, however, because the catheter was held in place by a balloon filled with water in the bladder. I finally put enough water inside that balloon to prevent her from trying to pull it out again. Another problem solved.

Then late one night I heard Peggy screaming. Maxcine was off duty, and I was sleeping downstairs. I flew into her room. She was absolutely panic stricken.

"Peggy, wake up! What's the matter?"

"I am not asleep. The plane is going to hit us," she screamed.

Since we were close to an airport, I did look out the window onto the bay and saw nothing. I tried to convince her there was no plane, but she continued screaming. Finally, she stopped and settled down. I knew the medication she was on would cause hallucinations, but the plane was real for her.

Several nights later, as we watched TV in the family room, John suddenly jumped up, followed by Mike. What had they heard? Mike shoved Alyssa and me out the front door.

They both screamed for us to run. RUN? Run where and from what? We ran, but why? Terror filled me; my heart was pounding, and I was shaking even as I ran. But what did the men know that Alyssa and I didn't? What was happening? John was still running up the street, but I was so out of breath, I couldn't run any more. Besides, Alyssa had fallen, and I went back to help her. Where was Mike? I didn't see Mike. Then I remembered my charges and began running back to the house.

Suddenly, I heard a deafening noise and knew instantly it was the engine of a plane.

"Oh, my God!" I screamed. The plane barely missed the roof of our house, hit the power lines, and went down in the bay.

Quickly, the streets were filled with hysterical neighbors, everyone talking at once, no one quite sure what had happened.

As I pushed through the crowd, I could hear sirens approaching and thought to myself that it was the Coast Guard the people on that plane in the bay needed, not ambulances, not here. The police were busy trying to keep the people away from the sea wall and the streets adjacent to the water and the downed wires.

Finally, I reached my house despite the downed wires, the efforts of the police to keep me from getting there, and the frantic neighbors rushing in the opposite direction.

Because of the downed wires, everything had gone dark. The house was eerily quiet. I went in, found a flashlight, and rushed to the bedrooms, but all my *babies* were fast asleep, oblivious to the chaos. I paused and leaned on Peggy's doorway, remembering her prophecy just a few nights before and feeling amazement. How had she known? Her nightmare predicted the plane actually hitting the house…did she somehow effect the narrow miss? I shook my head and shuffled down the hall in a daze.

It was then that I remembered reading in the newspaper that the control tower was unmanned, and a big ruckus was going on about it. From what the experts said it took a good pilot to bring the planes into this small airport because the runway was surrounded by water on three sides.

After several hours, the electricity was restored. Soon a policeman came back to tell us the pilot had been alone and was alive. He had been too far into the landing before realizing the runway was on the next finger of land. By then it was too late to pull up and go around.

Chapter Five
Shoreline

Peggy would be leaving soon since the house I had leased up the street was going to be licensed as an Adult Living Facility (ALF). An ALF is for adults who need minimal assistance with day-to-day care, such as baths, caring for clothing, taking medications, exercise, and transportation to church, stores, or banks. Meals are prepared for them. I found out that I could get a license for seven persons there, and Peggy could not be one of them because she needed more care than an ALF would provide.

I worked diligently trying to get what would be called Shoreline open. But my time was precious with four residents to take care of. I found some relief with part-time morning help but mostly took care of them myself. Even with a small staff of four, payroll was now up to $1700 per month, reason number 200 why I would never get rich and reason 500 why I questioned my own sanity every day!

The stress and fatigue caused by trying to open an ALF in Florida is almost more than the average owner can cope with. Relations between Health and Rehabilitative Services (HRS) and the owners of the licensed homes is tenuous because the owners often feel threatened by people in authority at HRS, who often attempt to intimidate rather than help. In my opinion, illiteracy, stupidity, and power plays caused most of the problems. Conditions never improved during the next five years or so, especially as far as my relationship with HRS was concerned. The hassles were numerous, and I and other owners lived in the fear an inspection would end in fines or worse. The livelihood of the owners was in the hands of some surveyors who were not fit to hold public jobs. Also, it seemed that some owners who were only out to make a buck and couldn't care less about rules that were written to protect the elderly could operate without impunity. I never quite understood why I was singled out to do everything by the book unless it was because HRS surveyors knew me when I worked in nursing homes and considered me a trouble maker. I had been outspoken about deplorable conditions, and you would think that HRS would view my caring about the residents as positive, but I'm guessing they saw it as a threat.

Until about 1985 or 1986, anyone could apply for a license. A high school education was not even required. HRS insisted that everyone applying for a license would have to be screened, but I knew of people with criminal records who were licensed and operating homes. The illiterate owners depended on those who could read to get them through the regulations, and what a handicap that was! They were just clobbered by the surveyors and had no idea why.

The Federal Registry is one screwed up piece of literature. This is the rule book (laws) to determine the optimal health care an elderly or handicapped person must receive, but the law makers had no clue as to the real needs. An average person could read it with good intentions of understanding it, then not learn a thing. In order to obtain a license, a person had to be able to interpret this document as well as implement the laws. Just to figure out what had to be on the bulletin board required a month of sorting through the document. Policies had to be written, then a procedural manual telling how policy would be implemented. Something had to be written for almost every section of the Registry.

Additionally, fire protection had to be complied with, dietary standards adhered to, and personnel policies followed. Physical plant and maintenance of the building were top priorities, but above all were the standards for resident care.

After I broke everything down into categories, it was easier to sort through the rubble. It was one thing to write a policy but still another to show the end product. However, I was ready to open by the date I projected. HRS was supposed to inspect every new ALF. Sometimes they did, sometimes they didn't. In my case they did. The teams who came out were usually washed-up nurses and other personnel who could not hold a job doing anything else. They didn't know their jobs and certainly not the regulations. In many instances they bluffed their way through and never acknowledged it if the owner or administrator knew his/her own business.

When they made an appearance, I had everything ready. It was hard for them to find fault, but they did, nit picking things that could easily be corrected. They gave me a conditional license for eight persons. For this I was glad because I had ten lined up to come in. I could go ahead and take residents, and they would be back in 60 days to see if the deficiencies were corrected. The outcome really wasn't too bad; I fought them on only one point and won. It was over giving prescription drugs. According to them medications could not be given by anyone in the home. A bottle of medicine could be opened and handed to the resident but any other procedure was TABU. However, I was an R.N. and, therefore, governed by the board of nursing. I told them I could give any medication that was prescribed by a physician. This meant I could take it out of the bottle and give it to the patient. They didn't like admitting they were wrong. I informed them I would have to practice nursing according to the Nurse Practice Act unless the physicians wanted to make a written protest denying me this right. Finally, they settled in my favor.

After handing down their list of required compliances, they departed haughtily, leaving me feeling threatened and anxious. But I knew I could meet their requirements with no problem. I was not one to bully easily!

When I went to the hospital with a medical emergency, they came back for the follow-up, 60-day inspection. My staff knew what to do and how to handle them. Or so I thought. No matter how many times I had drilled my staff, they could still become intimidated during inspections.

The inspectors found a problem, which they said I had not corrected. First of all, it had not been listed on the first list of deficiencies. The problem did not exist. Grab bars are mandatory in all bathrooms, and they were installed three months before I opened. The inspectors listed "no grab bars", but Sam, one of my employees, told me they did not open the shower curtain to look.

I wrote a letter of complaint to the governor's office and sent copies of my receipts along with a copy of my deficiencies. I was ignored and ordered by the state inspectors to correct the deficiencies within 24 hours. At that point I threw up my hands and let Sam handle it. HRS was there in 24 hours to inspect again. The inspector went to the bathroom where he promptly stated that there were no grab bars. Alyssa and her husband, Tom, took a picture of the inspector and Sam in the bathroom clearly showing the grab bars. They told me the inspector wasn't upset, and yet he continued to say, "There are no grab bars." When HRS inspectors got something in their heads, there was no changing it. I felt as if I were in the Twilight Zone!

This was a typical example of the frustrations we administrators had to go through. I ended up paying a $1000 fine for noncompliance, and it remained a matter of public record. During the next yearly inspection, the same grab bars were there in the same places. The inspectors made no mention of them.

One aspect of the inspection was particularly important to me—fire prevention. I agreed that all window dressings had to be flame-resistant. It was a costly compliance but worth the money, nearly $200 for the draperies in the Florida room alone. I took down everything on the other windows and put up mini blinds. They were clean, colorful, and they let in whatever light we wanted. So, the problem was solved. Right? Wrong! The company that had done the flame-proofing was unacceptable to the HRS. The flame-proof company representative had given me a certificate of flame proofing, and that was all that was required. Nope, HRS would not accept it.

I was getting tired of playing games, so, while the surveyors watched, I went into the Florida room, took down the drapes, put them in a plastic bag, looked for a box to pack them in, found one, addressed it to the governor, and wrote out a short note requesting an opinion as to whether the drapes were flame proof. I sealed the box and addressed it as they watched me. I sent Sam to the post office while they sat with their tongues hanging out. This was the only way to settle this matter. My note was on letterhead stationary and stated the discrepancy had been noted during an inspection and that a copy of the deficiency report would be forwarded.

My drapes were mailed back with a letter that said they had been sent to a state fire inspector, who had approved them as being flame-retardant and certified for use in an ALF.

It seemed I would always have a fight on my hands with HRS if I remained licensed. In any event, it was difficult to stay ahead of the game by anticipating the HRS surveyor's every move.

When I thought the time was right, I started moving in the residents who would take up homesteading at Shoreline. First I wanted to move the ones from my private home, but it was not to be. Nancy's family did not want Nancy to move. I did not want to move Walter. Margot, I wanted to send elsewhere, and Peggy was not suited for the new place. They had already ruined the carpet at my house. Why tempt fate by moving them to Shoreline with its new carpet.

Instead, I concentrated on bringing in the people I had on a waiting list. They were Marie, Gig, Hannah, Maggie, Stuart, Jock, Prudence, Bea, Vera and Laverne. I had to increase the staff in order to help care for the residents at my home because I would be spending most of my time at Shoreline.

It was now time to schedule the new arrivals. Since licensing, I had to do everything by the book. I had resident files all made up and a detailed instruction sheet on how to do an admission. If a form wasn't filled out completely, it was ultimately my responsibility. For the most part the employees did a good job. However, often the responsible member of the family or the legal guardian failed to fill out these forms. It seemed that the person legally responsible for the resident felt he or she would be giving away family secrets. Sometimes I would have to literally force those responsible for the residents to fill out the paperwork when they visited the first time because they seldom returned.

The first one on the waiting list was an 83-year-old gentleman named Gig. He was well dressed—unusual for men of his age. I say this because during the many years of taking care of the elderly as a nurse in homes or adult living facilities, I used to cry over the appearance of the men. No matter how hard we worked, they never looked good. Even the best shave was shaggy. The best clothing would be wrinkled and never fit right. I remember being annoyed with the low level of care of men's clothing in laundry departments in nursing homes and in private homes. I always thought clothing should not only be wrinkle free, but also mended, if needed, and fairly new looking. Caring for Gig taught me a very valuable lesson and turned my thinking around.

Ever mindful of how he preferred to look, Gig took care of himself rather than depend on someone else to do the job. He bathed and dressed himself and seemed to appreciate our laundry staff's dedication to clean, unwrinkled clothing. He primped in front of a mirror and made sure he looked just right. The difference was physical or attitude or both. Unlike Gig, most elderly men were unable to take care of themselves due to handicaps or apathy. A man can lose his dignity very fast if he's no longer in charge of his life. After all, he's accustomed to being the strong one, the man of the house. I discovered that men resented being taken care of and sometimes refused help, perhaps out of pride; that was the main reason for their sloppy appearances.

On the other hand, Gig exhibited lovely old-fashioned manners that charmed the ladies. He would converse after meals as long as he liked the conversation. If he didn't, he would politely take his leave with a bow.

Gig liked to walk around the neighborhood, always alone. It was safe and he enjoyed himself. One morning a few weeks later, while in the garage, I noticed a lot of lawn care tools hanging on the wall. At the time I was busy and didn't realize they looked unfamiliar until one of my employees, Kris, asked me if I had been going to garage sales. I certainly would have liked to but told her I never had time.

"Carolyn, this garage is full of tools that weren't here when we moved in, and the supply keeps growing," she said.

As I looked around, I saw what she was talking about. I asked Mike and John if they had brought the tools there, but neither knew anything about them. Usually things vanished rather than mysteriously appeared from our homes. Maybe one of the residents' relatives was buying the tools as a hint that we should do lawn work, but I doubted it. The front lawn had to be reseeded, but I did have that scheduled. I guess we would just have to watch everyone to solve the mystery.

Later as I was putting dishes into the dishwasher, I looked out the window and saw Gig coming up the street. He was carrying some hedge shears. I watched as he went over to the garage side door and opened it. I opened the door leading to the garage to watch him. He picked up a hammer, found a nail, drove it into a stud, and hung up the shears.

Well, the mystery was solved. Now what would I do about it?

I finished what I was doing, washed my hands, and told Kris I was going for a walk. I knew the neighborhood well and most of the people in it. In the first open garage, a man was working at his tool table.

I asked him if Gig had been there that morning, and he replied laughingly, "Do you mean the elderly gentleman who walks around all of the time?"

I said, "Yes." Apparently he found this funny, for he was smiling at me as he asked me how long Gig had been living with me. I told him only a few weeks.

In neighborhoods like this one, people were usually leery about the presence of homes for the elderly. They considered them to be businesses, which they were, and were really afraid of their own property values decreasing. I turned around to ask him if Gig had been taking his tools.

"Yes, mine and everyone else's," he smirked. "He walks in, takes what he wants, and carries it home."

I told him I had watched him bring in some hedge sheers and nail them to the wall just a few minutes before.

"Well, sometimes he brings them back, too. He might not get them into the right garage, but we know what belongs where, and we just exchange them." He still thought it was funny. I assured him I would talk to Gig, but the man said, "Just leave him alone. The poor bastard doesn't have much left so, if this gives him a sense of belonging, let him have it. We will watch out for our tools and will come for them if we need one." I thought I was hearing things. Usually, people weren't this nice anymore.

I had to laugh when the man told me about the garden hose. He and his wife had been looking out the window as Gig took the garden hose off the faucet and carefully rolled it around his arm and carried it to Shoreline. They were not worried about it, but in a few minutes they watched him hook it up to my outdoor faucet, screw on the nozzle, then turn on the water. Water went everywhere. He turned it off, took the nozzle off and again rolled it over his arm, and headed down the street to their garage. They overheard him say, "I don't know who punched holes in my hose, but I will catch them sooner or later." It was a soaker hose.

As long as Gig lived at Shoreline, he continued this habit. He never hurt anyone and eventually all the tools were taken back to their rightful owners except for the big saw. When Kris screamed one morning, I saw the only palm tree in the front yard falling down. Gig had cut it down and yelled "TIMBER!" as he laughed. For him this was the accomplishment of lifetime.

After Gig was gone I realized if I helped the men who came to Shoreline to regain dignity and pride, they would also be happier and take better care of themselves. This proved to be true, and one of the ways I used to accomplish this was to help them be more independent of all of us at Shoreline. To do this I would take them up the street to a neighborhood restaurant where they could sit outside and eat one of the damnedest burgers you ever saw or tasted. I always left them money for a couple of beers, and you would have thought they'd won the lottery because going out brought them so much pleasure.

Shortly thereafter I brought in two ladies, Vera and Bea on the same day. Both had been referred to me by the hospital and had been waiting awhile for a home. Vera was truly sweet and adorable. She was tiny and squirmy with a dash of white hair. She could walk and talk a little, but her vocabulary was limited. We did all of her care as she was unable to care for herself.

Bea was alert and a little overweight. She walked with a walker, though she could walk as well as anyone and didn't seem to have a problem with balance. Perhaps using the walker made her feel sure of herself. However, I had an instant dislike for Bea's daughter. She was too anxious to leave and tried to evade completing the paperwork. As she prepared to go, I said, "This paperwork is required by HRS, and, unless you want one of the inspectors at your doorstep, I suggest you take the time to do it." This was the second set of papers I had given her. She had misplaced the first ones. When she first applied for Bea to come in, what she filled out was vague and gave nothing about Bea's background. I just knew I had made another mistake by agreeing to take Bea, but I was wrong. Bea proved to be a peach. It was her daughter who would be trouble.

I charged her only $900 a month because her daughter said she could not afford anymore. The daughter gave me a check for $1,800 and left. That was the last time I received any money without threatening her.

For the life of me, I could not figure out these people. The money usually belonged to the residents who had worked hard for it all their lives. The sons and daughters could not stand for a dime of the money to be spent, but they sure as hell didn't want to take care of their parents either. I often wondered what would become of Mike and me if the time ever came for us to be farmed out to an ALF or nursing home.

Several months later while preparing a beef dinner, I opened the liquor cabinet to get a bottle of red wine. There were no bottles of anything. I was puzzled. I asked one of my workers, Kay, if she knew what had happened to the booze. She just shrugged. The only other employee to ask was Maxcine, who worked nights, but she knew nothing either. I then called Kris at home. I told her what had happened, and she not only knew nothing but was appalled. At the time, she and Maxcine were the only two employed long enough for me to know they were trustworthy.

Yet I felt that the staff and not the residents were responsible for drinking the booze. I went out to the dumpster and in the bottom, buried in a bunch of grocery bags were the empty bottles. At least I had the evidence.

As a last resort I decided to ask Bea about the booze and if there had been any parties lately. She was alert when she wanted to be. She had to think about it but finally said, "Do you mean where we have snacks and stuff?"

"Yes, and cocktails, too," I said.

After a few minutes she came to life and said, "Oh yeah! The girls who work here were really mad at you last night. They were talking awful to us about you."

"What were they mad at me for?" I asked her

"They were pissed because you didn't pay them." Sometimes I did pay employees late when the families didn't pay me, but it had not happened recently.

"They didn't feed us either," Bea complained.

I went to the kitchen, checked on dinner, and picked up the phone. I called everyone but Kris and Maxcine and fired them. I wrote a termination report on each of them and sent John to get copies and to get me some money for their final paychecks.

I finished dinner, fed the residents, and then sat down to look at the schedule. I would be putting in some drastic hours. Maxcine already worked six nights a week, and Kris had another job. Oh well! Being short staffed was better than employing thieves.

It was Maxcine's night off, so I had to work the night shift. It was then that I found out why Vera slept in a chair in the living room. It was a reclining geriatric chair with extra padding in it. Before this night I had put her in her bed a dozen or more times and she would not stay. I was unusually tired and feeling very frustrated because I could not find suitable help, so I put Vera in her chair and told her to stay. She did. But all night she sang, "A, B, C, D, E, F, G, H, I, J, K, L, M, M stands for Milky Way, Vera wants a Milky Way." Over and over again, "A, B, C, D, E, F, G, H, I, J, K, L, M, M stands for Milky Way. Vera wants a Milky Way." Of course, I never slept. When I asked Maxcine about Vera's singing, she said after a few nights she just didn't hear it anymore.

The thing that frightened me the most while running these two homes was the thought of a fire. I trembled when I thought of what could happen if there ever was one. My fire disaster policy and procedures left no room for error. I drilled the staff and residents so much that when the door bell rang, they ran to the porch and tried to get out. Drills were conducted several times a week until the house could be evacuated in less than three minutes.

Bea always had that walker with her and used it at all times until I pulled a drill one night at about 11:00 p.m. Everyone went flying out, with Bea carrying her walker and yelling, "Come on, let's get this thing over with so we can sleep." She went all the way to the front porch before she realized she was walking without her walker. The walker was simply a pacifier.

Bea was an ideal resident, always pleasant and agreeable. She ate whatever food was set before her and seemed to encourage others to do the same. The residents liked her, and frequently I would hear conversations about who was going to sit next to her. One would say, "You sit next to Gig this time. He likes you."

Another would say, "Scoot over honey. I'm more comfortable in this chair."

Yet another would say, "Get your own damn chair, I'm not moving." Everyone loved Bea.

Bea's daughter, however, tried to drive me nuts. This was my rule: THREE DAYS LATE AND A $10 PER DAY LATE CHARGE WILL BE AFFIXED TO THE BILL. This woman owed me her soul in late charges. I had to threaten her each month, call the school where she worked, call her husband's work, and even wait at her apartment for her to come home at night. I sent her late notice letters every month and finally sent one that said I would notify HRS to file legal guardianship if she didn't start paying me on time. She brought the rent right over.

The next month she disappeared. Her apartment was empty, and she was on an extended leave from school. When I called her husband's place of work, they said he had gone to New Jersey on vacation. These people really knew how to disappear.

I was frothing at the bit. HRS was formally notified that Bea needed a legal guardian because her daughter did not have her best interests at heart. They came out, investigated, and agreed with me that they had apparently abandoned her to my care without pay. So they began the procedure to appoint a total stranger as her guardian. If this was what the daughter wanted for her mother, it would be just what she got.

On the 12th day of the month, the daughter called me from New Jersey. She was stupid enough to tell me that she and her husband had gone on vacation and that she just forgot to pay me before she left. She said she had to have emergency surgery while there. She said she was calling from a certain hospital that she named. Before she hung up, I managed to tell her that, if payment was not on Western Union wire service within the hour, I would notify the principal of the school where she worked to say that she had abandoned her mother. After her call I called directory service to verify that the hospital she named existed. It didn't.

I waited a couple of hours and called Western Union. The money was there. I went after it before she could take it back. It would only be two weeks more before payment was due again, and I would have to repeat this dreadful process.

A few days later the daughter arrived with some papers in hand. She did everything she could to get her mother to sign them, but she had hit a sore spot. There was no way that Bea would sign those papers. I had no idea what they were and didn't ask, but Bea got up off the couch and headed for the bedroom, shaking off her daughter's hand on her arm. The daughter was furious. She tried to follow her, but Bea was ready to wrap the walker around her neck, so she backed off.

I was indignant when the daughter asked me to get her mother to sign the papers. Where did she get her nerve? The way she had treated me and her mother was loathsome and now to expect me to do something for her! I refused.

When she asked Kris, Kris said, "Just leave them, and I will see what I can do." As the daughter was leaving, I reminded her that rent would be due soon.

That afternoon her husband arrived, threw a few sheets of paper and money on the floor, and left without a word of explanation. I picked up $1,800 off the floor in $100 bills. He didn't even ask for a receipt. Well, that would take care of the next two months without a fight.

The papers were for the purpose of giving her daughter power of attorney to sell property in Atlantic City. I asked Bea about the property. She was adamant about not talking and walked off.

In a few minutes she came back into the living room crying. "I was born in that house and my mother before me, and I will not sell it," she said. As I further questioned her, I found out that there were 30 acres and the frontage was on the Atlantic Ocean. She told me a man by the name of Harrah had been waiting to buy it to add on to his gambling joint.

It just so happened that I knew that Bill Harrah was one of the biggest gambling moguls in the world. That property was premium. No wonder the daughter wanted to get her hands on it.

Bea still refused to sign the papers.

I did what I thought was right and let her alone.

When the next month rolled around, to my surprise, I received a check in the mail for $900 shortly after the first of the month. Bea's daughter obviously did not know her husband had brought over money. I would still be secure for two months in advance.

I realized the address on the check was one I didn't know. I called zoning to find out who owned the property at that address. It was her daughter and her daughter's husband. The purchase price was $178,000.

I drove to their house, which was beautiful. There were three new cars including a full-size van, a Buick, and a Jeep Cherokee. I wrote down the license numbers to check out the registrations and found out the vehicles did indeed belong to them. The husband sold insurance and she taught school. Something was wrong; their own finances couldn't buy the property and vehicles I saw. I was willing to bet they had forged those papers and sold that property.

I called HRS again to find out if a legal guardian had been appointed for Bea. As usual the agency was dragging its proverbial feet. To my question the response was, "We'll get around to it as soon as we can."

I decided to hire my friend Harry, who was a private detective. I was ahead $1,800, and I was going to spend some of it for a little detective work for Bea. When I called Harry, it just so happened he had a case that would take him to New Jersey, and for no pay he would try to find out who was involved in the transaction of Bea's property.

A few days later my detective friend called me from Atlantic City. He said Bea's property had been sold, and the mortgage company held a power of attorney (P.O.A.) document she had signed. Of course, I knew it was forged. I asked him to get a copy, but he already had all of the transactions. He asked me if I was interested in the purchase price and, of course, I said, "Yes." Almost $2,000,000.

Around the first of the month, another check for Bea's rent arrived in the mail. I tried to call the daughter, but her phone was unlisted.

Not long afterwards Bea became ill with pneumonia, and the antibiotics were not kicking in. I decided not to tell her what had happened. Fearing the worst, I called her doctor and asked that she be admitted to the hospital.

HRS came out to check on her status. I gave the HRS representatives a copy of all the papers Harry had brought back. Among these papers was Harry's certified statement that he alone had brought back the papers and that he knew what the papers from New Jersey contained. They took statements from my staff, verifying that Bea had not signed any papers and had not left the facility. I guess HRS was finally going to take some action.

One of my policies was that when a person left the facility temporarily for any reason, the bed would be held at the room rate unless the family, guardian, or resident signed a form stating the bed should not be held, in which case the belongings were moved out. Since I could not contact Bea's daughter, I held the bed with the money I had.

Her daughter's house now had a FOR SALE sign in the front yard. When I approached the realtor, he said he only had a P.O. Box in New York.

Mandy, the hospital social worker, was mortified when I told her what I had been through with the daughter. She called HRS in to sign the papers for the hospital. HRS didn't give me a hassle because Bea went into a coma and would have to be placed in a nursing home.

To my knowledge no one ever found the daughter or her family. Bea was sent to a nursing home from the hospital.

I saw her obituary in the paper a few months later. Several of us wanted to go to her funeral, but there wasn't one. She was cremated because that was all the state would pay for. God alone knows where the ashes went..

I saw greed and wicked behavior toward the elderly repeated again and again, seemingly winning out over love and caring.

My philosophy on Alzheimer's disease varies considerably from that of the so-called experts. I strongly believe that senility is mainly due to hardening of the arteries, thereby restricting the flow of oxygen to the brain. There are many symptoms that reflect virtually the same diagnosis, but diagnosing these symptoms as Alzheimer's is often too simplistic. The fact is that at a certain time in one's life, although there are exceptions to the rule, there is an interruption of rational thought. Some become worse than others. Maggie was one of the worst ones.

Her case was typical in that her family had suffered in trying to accept her diagnosis of Alzheimer's and effectively dealing with it. My first encounter was with the daughter. She had flown in from California to insist that her father place her mother, Maggie, in a home. She was honest and blunt, making no qualms about her feelings. She let me know that she had lost her mother years ago, but she felt a strong need to make sure her mother was taken care of for the remainder of her life.

My next encounter was with Maggie and her husband. He was a well-dressed gentleman, who was active in civic affairs and golf. He certainly did not look his age of 78 years old. Most of his activities had been sharply curtailed recently because of his utter devotion to his wife in her increasing need for care. Maggie, on the other hand, looked 90 years old. She was literally lifeless, zombie-like. Her hair was unkempt, her skin dry and colorless, and her clothes were a mess. Surely he could have afforded to hire someone to take better care of her. I tried to communicate with her, but there was no response.

We agreed to a rent of $1500 a month. We made arrangements to move her over that same day, which was fine with me. She would need total care, and we were well equipped and well staffed to handle total-care residents. I had asked a lot of questions about her history because I needed to know when she quit walking and when she quit communicating and eating. It was important to know when she ceased to function. I had pulled off a few miracles and maybe she would be another one.

Once she was settled in, we had time to give her a bath, shampoo, and a Kwell job before I started dinner. She seemed pleased, once taking the washcloth and rubbing it on her legs. This woman probably had not been put in a tub in a good while. She enjoyed it. We dried her hair, curled it, and put on some loose-fitting clothing that would look good on her in the wheel chair.

I don't know why, but I wanted pizza for dinner. I would be at Shoreline until 10 p.m., and the family could either come up there to eat with me or get what they wanted at home. I ordered enough for my family, my staff, and the residents. Then Kris and I sat down for a cup of coffee.

Maggie's daughter drove up, came to the door, and gave me a check and the paperwork. She told me she would be calling her father that night at 7:00 p.m. She wanted to know if she could call me the same night to see if things were OK. I assured her she could and to feel free to call at any time.

"I will call only this once. You will receive a check each month until she dies. Here are the funeral arrangements." With that, she turned and left. Kris, who had a heart as big as the moon, just sat there in her chair and began to cry.

"How can people be so cruel, Carolyn?" I had no answer for her.

The pizza arrived. We brought the residents and staff to the table and poured some cola. I even had ice cream for dessert.

I wondered if I would have to puree food for Maggie, but by the time I pulled her to the table, she was smiling and said, "Boy, I haven't had pizza in a long time."

Kris and I looked at each other with tears in our eyes. We had moved her to a geriatric chair with a tray so she could eat. She wanted to be at the table with the others, so we quickly pushed her up to the table.

Maggie was going to be fine. We didn't treat people with mind-altering symptoms any differently from the others. Maybe this is why they responded to us so well.

The smell of the pizza drove all their taste buds into action. Gig ate five pieces and Vera ate three. I had to cut hers up, and she devoured them completely. Little Miss Maggie ate five pieces, but I wouldn't give her anymore for fear it would make her sick. She and the others were absolutely delighted, and their eyes about bugged out when they were served ice cream as well.

Around 7:30 p.m., I received a phone call from Maggie's daughter. She and her father had agreed that she would call around 7 p.m. after her plane trip. She was upset because he did not answer the phone. She wanted me to go over there to make sure that he was well. I called Mike to come up and stay at Shoreline while John went with me to her father's house. I knocked on the door and rang the doorbell, but her father did not come to the door. I looked under the mat and found a key. John opened the door as a neighbor came across the lawn. I introduced myself to him and told him why I was there. He looked confused but came in with us. We were too late. Maggie's husband was lying dead on the floor and had been dead for a few hours. I called 911 and waited for the ambulance. I answered their questions, and then called the daughter to give her the bad news. She was understandably distressed and agitated. I asked her if her husband was home, but she had apparently given him the phone, for he asked me what happened. I told him.

All he could say was, "She killed him. She finally did it."

I offered my condolences, and then handed the phone to the paramedic. When he was finished talking, he handed the phone to the coroner. I heard him tell them that her father had been dead at least four hours, probably from a heart attack, which meant it happened shortly after I left with Maggie and the daughter left for the airport.

How ironic! He had devoted his life to caring for his beloved wife rather than to get help, and now he had died first.

Maggie did well for a few weeks. She learned how to walk again and talked to us all of the time. She could feed herself and carried on conversations with the other residents.

Several weeks later Maxcine called me in the middle of the night to say that Maggie was burning up with fever. Her temperature was 106° by mouth. I told her to take it again rectally, which was more accurate.

It was 109°. I had never heard of a temperature that high. I called 911 and drove up the street to Shoreline. The paramedics arrived as I pulled up.

The hospital called me an hour or so later to tell me that she had died. Her doctor thought she had suffered a stroke in the hypothalamus region, which had knocked out her thermostat. Her temperature had risen to 110°.

Even I, a nurse, didn't realize what the result would be if a stroke took place in that region, but it made sense. How mysterious is the human body! I was discovering that owning and running my own home for the elderly was schooling for me because I was constantly learning. I wanted desperately to be able to ward off these strokes among my elderly patients, but how to do it? Unfortunately, I had little time for speculation and reflection.

Another empty bed needed to be filled, and I had to get busy.

Hannah, one of the ladies on the waiting list, couldn't wait any longer. I had not visited her and had no idea what she was like; however, she was in the emergency room at the hospital and was being released. Her sister called me to see if I could help. I hesitated because I didn't like being rushed into making a decision about whether to take her or not but knew this lady needed help.

When I arrived at the emergency room, I never saw such a mess. One of the nurses I had known for a long time was there and started laughing. "Wait until you see this one!" she said.

What I saw was a little shriveled up piece of a human being who looked up at me. "Well, who are you?" she asked. I introduced myself and asked her if she would like to come home with me.

She didn't say, "NO!" she said, "HELL NO!" I sometimes got this reaction the first time I met potential residents. After all, I was representative of a drastic change in their lives. No wonder they resisted. Also, I've been told on occasion that I had a frightening, authoritarian look. I smiled at her.

Hannah's petite and perky face was rimmed with not one but two wool stocking caps. One was solid red and the other, blue and green striped. Her feet were wrapped in wool, and she had on a pair of too-large, hand-knitted slippers. Her body was covered with rags under a shabby, brown wool coat. Where had she found these excuses for clothing? And wool in Florida? Her filthy fingernails had not been cut for a long time. I would guess at two times in the tub before the dirt would soak and scrub off. Only then would I let her meet the other residents and socialize. I asked the nurse where she came from.

While hugging Hannah, she laughed and said, "The same place they all come from. Somebody calls HRS, they go out and root them out of their own homes, and they end up with me." She went on to say that Hannah's house was so bad that no human could live in it. They lost track of the count of cats, for when they opened the door, they ran. Hannah would not let the cats outside. The entire little house was their sandbox.

Hannah ate only because a neighbor would put a plate of food on the screen porch once a day. Hannah would not come out where anyone could see her. As a matter of fact, it had been a year or more since anyone had seen her, including her sister. Hannah was a weird one, that's for sure.

The nurse covered my car seat with disposable blue pads before we placed her in the front seat. She said little on the way home.

I called Lillie, the new girl I had recently hired, and asked her to have the bathroom ready with all the supplies we would need to give a ten-year, over-due bath. She laughed. I guess they all laughed at me, for I could really find the derelict ones. When we took Hannah into the house, we went straight to the bathroom and what a scene she created. It was pure pandemonium just to get her clothes off. They went straight to the dumpster.

All except for the wool hats. I told her I would wash them, but she didn't want to let them out of her sight. I carefully examined the caps for lice. There were none visible, but nonetheless they had to be washed immediately. After convincing her that her caps would be returned, I took them to the laundry. Next would be the bath. Hannah was none too pleased to get the bath, but a bath she would get! Her toenails were so long—at least two inches—I was afraid to cut them. It would take a podiatrist to get those nails off. After she soaked awhile in the tub, I used a brush to scrub off the crud. Then we cleaned the filth out from under her fingernails and cut off a half an inch. She didn't look much better when she was clean, but she smelled like a rose.

This lady was scrawny and crooked looking, bent like a dogwood tree. Because her toenails got in the way, she walked on her heels. Her belly stuck out, and she was sway-backed. Everything hung and swung—typical results of gravity. Somehow I felt we would have some good times with this neglected lady.

The next day her sister showed up in a Cadillac. She lived fairly close to me in a lovely home. I wondered how she had been able to allow her sister to live in squalor. How cold and calculating she seemed! I asked her to sign the papers, which she did, but she didn't want the responsibility of paying me. Certainly, Hannah didn't have the money to pay me, or so I thought. Then the sister produced a checkbook in Hannah's name, but no checks had been written in several months, nor were there entries or a balance. At this point, the sister realized she would have to straighten out Hannah's finances. She wrote me a check from her own account.

Hannah turned out to be a sweetheart. She was no trouble except at night. She would not use the bedside commode and would not wear a diaper. Maxcine had a time with her trying to keep her dry. She may have been a problem at night, but during the day she was a joy.

One day I watched her doodling on a piece of paper and realized she knew what she was doing. I bought her charcoals and paper to work on. For a while she continued to doodle but soon gave up any notion that she was going to draw, even though she had been an artist at one time, as I discovered.

Very soon I knew that something had to be done about her rotten teeth and terrible bad breath. I asked her sister if there was any money to pull her teeth but, of course, there wasn't. I found a dentist who would pull her six or seven teeth for only $200. If I had to, I would pay for the dentist in order to keep down odors and prevent infection in her body.

As it turned out, I was the one who paid the bill. I had a suspicion that

Hannah had money, but if she did, I would never know about it, and her sister was not going to spend a dime more than she had to on her.

Hannah mentioned her artwork was displayed in her sister's house. When I asked if we could go and see it, Hannah snorted and said she was not allowed in her sister's house. It seemed a feud had been going on for years. If Hannah couldn't go in, I was certainly out of luck.

In time Hannah became a little social butterfly in the home, entertaining the other residents with her witty conversation and small jokes. Happy hour was her favorite time of day.

All too soon her time with us was cut short. Several months later she died from complications of pneumonia, which developed suddenly. All of us were saddened to see her go. She was one of a kind, and, thankfully, she spent her last months in peace, dying with dignity.

Shoreline was a happy place. We had our share of tragedies but mostly there were good times, and the residents enjoyed themselves. They ate well, even though their families wanted reduced rates because they felt that their relatives at Shoreline wouldn't eat much. They would say, "Mom and Dad have always had small appetites. They won't eat what the others eat. Why should we have to pay for food they won't eat?" Contrary to what their relatives thought, the residents loved what we cooked. And their diet was one of the prime factors in increasing their mental capacity. I scoured the cookbooks looking for recipes that would please this diverse group with such varied taste buds. Thankfully, the Yanks soon learned to love beans and cornbread, and the southerners learned to love boiled potatoes if they were spiced well. They ate high protein, low fat, some complex carbohydrates, and a minimum of sugared desserts. I was very proud of the outcome.

Also, they slept without the aid of sleeping pills, and, I might add, their medications were limited to what the doctors felt they absolutely had to have. As a result most residents' minds became sharp and clear, though some were so confused, no amount of medication reduction could help them.

In addition to the other health-giving changes in the residents' lives, exercise was an integral part of the everyday routine. One of their favorite activities was a rhythm class. A volunteer missionary came in three times per week, bearing rhythm instruments, a keyboard, and a boom box. She would give the residents instruments, and they would sing and laugh, all the while keeping time to the music or rhythm. Even Timmy, my grandson, got into the action by directing the chorus.

Another aspect of everyday life in my home included freeing many of the residents from their drug dependencies. Usually, upon admission, I would be handed a huge checklist of the current medications for the patient, many of them, pacifying, calming drugs. I disagreed with pacifying the elderly through drugs, but received heavy-duty opposition from the doctors and the social workers.

They would say, "Be careful. If they aren't at least somewhat sedated, they will need much more care." Another doctor would say, "You are the one who has to take care of them," and "If I were you, I would want them calm," or "Why would you want to take them off the drugs? They are working."

I received similar responses from all of them. The doctors were totally against taking them off tranquilizers and sedatives. Granted, there are those who do need medication to calm them down, but not everybody over 65 years old needs to be calmed down. Finally, with doctors' reluctant agreement to reduce or stop giving tranquilizers, I felt ready to take the consequences because I was convinced most elderly people were over medicated.

As soon as I would get their systems cleared out, I could see improvement. They suddenly realized they had a name. They could remember the last place they lived, and eventually they could remember their mother's maiden name. This last bit of information had to be filled out on the HRS forms.

It was horrible what had been done to their memories. The tranquilizers had been prescribed because…"Mom won't sleep at night"…"Dad thinks he has to walk the streets"…"Can't you give her something so that I do not have to worry all the time?"

Even in nursing homes…yes, they are the worst. Before I became a home health nurse, I had worked in nursing homes, first as a nurse and later as administrator. I knew first hand that the night shift wouldn't come to work unless all the residents had a sleeping pill or tranquilizer because they wanted them in bed at a certain hour, so they didn't have to "fool" with them. One of problems was that there was never enough staff to make sure the patients would not wander around all night half naked, singing, muttering, or even yelling.

During the day administrators and directors of nursing wanted all residents looking good and calm in case someone important came in. In answer to a nurse's complaint they would ask, "Why don't you talk to their doctor about prescribing a mild calming medication for the patients?" Mild usually turned into wild doses far exceeding the maximum limit. The mood-altering drugs of choice included Malarial, Elavil, Thorazine, and, up to a point, Valium; to them add the heart medications, blood pressure pills, blood thinners, beta-blockers…the list goes on and on. The end result? An entire population of elderly rejects, zombies allowed to live only if they didn't bother anyone.

The prevailing attitude among the heads of the nursing homes and, in many cases, the doctors, was that "larger does are OK because the patients build up a tolerance and, therefore, need higher doses." Not true! The older the person is, the lower the dose of most medications should be because the elderly become more sensitive, not less sensitive to drugs.

As a nurse I had seen the bad effects of over medicating, including serious problems with medicines interacting, and these problems had always been a thorn in my side, so, once I was in a position where I could make a difference, I weaned my patients off as many drugs as possible and altered their diet to bolster mind and body functions. The changes for the better were profound and amazing. I wished these changes could have been done industry wide.

Now we had six residents at Shoreline, and I still had two on the waiting list. I had deliberately waited some time between accepting each of them because I needed to have an adjustment period with the new resident before admitting a new one. The next resident to come to live at Shoreline was Jock. His son in law filled out the appropriate papers and left as quickly as he could. Uh-oh! Red flags went up. Surely enough, Jock wore out his welcome fast.

It didn't seem he would cause trouble because he looked to be such a gentleman. He was different from most incoming residents in that he was impeccably groomed, tall, and tanned. He might have even been called good-looking. Since I had never had a man of his obvious caliber in the home, I felt there would be times when I would not know how to entertain him. In spite of my high regard for him, I would soon find out he had an ugly side.

One of our newer residents, Marie, was very pretty and meticulously dressed. Her hands were beautiful and well manicured. She walked like a debutante and spoke like Boston Knob Hill. Marie had been the heart of society before her mind started escaping her. She also had a beautiful Persian cat about half-grown.

Her kitty quickly became everybody's sweetheart until Jock beat it to death with his cane. The entire household was tremendously upset, and Marie was losing it. I had to send her to the doctor for medication to calm her down. She was frail and could not cope with violence. I sentenced Jock to his room and tried to reach his family, to no avail. The isolation worked…for awhile. I wondered if I should evict him, but with no family, my hands were tied.

Soon Jock became very agitated and angry; I didn't think I was going to be able to control him. The doctor was of little use. When I asked him to come to the home and adjudicate Jock as harmful to himself and others, he informed me he didn't carry a little black bag nor drive a horse and buggy. Having the doctor come to Shoreline would have been the easiest way to admit Jock into a state mental institution. I tried to transport him by ambulance to a psychiatric center, but the ambulance could not move him without his permission. He spat in the face of one of the attendants. I called HRS for their advice. The person I talked to didn't know what to tell me. I knew I was bound by law to remove anyone of his nature immediately. I called the police. A policeman came to Shoreline and saw the dead cat, but, because he didn't see Jock kill it, he could do nothing. He said he was sorry, and, besides, it was twenty minutes until 11:00 p.m., his quitting time.

Jock wouldn't go to bed and wanted to walk around. I was afraid he would harm someone since he was still highly agitated. Because I felt that he needed to be restrained, I asked John and Mike to come up from our house to help me. We sat him down in a recliner, tied his arms together, his feet to the bottom of the chair, and secured his body with a sheet wrapped around the chair. It took four of us to do this, and I did not feel secure that he would stay there. He was fighting mad but remained quiet.

It was about half an hour before he got his feet loose. Eventually he got his arms loose and none of us could keep him down. He turned the chair over on its side leaving us in harm's way while trying to upright him. Finally, after Jock gave John several blows, John asked me to turn him loose. I questioned his judgment but nothing else was working. I went behind him and untied the sheet. As he stood up and started to walk towards Mike swinging, John tripped him deliberately. He fell to the floor and struck his head on the baseboard. I checked him as John called the paramedics to tell them we needed assistance with a head injury. He just lay there. His pulse and respiration were good, but he was OUT! Suddenly I was a little frightened. I knew why John had tripped him. It was the only way we could get him out of Shoreline and into a mental-care facility, but, if the news ever got out, we were doomed.

The paramedics arrived in record-breaking time. Jock was conscious now and had a bump on his head. I asked them to take him, but they refused because the injury was not serious. I explained what had happened all afternoon and night. One of them radioed for police. They came. We all conferred on what I needed to do, but I explained to them that no one was cooperating, including the other police officers. We walked back to where he was sitting and he swung his foot with all of his strength and kicked one of the officers where the sun didn't shine. The policeman remained remarkably calm.

Jock was cuffed, placed in the back of the police car and the uninjured officer said, "Let's take a little ride, sir!" Although I left messages with Jock's family, no one ever contacted me. I often wondered whatever happened to him.

I could now turn my energies to the needs of the residents. Marie was broken hearted about her kitty…for a few minutes. She had the attention span of an ant. We approached her about a new kitty and her response was "Oh, where is the kitty?" Enough said about the cat.

Another new resident, Stuart, was referred to me by the hospital. His legal guardian was a private detective. I sensed right away that Stuart was not what he seemed, and that Harry, his guardian, was being evasive about something. They were both nice fellows and I enjoyed their presence. I was told Stuart did not have any family. In one way this was sad, but in another it was a blessing. No family, no heartbreaks.

I introduced him to Gig. They got along fine and frequently shared a beer. I could trust them to sit at the hamburger joint up the street for an hour or so.

Then Stuart started getting some strange visitors. Some were doctors, some were attorneys, and one was a judge. I called Harry to ask if there was something going on I should know about. He was stunned and knew nothing about all the visits. He came to see me the next day and finally told me the truth.

Stuart was one of the heirs of a large corporation, and was worth millions. He had been declared legally incompetent by the courts, and Harry was his guardian. The declaration was made because he had no family to manage his assets.

Apparently, some distant family members had crawled from under the rocks and were in the process of trying to seize Stuart's guardianship. My phone call was the first Harry had heard of their attempts. He told me not to let anyone visit Stuart without his permission. I honestly believed Harry cared about Stuart and was trying to protect him.

Unfortunately, the protection didn't last long. The next few months were disastrous to this little man. Although I could keep people from coming into the house, he was summoned to court over and over again. Lawyers and judges hounded him with questions, and poor Stuart became more and more confused, falling right into the incompetence trap his relations had lain for him. I watched a fun-loving man turn into a mere living shell, and there was nothing I could do.

In the end, the family won. They hauled Stuart off like a common criminal and placed him in a court-appointed institution to await his death. They didn't have to wait long. I read his obituary a few months later. No service was listed, just a request to donate to his favorite charity.

I was about to throw Margot into the bay, figuratively speaking, of course. There were times when she stretched my patience and sense of good will with her meanness and nastiness. I had to rotate the schedule so that someone was at my home both day and night. The staff hated to go down there because of her. Furthermore, her deposit would not even begin to cover the costs of the chairs and the carpet that would have to be replaced. I just had to find another place for her. So far Mandy had not kept her word about placing her somewhere else.

After I computed my loss with her, it meant I would have to get her out of there by the fifth of any one given month and not refund any of the rent that was paid for the month and keep the entire deposit. How frustrating!

Peggy was also a royal pain because she so closely mimicked Margot's toilet habits, but now that she had consented to wearing diapers, she could be tolerated. Somehow I knew she could do better and would do better eventually, but for now, she had, with the able assistance of Margot, totally ruined the carpet, so I would not let her go anyplace where there was carpeting. On the other hand, Nancy and Walter were pleasant to all of us and appreciated everything done for them. Their eyes revealed their pleasure as they twinkled all the time.

I had long since decided that this business definitely would be lucrative as long as I was willing to work and stay on top of things. This is why I looked twice at a stunning Victorian-style building while driving down toward the bay. I swung around the block and parked in front. It was for lease.

What I could see looking in the windows was enough to make me want to see more. It was huge inside and beautiful. The outside had wrap-around porches and a round tower. Suddenly, I had a dream! With a little work I could have a show place. The name "The Grand" popped into my head, and I knew I had to have it. I wanted the best place that could be had for the elderly, not a large place but one that would be stylish and upscale, one that I would be proud of, and possibly one that would become a legacy for my children.

I talked with Mike and John that night. They thought I would be biting off more than I could chew, and perhaps they were right. I was always on the lookout for a challenge, but I would learn sooner than later that I had created a greater challenge than I could possibly have foreseen. But then, in my innocence and enthusiasm, I honestly believed I could do the job, and perhaps I could have, had I gone at it slowly. Going slowly at anything was not my style and, as usual, I plunged right in. It would prove to be more than I could cope with, but I didn't know that then.

I had been able to build a waiting list for Shoreline, but I had heard the market was becoming saturated. I would have to do some research on this possibility before I could make a commitment to lease another place.

I returned home with my head full of Victorian dreams and came back to reality when I thought about Margot. She would have fit well into The Grand if she had not been depressed. I knew that her toilet behavior was not only continuing, but becoming worse. She could not make our lives any more miserable unless she tried to drown in her own excrement. This she almost succeeded in doing. It appalled me that a person with her fine head and education could develop such a despicable habit. She made the situation worse by rejecting the only friends she might have had by demeaning those who took care of her. I could have easily been her friend, but not under those circumstances. She was not senile as one might expect, depressed, yes, but not senile. This is where her depression had taken her.

When I went into Margot's room I thought she was sleeping, but she was almost comatose in that chair. We couldn't move her, and she would not or could not help us. Her vital signs were fairly normal, but there was no physical response. She seemed catatonic. I suspected she had had a stroke. When I called her doctor, he asked me to send her to the hospital.

A stroke was indeed the diagnosis. She died two days later.

I honestly felt relief that she had made her transition, mainly because her life had become so meaningless, but also because, as cold as it may seem, I wouldn't have to clean up after her anymore.

Now I needed to work on Peggy to help her change her toilet habits. If she improved, I thought, she could go to The Grand. Go to The Grand? Did this mean I had made my decision?

Chapter Six
The Encroachment

There are times when God outdoes Himself. I couldn't know ahead of time how much more I would gain over what I gave in caring for my newest resident, dear, sweet Laverne.

Her niece and nephew, who lived in Pennsylvania, were waiting for me to have an opening. As soon as I did, I called them, and they flew down to move her in.

They seemed to be devoted people. They were either sincere or trying to pull the wool over my eyes. Time would tell. Laverne, a feisty, little bitty thing full of hell, was delightful. She was also visually challenged. From future conversations with her, I would learn that she had combed the world.

On moving day, Laverne's nephew, Dan, backed a U-Haul truck up to the garage at Shoreline. The truck was full of furniture, clothing, appliances, a vacuum cleaner, boxes and boxes of pantry-shelf food, and at least ten grocery bags of food just bought. There were new sheets, blankets, spreads, new pillows, and mattress covers. Things were coming off the truck so fast I couldn't get in a word. What was I going to do with all of it?

Her niece, Arlene, just kept saying, "Laverne asked me to do this." I was overwhelmed with gratitude.

Arlene unpacked the groceries, and Dan brought a large box into the kitchen full of wine, champagne, scotch, and soda water. Arlene told me to go ahead and do whatever I had to do as she was going to fix food for a party, which would serve as our dinner. I made Laverne's bed, putting on two of the beautiful pink blankets and two of the pillows that had been brought. I took all of her clothing to the garage and explained that it would all be marked and washed before going into the closet. She didn't object to a bath and a Kwell treatment. I dried her short curls and put lotion on her body before taking her to the living room.

By now I was exhausted. For over two weeks I had been extremely busy interviewing for extra help, but not one person was qualified to work. I suppose I was just too picky. Kris helped a lot, and I knew Maxcine would be there faithfully for the night shift by 10 p.m., but I would really have to find more help soon.

Arlene brought Laverne a scotch and soda. I took a glass of wine, and sat down in the kitchen to watch Arlene. I couldn't believe the food she was preparing. She must entertain a lot, for she knew how to prepare food for a party and was a good hostess.

There were delicious-looking vegetables and a special dip I watched her make. On a large platter were cheese and crackers, pâté, chips, and various kinds of hors d'oeuvres. She had also thought to bring pretty party plates, cups, and napkins. The food was set up beautifully, and a tray held wine glasses bubbling over with champagne and sparkling soda. When Kris came in to work, she was astonished at all the food and how it was prepared. The punch bowl, full of fresh fruit, sat in the center of the table with small plastic bowls stacked neatly on one side and dishes of rolled ham, cream cheese, and meatballs in sweet and sour sauce on the other. For dessert there were custard pastries and fruit. I called Mike and John to come up. What a feast!

We did all of the paperwork, including the burial arrangements. The latter was never a good sign. It had been my experience that I would never see the family again when this happened. I was seldom wrong.

Later that night before leaving, they told me they would be back at Christmas but would send packages often for Laverne. I received a check each month; however, no letters, cards, or packages ever arrived for Laverne.

Everybody loved her, not only for her bright spirit, but especially for her entertaining stories. This lady had lived a life few would ever experience. She had been a chorus girl in both Goldwin's and Ziegfeld's Follies and prior to that was in Vaudeville. Then she went on to become a cruise director of the Queen Mary and the USS Constitution, serving on them for nearly thirty years. The world was her home, for she traveled almost the entire surface. I asked her once why she had never married.

She told me, "Now why would I want to mess up a good life? I could brag that I had made love to a man in every country in this world. I loved my life." With that I couldn't argue.

The months rolled by until December, the month of gift giving. You would think I would be grateful for my blessings, and I would have been if I wasn't losing the Shoreline residents for various reasons. Now the only one left was Laverne, and, as a result, my income was severely curtailed. Three persons were scheduled to come in January, but this was Christmas. Even with curtailed finances I felt I had to hire another person for the January influx of residents. I hired Janice to help out on the day shift. She was fairly good but did not want to do everything that had to be done such as working on Christmas Eve. In this she was not alone, but I was. I was alone with Laverne at Shoreline on Christmas Eve when I should have been home with my family. I asked Laverne to go home with me, but she wouldn't go. She told me what she wanted to do, and that was to stay at Shoreline. We stayed.

We watched *Holiday Inn* with Fred Astaire and Marjorie Reynolds. She knew the entire score and frequently sang along. During the movie she made the comment: "That Ginger Rogers can really dance." I wasn't sure if she had seen the movie so many times years before when she *could* see or if she was truly seeing the dancing at this moment. I told her it was not Ginger Rogers who was dancing. She leaned forward and gazed at the screen and said, "Yes, I can see now. It's Marjorie."

It took a few moments to make me realize that she might actually be able to see. I asked her what she was watching and she replied, "They are playing in the snow. Can't you see?" Yes I could see. They were playing in the snow. I was astounded.

When the movie was over, she looked up toward the windows that surrounded the Florida room and stood up a little. When I reached to help her, she said in a small voice: "Carolyn, they have turned on the lights for Christmas."

I walked with her over to the windows where she could get a better view. It was then that I knew for sure that her vision had returned. She really could see, I finally realized, as she pointed out the many lights in the neighborhood. I had goose bumps all over my body. I called home and asked my family to come up.

When they walked into the room Laverne was saying to me: "Carolyn, I have done everything I ever wanted to do, have seen everything there is to see, and have loved my share and been loved back. Being able to see tonight is a message from God."

Alyssa said, "Ma, can she really see?" I walked Laverne to the windows again. She pointed to the pier and remarked about the different colored lights on the boats.

"Does that answer your question?" Laverne asked.

"Yes, indeed it does," I said, marveling at the miracle.

"Carolyn, I would like to have a radio in my room tonight so that I can listen to Christmas music." She could have asked for a sleigh and reindeer, and I would have tried to get them for her.

After my family left, I walked Laverne to her bedroom to prepare her for bed. I placed the radio by her bed and set it to a station that played Christmas carols. The radio played all night, and a light was left on in the bathroom.

When she was asleep, I went down to my house for a few minutes. My other daughter said she would go up for awhile to allow me to enjoy a bit of Christmas in my home, but after the miracle of Laverne's vision returning, what more could I enjoy?

We ate and listened to music before I went back.

When I awoke on the couch the next morning, Janice was just arriving for work. It was really early, but she wanted to relieve me so I could go home for the day. What a nice Christmas gift.

Laverne never ate another bite of food and only had fluids to keep her mouth wet. She was put in the hospital for the entire month of February and part of March. While she was able to speak, she told the doctor not to give her IV or tube feedings because she didn't want artificial means of keeping her alive. The doctor honored her request.

For every day an elderly person remains in a home for care, she or he is subject to a miscarriage of justice. It is unfortunate that many of the elderly are not allowed to die with dignity. Compassion would compel me to bring Laverne back to my home, who I knew would be dead in a few days. I felt I had to take her out of the hospital, even though Medicare refused to cover her expenses at Shoreline because she was no longer eligible for benefits. The hospital could have kept her and eaten the charges. After all, she had already been there for a month and a half, but no, the hospital was discharging her. In essence she was being sent out to pasture to die. The family could have agreed to pay for the few days she was back in my care before she died if they had cared to do it. Where were these good people who loved her so much and were going to take care of her so well? I hadn't heard from them since I called to tell then Laverne was in the hospital. Prior to that, I had called to ask where the Christmas box and card they had promised to send were. When I phoned, they were too drunk to talk to me and placed me on a speakerphone so that I could hear the activity of a house full of people. Finally, Arlene spoke to me. She swore she had sent the box. We never received it. This happened a week or two before Laverne went to the hospital. This was when Laverne started to feel she had outlived her usefulness.

Laverne arrived at my private home from the hospital in an ambulance. The doctor had warned me that Laverne would be emaciated, so I knew what she would look like. The other residents would not be allowed to see her.

I put her into a spare bedroom, one that was rarely used, and in a bed padded with sheepskin covered with blue waterproof pads in case she was incontinent. It was highly unlikely because she had taken nothing by mouth, tubes, or IV's in over a month.

She was covered with a blanket when they brought her in. All I could see was her face, which was shallow, sunken, and gray. Her hair had turned from brown streaked with gray to all white. She had lost so much of it that there was barely any to see.

When the ambulance attendants laid her down in the bed, one of them remarked that she was so fortunate to be able to die with dignity. I started to correct them, but what was the use? I pulled the sheet down to look at her body. One of them turned his head and grimaced.

The other said, "Oh my God!"

Her body was mottled with black, dark blue, purple, and cream spots. There was only a skeleton frame, no muscle. The veins and arteries were lying on top of the bones and were prolapsed. I could even see the sciatic nerve. It was sad she couldn't have died sooner. I knew she had wanted to die months before now.

It was unusual that her body didn't emit an odor. This was good as my family wouldn't be able to complain. Instead I heard these words: "You aren't even being paid for this!" However, for me, money was not the issue, as I could not let her die with strangers. She had no one but me now. I would not let her down.

I wouldn't let anyone else take care of her because of infection control. By morning, what flesh was left was falling off her body, leaving open sores I couldn't treat. I tried to turn her, but doing so was difficult and became more and more so. Any part of her body that she lay on was down to the bone by the time I turned her again. I didn't know how much longer she could last, but I prayed it wouldn't be long. She did not deserve to live like this.

The doctor was in contact with me daily, and she would have done anything to help me. When death came, it was of the utmost importance that she would tell the paramedics that she would sign the death certificate. She was fully cooperative.

There was a strict procedure I had to follow when I had a death in the home. First, I had to call the paramedics. Doing this seemed odd to me. In Florida it was against the law for an R.N. with a bachelor's degree to pronounce a person dead unless the R.N. was also the director of nursing in a nursing home. However, paramedics with only certificates could pronounce a person dead. Does this law make sense? Second, the paramedics had to call in the police, and the doctor had to sign the death certificate. If it was an expected death the mortician was then called. Third, if the doctor could not be reached or had not previously agreed to sign the death certificate, and, if the death was unexpected, the coroner was required to go to the deceased. When he or she was finished, the mortician would be called.

A hard and fast rule is to get Hospice involved when you suspect a person might be terminal. Hospice doesn't have to call anyone and is allowed to pronounce a person dead. The person doing the pronouncing may or may not be a nurse. The person could even be a volunteer—a volunteer for God's sake! This law would be hilarious if it weren't so illogical and ridiculous.

The second day Laverne was with me, I knew death was imminent. I called the doctor to let her know. She asked me if I had called Laverne's family. I told her that I had not heard a word from them after leaving a message on their machine the day Laverne came back to me.

She said, "The daughter and her husband sure are a strange pair, aren't they?"

I could only agree, but I reminded her that the checks they wrote to pay me and her were still in Laverne's name and were written on a local bank. "You can bet they will be here when she dies," I said. We both laughed a little, knowing how right I was.

I cleaned her up as well as I could and covered her so she looked good. Strangely enough, her face had not been affected by the blotching. I talked to Laverne as if she were there with me and always gave her a kiss on the cheek when I left the room. She continued to breathe until 11:05 a.m. on March 18th, two days after I had brought her into my home.

I called the paramedics and told them it was an expected death and then called her doctor. She told me to have the paramedics call her when they arrived.

I recognized the paramedics as they had been to my house before on other errands. I took them into Laverne's room. They listened for a heartbeat and checked the carotid pulse. Of course, there was none. When they saw her body, the only reaction was to ask me how long it had been since she had taken any nourishment. I told them and then handed her chart to one of them. They looked it over and went to the kitchen to call the doctor, who confirmed it was an expected death. She told the paramedic she would sign the death certificate.

Next, a police car with two officers arrived. I showed them Laverne's room. One of the paramedics followed them in.

I overheard one of the officers say, "This looks more like a homicide than an expected death."

The paramedic argued with him; right then I knew there was going to be trouble. This time I picked up the phone and called my lawyer, Barnaby. He said his assistant, Charley, would be right out there. I sat down at the dining room table with the other paramedic. He was embarrassed because he knew my reputation was good. He fidgeted over some paperwork, and, before I could say anything, he radioed for his lieutenant to come out.

In a short time he arrived, and I was grateful that it was someone I knew. He asked the paramedic what was going on, and they walked toward the bedroom. The paramedic told him the police didn't want to accept the fact that this was an expected death and that the lady had starved herself to death. He shook his head and opened the bedroom door.

Although their voices were lowered, I heard one policeman say, "I'm taking the owner in. I don't like the way this woman looks."

The lieutenant responded, "I'm telling you this lady died of natural causes. The doctor has already confirmed it. This lady starved herself. She looks like she has not eaten or taken fluids in a month or longer. What more can I tell you?"

They were really arguing now, and it appeared the policemen were not going to accept the lieutenant's word.

As they walked out of Laverne's room the lieutenant said, "Make up your damned minds! I don't have time to put you through med school, and I have known the owner for years. Besides, residents are no good to her dead. She only gets paid if they are alive."

From where I was sitting, I could see them walking down the hall toward me and, at the same time, I could see Charley at the front door.

I let him in. He went straight to the policemen and told them to either charge me or drop everything.

One of them said to the lieutenant: "We're going to take you at your word and you'd better be right."

I guess they had phoned the coroner from the bedroom, for he was the next to arrive. He walked in to the bedroom and said without hesitation, "She thought she would die fast if she stopped eating, huh?"

He walked out shaking his head sadly and told me to call the mortician. I did and then sat down with a stiff drink.

The paramedics left. The lieutenant stayed a while with me until the mortician finished. He took Laverne away in a black bag.

I called the doctor back to tell her what had happened. She said, "Carolyn, there is a God...and there are jerks! You have just been exposed to both." The lieutenant left. I thanked him and expressed my appreciation.

Afterwards I cleaned up the room, stripped the bed, and put Laverne's clothing in a box. The doctor had contacted Dan and Arlene. Apparently, they were going to come down the next day.

All I had to do now was find a way to keep my family from finding out she had died in the house. I had promised them it would not happen. I ended up telling them she died in the ambulance as I attempted to send her back to the hospital.

As expected, Dan and Arlene arrived the next morning. They immediately asked for the deposit back. After I handed them the check, they gave me a small pile of envelopes.

Arlene said, "These are thank you notes from Laverne. Would you see that they get to your employees?" Each one contained a measly five-dollar bill. A five-dollar bill was adequate thanks? I guess they thought so. I didn't.

They wanted nothing of Laverne's. Dan shook my hand and they left. Neither of them thanked me. This man ran a major airline. I'm sure glad he wasn't my boss.

Chapter Seven
Ilga

Shoreline had only six residents. If I was giving any thought at all to opening up my Victorian dream home, I needed to show more motivation. Because of fatigue and stress, I had become apathetic about admitting new residents. The three at my home and the other six would not provide enough income for me to open The Grand. I needed a waiting list of at least fifteen people. I had not pursued the idea of acquiring my dream home as yet but surmised it would safely hold thirty-five or forty people.

One of the social workers called me looking for placement for a 90-year-old female. She sounded as if she would be pleasant and fairly easy to care for, so I agreed to come and see her. I liked these pre-admission inspections. They were fun and usually challenging. I took whomever they had most of the time because I was always in need of money, and the ones I inspected weren't usually the troublemakers.

As I pranced into the room, a very tall lady stuck out her hand to me. In a very strong accent, she said, "I'm Ilga, and who are you?"

I introduced myself and asked how she was. Once she started talking, she didn't stop. This should have been an obvious clue to trouble for this administrator. You might even say I was stupid! I would live to regret saying yes…again. I seemed destined to destroy my sanity.

Her accent was thick with a European tongue. I knew immediately she was simple and somewhat pretentious but, at the same time, someone I wanted to protect. You might even say I fell in love with her from the start.

When I asked her if she would like to come home with me, she said, "Aya. Do you live close to me? Can we go dancing and out to eat?"

My knowledge of this femme fatale was limited at this time. It would appear that I would have to start digging for more information. She was sure to have an interesting history.

Although she had a legal guardian, she became my responsibility the moment she entered my door. It only took me less than a month to fully realize that her graceful, slender body didn't just happen. She had developed it over years of walking and eating meagerly.

The first time she left home, I was totally amazed at her strength. One day she walked nearly five miles barefoot. At the entrance to a Dali museum, she was recognized by a security guard. She had frequently gone there and apparently followed her nose. The police were called, and they brought her home. They had been looking for her as long as we had, which was for several hours. Thus began her rap sheet, which would grow into a book before her life was over.

There was no way to discipline her. She could not understand that she had done something wrong. Her feet were badly blistered, which needed my immediate attention. Then I wrote a plan of care to prevent this from happening again and again and again!

Ilga's escapades seemed to have purpose. She loved a good time, so perhaps she searched for the source of her memories. Or maybe she longed to find her beloved spouse who had died several years before. No matter what she seemed to be looking for in her mental and physical wanderings, she would never find it on this earth. As time went on, only constant monitoring prevented her from wandering away. Even so, she was not always safe or out of harm's way.

At night we put large cowbells on the doors. I was not allowed to put chains or deadbolts on them because they were against fire regulations. It was okay for the elderly to walk out of the door and get hit by a car or for undesirables to enter the home because it was easy prey, but, according to HRS, a dead bolt or a chain would prevent them from getting out in the event of a fire. The cowbells made a loud noise, but she managed to escape in spite of them on several occasions. I also put a smaller one around her neck so that it looked like a necklace. She was so graceful she could walk all over the house and there would never be a sound from the little bell. I put a bracelet I.D. on her. She would remove it once out of doors. I took her picture as I did with all residents and kept several copies in a file for the police so that they would know what she looked like. The police were grateful, but, after a while, they didn't need a photograph. They all knew what she looked like.

She scared the hell out of me. The bay was in our backyard and there was a certain part of town she should not be in if she accidentally turned the wrong way. Restraints were not the answer. She was obviously trying to get home.

I brought some of her belongings to the home thinking she would adjust to them and think she was home, but she would just look at things and smile. She could not comprehend anything beyond the moment.

All of the staff did things to keep her busy and tired. Sometimes she slept; sometimes she was awake for days without sleep.

Ilga would dance all day to music. I looked forward to the evenings when the residents were finally all in bed. If I was on duty, I took my time and tried to relax them with soft music and hot tea or cocoa. They always had special snacks before going to bed. All of them were usually ready to call it a day except when Ilga wasn't sleepy.

I remember one particular evening when I was looking forward to crashing on the floor with the movie I wanted to watch. Things were going pretty smoothly with bedtime, and I was making good time with my chores. When I finished, they were all sleeping as I closed the doors and turned the TV on. I grabbed several pillows and made myself a nest on the floor. It didn't take long before I was thoroughly engrossed in the film and oblivious to what was going on around me.

After a while, despite my focus on the film, I felt a presence in the room. Nothing I wanted to leave the movie for, but something was trying to get my attention. I quickly turned my head around in time to see a black cloud pass over me. I was so startled, I jumped up, my heart pounding, and turned toward the 'apparition.' ILGA! She was swinging her legs so high she would be competition for the Rockettes. She had dug out one of the black chiffon dresses I had kept for her in order for her to feel more secure. She called these dresses her dancing dresses. They had very full skirts, and she loved to twirl in them. The tails of the skirts were what had gone over my head.

The next day I moved her to my home thinking that there were more people to watch her there. She moved in with Nancy and Peggy. Also, I figured that I could put chains and bolts on my own doors. It did work out better until my little three-year old grandson, Timothy, caught Ilga trying to get the front door open one day. Ilga was pulling with all her weight but that door wouldn't open. Timothy very politely dragged a chair to where she was and said, "Ilga, climb up there and take the chain down." She didn't understand him at first, but his little mind kept on until she did.

I was washing dishes in the kitchen and didn't see what was going on. Timothy came into the kitchen to me to tell me Ilga was outside. By the time I dried my hands, she was almost out of sight and had those black dresses thrown over her arm. I ran up the street, retrieved her, and once again brought her home.

Normally, I did not have employees at night at my home. There had not been a need until now because I slept in one of the guest rooms close to the residents; however, now that I had Ilga, I was scared she would get outside, so I put one of my employees on duty there at night. I put a twin bed against the front door and asked the employee on duty to please sleep on it to prevent Ilga from getting out the door. Ilga had not the vaguest idea of how to open the glass sliding doors, and the door into the kitchen was locked at night. This was the only way she could get to the garage door. I did feel more secure than at the other house.

All this was not as good as it sounded, for in the daytime people were in and out and she had to be watched closely.

Ilga would be with me for a long time. She touched the lives of all of us and was loved by all despite her escapades, which, by the way, did not end here.

Chapter Eight
Naomi

I respected the social worker at the hospital where I received most of my admissions and realized that she had a job to do. Her priority was to place patients who had been in the hospital so long that Medicare disallowed any further coverage. This meant that the heat was on for the social workers.

Nursing homes charged an average of $4000 a month plus expenses for private pay. There aren't many elderly who can afford this amount, and few, if any, have insurance eligible for nursing home care. For them to be eligible for Medicaid—the state insurance program that provides medical care to the indigent—their income must be at or below poverty level. Then there are the in-betweens who have too much income to qualify for Medicaid and not nearly enough to go into a nursing home at the private pay rate. This is where an Adult Living Facility comes in to play, that is, if the residents do not need much care. They are allowed to have assistance only. The problem is that the people who write regulations have obviously never taken care of an elderly person and in all probability have not ever been around anyone elderly. It is incredible what can be interpreted from the regulations, and a person needs to be a college graduate to implement them.

The social worker called me when there was a tough one to be placed, and, if I could, I would take the person. This business is no different from any other. It takes back scratching to survive. By helping her, I knew when a good paying one came along, I would be the first one called. Also, I did my share of public relations. I was not afraid to send flowers for special occasions or to take down a basket of fruit and goodies to thank the department. If they wanted imported beer, that's what they got. It was a dog-eat-dog world out there, and I intended not only to survive but to succeed in it.

When I was called about Naomi, I felt sorry for her. The social worker associate who called described her as a little bit of a lady, weighing barely sixty-five pounds, with a wisp of white hair and big brown eyes. She could walk and feed herself. This met the basic requirements for placement into an ALF. She was on no medications and went to the bathroom with assistance. This was a relief. I surely didn't need anyone else in diapers. Naomi's rent would be paid by a legal guardian, and he had agreed to my usual fee of $900 a month plus any expenses for diapers or bed pads. Her having a guardian was a relief to me because I could always depend on legal guardians to pay on time and to take good care of their wards.

My procedure was to have the guardian inspect the facility and meet with me and the other residents to assure the new person would be able to socialize. While I was trying to explain this on the phone to the associate social worker, she sounded antsy about the placement and a little nervous as she asked me if I would phone her back that day. I told her I would call her as soon as possible.

The call to her guardian was pleasant. He said he would be over around dinnertime. This was appropriate. There had been so much bad publicity about the care and treatment of the elderly, one could never be too careful. Most of the licensed places barely fed residents enough to keep their bodies going, and he apparently was conscientious enough to care that his ward received good nourishment.

I had been unable to visit Naomi at the hospital as I was on duty and had to cook dinner. My policy was NOT TO ALLOW ANYONE IN, SIGHT UNSEEN. I broke my own rules this time, and my life would never be the same.

Mr. Anderson arrived on time. He was a rather good-looking man in his seventies, clean, well-dressed, and well-groomed. His mannerisms pointed to a quality background. We went through the formalities of introductions, and I asked him to wait for a few minutes until I could make sure everyone was dressed. Some of them have been known to strip when they were least expected to. The coast was clear, and I began to bring the residents to the dinner table. He watched every step I took. When they were all seated, I served the plates with the steaming hot food. Tonight it was stuffed peppers, mashed potatoes, ford hook lima beans, and a carrot and raisin salad. It was hard to get them to eat raw vegetables, but I had learned that if the carrots were grated fine enough, they loved them. There were also corn muffins and a fruited Jell-O with whipped cream for dessert. I was alone until seven o'clock when Linda came in, but I had a system and could easily handle serving dinner.

I watched Mr. Anderson as he took in the sights and sounds. Thank goodness the residents were behaving tonight. Everyone was pleasant and busy eating.

I escorted him throughout the home, pointing out various things that I knew he would not see in other homes such as matching sheets and comforters, only two residents to a room, and one private room. He was impressed with the fact that I was an R.N. with years of experience and great references. I gave him the menus to read and a packet with all the paperwork he and I had to comply with. While he was reading, I assisted those who needed help at the table. They were eating heartily tonight and were not screaming or throwing food. I thought of having a guest every night if it would maintain control! Mealtime was actually pleasant.

Mr. Anderson said, "Do you have enough for me to have a pepper?" I was thrilled to pieces that he would ask. Most guardians and family members would wait outside until the meal was over.

"Of course," I said, "May I fix you a full plate?"

He was delighted and replied, "My wife will probably have something to say about it as she is waiting dinner for me, but, yes, I would love that." I fixed two plates and we sat down to eat in the kitchen. We enjoyed the meal and he gobbled up all of his food.

We completed the paperwork over dessert and coffee. When he left, we shook hands and he made it clear that I could call him at any time.

I asked him if there was anything he wanted to add to what the social worker had told me and he said, "She has been in a mental institution, but the social workers feel she should do well in this type of environment." He thanked me again for the meal and was most complimentary.

I called the social worker the next morning to make arrangements for the transfer. Naomi had already been discharged and was waiting for me. On the drive to the hospital, I kept thinking of all that could go wrong, accepting someone I hadn't personally visited with and how difficult it would be to get rid of a person who didn't fit in or was unacceptable because of bad behavior. Had I made a big mistake?

One of the nurses took me to Naomi's room and called for a wheel chair to take her down to the car. As we approached the door to her room, I heard a blood-curdling scream. I know I was jolted back a foot or more. I looked at the nurse. She said nothing. The screams grew louder as we got closer. This was not uncommon with the elderly who frightened easily when away from their normal environments. However, these screams meant business. They were loud and sounded painful. What in the hell was wrong? The nurse still hadn't said anything, so I decided it was time for me to make a move.

"Do you have a problem, child?" I asked the nurse.

"You might say so." she answered

If I had had any brains, I would have turned around and headed for the nearest exit. There was something telling me that my meeting with Naomi would not be pleasant. It wasn't! That woman was yelling for no reason, and, when I did get inside the door where I could see her, she very clearly yelled, "You goddamn son of a bitch!" I would not forget this voice for a long time. I went to her and stood where she could clearly see me, although she tried to hide her face, and I spoke a phrase to her that I hoped would sink into her brain. As clearly as I could, I told her that I had no intentions of listening to her rotten mouth, and, as far as I was concerned, she could stay in the hospital.

With that, I turned and went out the door. The nurse asked me to wait, and the social worker was standing in the hall. I stopped. I heard the nurse say to Naomi: "You had a good home to go to and now she won't take you."

"Carolyn, don't leave. Let's go someplace to talk." said the social worker as she followed me down the hall.

Quite frankly, I had nothing to say. I couldn't take her home. They gave me a song and dance that could convince Frank Sinatra to marry Dean Martin. I was told to ask for more money and to put her in my private room. Money could not buy silence, and a private room would not keep her screams out of the rest of the house. They convinced me to at least go back into the room. I did. She didn't scream.

She looked up at me and said, "I'll be good. I won't scream anymore."

I took a close look at her. She looked like a shriveled up child in the fetal position. Her hair was white and tied back in a bun. She was clean. Obviously the nurses had been taking good care of her, for she had a glow to her face much like a model in an advertisement for face cream. Her beady brown eyes were staring at me, and she was trembling under the sheet. I suppose if I were 93 years old and stuck in a hospital with nowhere to go, I would be trembling, too.

I told her I would take her home with me. She opened her mouth and let out a bit of a squeal. I simply raised my eyebrows and she stopped. Well, that worked—this time. The nurse put her in the wheel chair, covered her up, and then handed me a small plastic bag that contained the only belongings Naomi had in the world.

As soon as the elevator door opened, she started moaning, and I could tell that she was about to start screaming. I said, "Naomi, if you open your mouth, I will walk out of here, and the nurses can take you back upstairs."

With this in mind, she screamed at the top of her lungs, "You mother fucking son of a bitch, you're not going to take me to your home for my money. God will strike you dead. Help! Help! Help! She is kidnapping me! Please anybody! Get this bitch away from me!" And again she screamed at the top of her lungs.

I looked at the nurse and said, "You can take her back upstairs. I will not tolerate this." I turned to walk away. As I did, I realized that the nurse had not said a word. Did she take me for some kind of fool?

Someone touched my arm. It was a doctor I had known for years. He had apparently agreed to follow her care at my home, but he sure had a perplexed look on his face. I turned to greet him, still hearing Naomi in the background for the nurse had not taken her back upstairs. She had probably been threatened with her job if she didn't get Naomi into my car.

"Let's go for a cup of coffee, Carolyn," the doctor said. Nothing was going to make me change my mind about that old woman. She was out for blood. However, a cup of coffee couldn't hurt.

He gave her history. She had been in a state mental hospital three times, each time discharged as suitable for a home situation. The first time she was forty years old and had a nervous breakdown because she had been jilted. The second time she was seventy years old and lost it again because she was left standing at the altar. Then she was rejected a third time, again at the altar. Her situation was truly sad and pathetic.

This is the story the doctor told me. There was a fairly young man, perhaps in his twenties, who lived in Naomi's neighborhood. Apparently there were a lot of elderly widows who lived on the street, and this young man helped them with their trash, yard work, and odd jobs. They paid him small fees for his help. Naomi wanted more. First she had him paint the outside of the house and then the inside. She paid him a small amount but not even close to what he earned. She was taking up more of his time than he could give. He tried to pull away, but, from what I was being told, she was a spiteful little devil. When she asked him to take her on a shopping trip to pick out some new furniture, he agreed.

When they arrived at a nearby store, she asked him to pick out what he wanted, for he would be living there. He immediately had a panic attack and took her home as fast as he could take her. I was told that he said he'd be going back to school and would be too busy to do anything else for the ladies. As in the old clichéi, "Hell hath no fury like a woman scorned."

The lady who had told this story to the doctor didn't stop there.

Apparently Naomi wasn't dissuaded in her goal to win the young man. She bought the furniture, a new wardrobe of clothing for him, and, for herself, a wedding dress. She made arrangements for the wedding, even though she knew the young man had left home. From the church where she was left standing for the third time, she was taken to Chattahoochee State Hospital again and from there to the local medical hospital. The State Hospital couldn't take her back because she was not harmful to herself or to others.

The doctor looked at me and said, "Carolyn, there is no place we can put her where she will not be abused. I trust you and your staff."

"But doctor, you've heard her. In all my years of caring fro the elderly, I've never heard such filth. How am I supposed to manage her?"

"I will give you all the medications the law will allow and will give you orders for IM (intra-muscular) injections when necessary, but I have a feeling that you can quiet her down without medications."

I sat for a while. I just didn't know what to do. This doctor was a saint, and the hospital had been good to me, but I knew what was in store for all of us.

In spite of my doubts, I decided to take her because I had already made a commitment and didn't want to go back on my word.

The doctor gave me a hug and told me he would tell the floor to bring her down.

I stood by the car as the nurse brought her over and attempted to put her in the car. She pushed herself down to the street and out of the wheel chair. I asked a stranger who walked by if he would just stand there to verify that we were not killing her. He laughed and gave me a business card. With all of our strength, the two of us got her in the car and fastened the seat belt. I gave the card to the nurse and asked her to give it to the social worker, just in case.

As soon as I started the car, Naomi began screaming again. After only a mile, a policeman stopped me, and he was not at all sympathetic He checked me out first and then called the hospital. When he came back to the car he was smiling. "You have some reputation lady. They think you are a saint."

"Are you sure they didn't say fool…I have her and they don't."

He wished me luck and drove off. I had no sooner started up the car when she started her damn screaming again. This time I stopped the car. I got out and told her that I would put her out on the street if she opened her mouth again. She spit in my face, and I, with my red-hair temperament, spit back in her face. She screamed and spit back at me. I ducked and the spit hit the seat. The screaming became much louder. All my life I had learned to walk away from situations I could not handle, but my temper had never been tried like this.

I got out of the car and walked back to a store half a block away and called the home for help. When Sam came, I was so upset I was shaking. He looked at her before I had a chance to warn him that she hated men. It was too late. She started shaking her fists at him and screaming profanities while trying to get the car door open.

"Carolyn, have you lost your mind? What in hell do you think we will do with her?"

I didn't have time to answer. Someone had called the police, and one was there. I had to go through all of it again. He called and found out I was not lying, that Naomi was certifiably nuts. I explained we only had a few blocks to go. He followed me home and went inside. Kris put Naomi to bed while I called in her medications to the pharmacy and said I needed them immediately.

Naomi would not only become a part of our lives, she would influence the residents into thinking they had already died and gone to HELL. We endured her only by the grace of God. There were times when I wasn't sure that God was a part of her life.

I found a wonderful lady volunteer who played the electric piano and sang. She put on a minstrel show of religious ragtime, using her tambourines and a zither. She taught the residents to keep time, which created a show stopper. This pretty little lady gave new life to those who were despondent. She was so well liked I booked her in three times a week.

She arrived one day with several friends she introduced to me and asked if they could visit the people there. I cheerfully invited them in. It seemed they were missionaries who were on their way to the South Pacific, and they had just brought their schooner in to the marina downtown to refuel and to get supplies. They had some wonderful stories to tell the residents, stories I thoroughly enjoyed. The music was loud and well received; everyone was bouncing around. I was so taken with these people that I had not noticed two of them were in Naomi's room.

While I was preparing some refreshments, one of them came into the kitchen and asked me if I knew that one of the ladies was possessed. I joked that all of them were, in one way or the other, possessed by someone or something. He looked exhausted as he said to me, "The lady in the back room is demonized." I was so taken aback, I couldn't respond.

"Ma'am, she is so possessed, I would be afraid to have her around other people."

I looked at him and replied, "Well sir, we have had her for a spell and the only way the others have been affected is that they want to kill her for that infernal screaming."

"Now, you see what I mean? They are already showing signs of the Devil getting them." This minister was white as a sheet. Could he be serious? His hands were trembling.

By now the conversation had to be changed, but he was not going to let this subject go, so I said to him: "You are a minister, why don't you either exorcise her or help me make arrangements. After all, God has to help the devil out of her, and he will need the assistance of a man of God." As I expected, he left me, rounded up his missionary brood, and hustled them out the door. An exorcism in a home for the elderly! Fraid not! I wanted to keep my license and could just imagine how quickly this news would travel to HRS.

Some of the staff had overheard him talking about possession and surprisingly agreed with him, especially Maxcine, who worked nights and vowed never to sleep again as long as Naomi was in the house.

Actually, exorcism didn't sound like a bad idea. We had a major problem with her, and maybe God freeing her from the Devil was the answer. I did have the house blessed by a Catholic priest, a Rabbi, and a Baptist minister. It certainly did no harm.

There were moments when Naomi acted half-way human. She called me on the phone during one of the times I had placed her in the mental hospital and begged me to come and get her. I'm sure one of the attendants dialed the numbers for her, but there was a conversation— yes, a two-party exchange.

She was pleasant and asked a pertinent question: "Do you think I could come back to your house if I promise to behave myself?"

I was afraid to be negative for fear of undoing whatever they had managed to do with her. However, I believe in treating people honestly, not glossing over the facts. I didn't want Naomi to believe everything would be OK, when I knew damn well situations could alter all that had been done. I told her I would have to think about it. There was no sense in trying to get a commitment out of her, for she would not be able to honor it.

She proceeded to tell me about the food, the exercise program, the group sessions, and the nice spirit of the nurses. I thought to myself, if they knew what was good for them, they had better be good to her! Times like this confirmed her diagnosis as a paranoid schizophrenic, but later we would find out much more about her diagnosis.

I always considered myself a working administrator. I would sometimes do everything that had to be done: cook the meals, bathe the residents, dress them, do all the personal hygiene care, clean the home, including the bathrooms, strip the beds, and vacuum. I could do all of this and have time to spare, but I had the incentive. It was my home.

On one such day, I was about to give Naomi a bath when a visitor came to see one of the residents. I knew her well, but I didn't know if she had heard Naomi scream before, and Naomi was sure to scream when I gave her a bath. I didn't know the lady had been there before when Naomi had a bath, for if I had known, I would not have been in such a tizzy. I'm sure she was laughing at me, for it was obvious what I had to do.

She finally said, "Carolyn, I have heard her before, and I know no one is trying to kill her. Just go ahead and give her the bath."

At this point Naomi started. She had been lying in that bed all smug and thinking, "Carolyn won't be able to bathe me today!" Out of her mouth came the usual filth in that squeaky shrill voice. She could put the worst cursers to shame with what spewed across the room.

"Damn her," I thought. "Why did I put up with her?" Oh well, the bath wasn't going to get done unless I just did it. I got her clean clothes, put her maroon slippers on her, and headed for the bathroom. She was screaming so loudly, I wanted to stuff a pillow over her face. I stripped her unceremoniously and placed her in the tub on the shower chair. I turned on the water to the right temperature and turned the hose nozzle to a gentle spray. I wrapped my left arm around her back and secured my hand to the soap dish to hold her on the stool. With my right hand, I soaped the cloth and washed her. She was pushing so hard that my arm felt like it was breaking. I admit I wanted to slap her because she was spitting at me, slapping me with both hands, and trying to bite me. Finally, I couldn't hold her, and no one was there to help me.

It just so happened that a neighbor next door, upset by the screaming, had come to the door to complain. The visitor had gone to the door for me but didn't know what to tell him. She came into the bathroom to tell me my neighbor was at the door just as Naomi was at her worst. I told her to tell the man that Naomi was getting a bath. She told him, and he seemed to be satisfied with the answer. I guess he had been through this before, and Tom had explained to him what was happening. When the visitor left the bathroom, I instinctively placed the end of the hose in Naomi's face. After all, water was thrown on dogs when they were hung up. She sputtered and fumed and tried her damnedest to lose her breath, but this was when I wet down her hair and put shampoo on. I had a few brief seconds when I could get something done without spit hitting me in the face. I had just about all I could take! I hosed her hair clean, turned off the water, and tried to free up my arm. As soon as I let go of the soap holder, she threw herself down to the bottom of the tub with the stool on top of her. I walked out of there crying. The visitor came to me and offered her help, but when she went into the bathroom and heard everything and caught the spit, she walked out.

Of course, I had to go back and help Naomi. I bent over the tub, removed the shower stool, picked her up with both arms, and quickly sat down on the toilet seat with her turned over on my lap. Then I proceeded to give her a good spanking. She actually stopped screaming. I dried her as best I could, picked her up, and carried her to her bed. I laid her down, covered her and left the room thinking she was going to kill all of us. My only recourse was to put her in a medical hospital and refuse to take her back. First, I had to find something wrong with her that Medicare would pay for.

It was becoming increasingly difficult to provide care to this woman. The few times she was quiet were short, and the times she raised hell were becoming more and more prolonged. I knew the staff could not handle her anymore, and it was deadbeat sure I couldn't. All of us were watching for something to justify a hospital visit, but it was not to be.

Although Naomi took up a great deal of my time, I was still trying to open up a place called the Inn and, of course, The Grand. I now had enough persons waiting to come in to fill both houses. The Inn would be ready before The Grand was, as it required less renovation, and the paperwork for it was already done. I had applied for a license and was just waiting for HRS to inspect. I had hired a live-in lady, Sally, to keep an eye on the Inn until we moved in, and then she would become part of the staff. It was a large place with a second floor. There was a small room that would be perfect for Naomi. The neighborhood was commercial, but clean and nice. There was no one to hear Naomi yell except for the home for retarded adults three doors down the street.

With that in mind, I decided to move Naomi to The Inn. Sally had no objection. I agreed to relieve her one full day a week.

Without further ado, Naomi was put into a car once again. She screamed all the way to The Inn. Fortunately, there were no policemen en route. I honestly believe she was happier in her new home. I came to realize she was terrified of people. Sally left her alone except for morning and evening care and her meals. She was quiet most of the time. Eventually, I had to move more residents there because Shoreline was becoming overpopulated.

However, the HRS had not yet come to inspect the Inn, even though I had repeatedly requested it over a period of a few weeks. We just lived on the wire with HRS. The agency was supposed to set an appointment before the first visit, but I had known the representative of HRS to simply appear. I did not want that to happen.

I don't know why I took a chance of moving residents into the Inn anyway, but I did. I guess I just liked to live dangerously. I had agreed to admit several people who did not need much care and who could afford to pay the set rent—that is, more than most of the others could pay. I could not turn them down because my operating expenses were skyrocketing. Bea and Vera moved in shortly after Naomi, then James, Ilga, and Minnie. Of course, I had to hire more help. We all took turns working the mornings until the work was done and lunch was over. Another employee would come over in the evening to help get the residents ready for bed.

The plan was to move them to my home during the inspection, that is, if we knew when HRS was coming ahead of time. If HRS showed up without our knowing ahead of time, we would just whisk the ladies out the back door into two cars. (There were always two there just in case.) Fortunately, HRS called me to set up an appointment. On the morning the representative was to arrive, we put the ladies into the cars with all of their clothing, stripped the beds and put clean linens on, and made everything ready. Honestly, you couldn't tell anyone had ever lived there.

The ladies behaved nicely except for Naomi. Her actions were totally predictable. I had medicated her with the maximum dosage of tranquilizers, explained to her why she needed to be quiet, and told her we would bring her back in a few hours. She seemed OK until we started to move her; then all hell broke loose. Jim, one of my employees, just picked her up, threw her over his shoulder, and put her in the front seat of his car. She bit Jim's shoulder and beat on his back. I didn't think to tell the manager of the condos where I lived that I would be bringing the ladies there temporarily. She knew what I did for a living, but I'm sure she didn't expect me to bring residents to my home. And, in fact, I had never brought any of them there before this time.

The other residents were having a good time. They enjoyed getting out and seeing different things. James and Ilga were hand in hand with James pointing out various things to Ilga. Bea was raving about the pool, Vera was doing the ABC routine again and poor little Minnie was just along for the ride. Several of the tenants of the condo had opened their doors commenting on how good I was to those people; they were smiling and some laughing.

"They're going to have breakfast with me for a change," I told them.

All good things must come to an end. Poor Jim arrived with Naomi. He came up the elevator with her over his shoulder, which was covered with puke. She had really let him have it. She had kicked him in all the wrong places and was biting his shoulder. Blood was oozing out of his shirt. Of course, she was yelping like a mad dog. I opened the door, let him in, and quickly closed it. He dropped her on a bed in the guest room and ran out. I medicated her again and in a few minutes she was saying hello to dream land.

I wasn't quick enough. The manager came to the door. I invited her in and told her they were there for breakfast. She was terrified they were there to stay. I showed her Naomi and explained how she was and that I could not do anything with her. She seemed to understand but cautioned me to let her know the next time because residents had started to complain.

The condos were upscale. The people who lived there were accustomed to having a life that included better things, not having to listen to a screaming woman.

It wasn't long after this adventure that we discovered Naomi possessed three distinct personalities. Kris recorded all three, but unfortunately the tapes eventually were lost. I studied the tapes listened to her with the intent of analyzing her conversations. I was truly interested in something Naomi was doing. Her personalities conversed with one another, usually about men but never in a social aspect. One would mention seeing so and so at the grocery store and the other would acknowledge this in a totally different voice. The nasty deep-throated voice would usually be the dominant one. One would ask the other two what they had to eat. The bad one would always say, "They are trying to poison me so I don't eat." One of the others would ultimately say she was hungry, and the food was pretty good. I knew that one personality liked egg salad and despised tuna. That same personality liked chicken soup and hated tomato soup. Any dessert would satisfy any of the three.

Naomi's bath time continued to be a riot. After the bath none of the personalities could do without her maroon slippers.

When Tom was working at Shoreline, he got up one morning and went to the kitchen to start the coffee and breakfast. When he saw a maroon slipper in the kitchen, he about lost it. We all knew Naomi could walk but only with assistance. She had the other one on. Now that we knew she could walk alone, we had to barricade the two doors to the kitchen each night because we feared she would attack someone during the night with knives and other items she might find in the kitchen.

Never a dull moment with Naomi around…

Chapter Nine
HRS Wreaks Havoc

Scabies (microscopic lice) is probably one of the most unpleasant surprises a nurse can come upon. They are highly contagious, difficult to cure, and impossible to live with. A person who is infected just might as well be in a leper colony.

In the South, it is something on everyone's mind, as the hospitals are full of them. To be fair, scabies is usually brought to the hospitals by people who work there and by patients who are already infected. God alone knows how the elderly get infected, for they are not physically active and usually do not go around touching others, which is the main method of contact. However, the itching, the sores from scratching, the isolation, and the associated stigma all have to be tolerated until cured.

One of the reasons for seeing a resident before admission is to discreetly inspect his or her body. Sometimes the rash is not evident as it is secondary to the lice, so a nurse has to look for other signs such as raised, reddened areas under the skin and, of course, the itching, especially of the hands.

When I interviewed Rosalie for admission, I found no signs of scabies and agreed to bring her into Shoreline. She was Italian and spoke with a heavy tongue, which was difficult to understand, and I liked her from the start. She was short and plump, had large brown eyes, and pretty brown hair with just a touch of gray. She sort of wobbled when she walked. She was happy in spite of her poor physical condition.

This was another charity case. I would only get $400 a month from her. She had had a lumpectomy of her breast and would only reside with us until the incision healed. Home health nurses would be coming in to do the dressings and to monitor the progress. We wouldn't be doing any laborious care for her, just personal care and meals.

Kris called me the day after she was admitted to tell me there was a suspicious rash all over her body. I was mortified and went into a panic. There is only one way to positively diagnose scabies. They are identified under a microscope, but first they must be found in a burrow on the skin and scrapped off and put on a slide. Doing this is quite difficult if you don't know what you are doing. I had had some experience and was fairly good at doing the test, but it was easier to simply start the treatment process, if you could call it easy.

All employees and all residents had to be treated at one time. This was the procedure: (1) strip the person of all clothing; (2) thoroughly scrub skin and hair; (3) apply prescribed lotion over all of the body, including all cracks and crevasses; (4) allow to dry; (5) dress in clean clothing; (6) strip the bed of all linens, including blankets, spreads, pillows and sheets; (7) wash in hot water; (8) wash all clothing and send to the cleaners what cannot be washed; (9) repeat this process with all residents; (12) the next morning bathe the resident, washing off the prescribed lotion, wash the hair again, put on clean clothes and change the bed entirely, and re-wash everything including the clothing removed from the resident. If luck was with the people doing all the work, this treatment would only have to be repeated once again in ten days. It is costly and humiliating to everyone.

When I told the employees what had happened, they were in shock. I had to instruct all employees to follow the cleansing procedure and have their entire families do the same. I was sure they would throw things at me, but they didn't. I had to absorb the expense of the lotion for them as well as for the residents. The pharmacist gave me a break, but with all included, the cost was over $400.

Poor Rosalie was good natured about having scabies. Because she had lived alone, she had obviously been infected by someone who came to see her. She laughed, but you should have seen how the tenderness of the home health nurse turned to terror when she found out about the scabies. Scabies is simply an occupational hazard to health care givers in the South.

I planned out how many extra people I would need on duty and began writing down the details and the schedule. We ended up with forty-three loads of laundry and a bunch of upset people. According to the residents, they didn't need baths two days running. They were furious to be jostled around so.

The madness went on for two days and then two more to complete the laundry. All of this to help out a social worker and for only four hundred dollars a month! The patient wasn't even a write-off for Uncle Sam.

It certainly wasn't Rosalie's fault. She didn't know she had scabies or how she had contacted them.

Unfortunately, her breast wasn't responding to the prescribed treatment. It drained constantly and had a horrible odor. The home health nurses were constantly calling the physician for advice, and we frequently had to change the dressings two or more times after each nurse left.

By the end of her first week with us, there was a marked deterioration. The physician had ordered an intravenous antibiotic. Medicare wouldn't pay for it in the hospital, so this meant it would have to be given at the home. An ALF could not be licensed to give intravenous deliveries. I was licensed because of being an RN, but I didn't want to be there twenty-four hours a day, and someone licensed was supposed to be present at all times. After talking to the home health nurses at some length, I finally agreed to administer the intravenous antibiotic, though I wasn't thrilled, but this was probably going to be Rosalie's last chance at healing. I allowed it after the staff had been thoroughly instructed about what to do. Actually, their job was easy. They just called a home health nurse if there was a problem. The medication would run for two hours. They had to shut off one valve and allow the other line to run.

There was little, if any, improvement during the course of the antibiotic therapy. Rosalie seldom engaged in conversation because of the language barrier, but I believed she was in a great deal of pain. I knew the physician well and called him for a report on her condition. He was not at all optimistic, even though the lump they had removed was benign. In my opinion, the infection had originated with the surgery.

Rosalie had visitors, but they were friends, never a relative. We knew she had a son who lived up north. However, he never called, and as far as I knew, there was no mail from him. I was unaware that the nurses had contacted her son until I found him on my front porch a few nights later. There was no car, and I had not seen a taxi. I went to the door. He introduced himself as Roberto, Rosalie's son. He was short like his mother, had dark hair, and talked with the same Italian accent. I let him in. It was late but Rosalie was still awake.

She was thrilled to see him. She rambled on in Italian, full of exuberance. They cried and laughed. What a wonderful dose of medicine for both of them. I overheard Roberto ask her if she had any money. She gave him some change. From what I overheard, he had ridden a bus from New York. He had no place to stay and no money for food. However, I felt it was good of him to come down here to be with his mother.

There was no reason why he could not stay here at the home. I could put him on the couch in the Florida room. Maxcine would have a conniption fit when she came in, but what else could I do? Surprisingly, she accepted him very well, although she was a little frightened at first. She even fixed Roberto a sandwich and a cup of coffee. I told him I had overheard some of the conversation between his mother and him. He was embarrassed but explained the situation to me.

"I haven't worked in several months. My wife works but she no make much. It is hard." I agreed. "I had to see Mama. The nurse called me and said she was no good."

With an approving nod from Maxcine, I asked him if he would like to stay here. "Do you mind sleeping on the couch in the Florida Room?" He cried as he shook his head and thanked me over and over. When he finished eating, he took another cup of coffee and retired to the couch.

I bid my farewell to Maxcine and went home. It had been a long day, but tomorrow would prove to be longer!

I didn't have to go to work when I awoke the next morning. It really felt good after many long working days in a row. I was forced to work this much because I simply didn't have enough dependable staff to do the job. The cause wasn't helped by my firing the four thieves, but, of course, I had had not choice but to do it. Eventually, the ones left realized my lack of tolerance for shenanigans. On the top of my list was theft: emptying out my liquor cabinet was just that. And to think my trusted employees emptied it in one day! That booze was for the residents. They enjoyed a cocktail and loved their little parties before dinner.

Before I got down the steps the phone rang. It was Sam. "Good morning Sam. Isn't it a beautiful day? I am going to spend a lot of time in the pool and my garden. How about you…?"

"Carolyn, I need you!"

"Oh no! What now?"

"HRS is here and they are not on a social call."

I threw on some clothes and headed up the street. They weren't due to come for months. I couldn't imagine why they were there unless there had been a complaint. By the time I opened the door and went in, I knew there was trouble. At least I was within my license status!

I said, "Hello" and asked them what I could help them with. One of the gentlemen I did not know asked if we could sit down. Sam quickly cleared the table for us.

"Would you like some coffee?" I asked.

"Sam is already getting it for us," one of the women replied.

"Good! Now what have I done this time?"

Before I could say anything else, the unknown man said to me in a nasty tone of voice, "We have a complaint that you are exceeding your license in this home."

I was really taken aback by this. For once, I was clean. I was not violating any of their damn laws. He had my dander up. I didn't like him because he was arrogant.

"Excuse me. I didn't catch your name." He introduced himself as Mr.

Southerly, an administrative officer with Licensing and Certification. "Thank you. I am Carolyn Connelly, the administrator here. Now, how can I help you with the complaint?"

"Mrs. Connelly, you are licensed for nine persons here. We have already counted ten." I looked around, wondering if someone had slipped in while I was gone. A quick count of heads only revealed nine people. I asked Sam and Kay if there was something I should know. They both shook their heads negatively and with confusion showing in their faces.

I quickly replied, "I only have nine residents here. Could we get the charts and physically count them?" The man was irate, but I wasn't going to let them file a complaint if none existed.

One of the ladies I knew said in my defense, "Let's go count together." I laid the charts on the table and we got up to count. We looked in every room except one, opened the doors and checked outside on the porch. We counted seven people. I knocked on Rosalie's door. I knew the nurse was changing her dressing and the woman with me was not a nurse. I was sure she would not enjoy the sight. I asked her to wait for a few minutes and assured her that no one would be going out the window.

The nurse opened the door in a few minutes and came out smiling. She said, "I am so pleased that Rosalie's son was able to make it down. He is such a nice person."

I agreed with her and walked into the room with the HRS lady. There was a strong odor. I reached for the room deodorizer and sprayed. Of course Rosalie's roommate had to have something to say about the bad odor.

"Can I leave the room? I feel like a prisoner here." I told her to be my guest. I introduced the HRS lady to Rosalie as I had with all the other residents.

"What is your count?"

"I have nine plus the man in the Florida room," she said.

"The man in the Florida room is Rosalie's son." She didn't need to know any more.

"It doesn't matter. He is a person taking up space."

As we walked to the table, I was thinking, "What in God's name are they thinking? Have they totally lost it?"

Mr. Southerly was writing and didn't look up when we sat down.

He handed me an administrative sanction, and was fining me five hundred dollars. I lost it.

"Surely you are not going to fine me for having a visitor in this place. He came all the way from New York just to see his mother who is dying."

"Does he use the toilet? You must have one toilet for every five residents." Mr. Southerly asked me.

"I hate to disappoint you sir, but I have two toilets for nine residents." He had to get out his regulation book to prove I was right. I could tell he thought I was trying to pull one over on them. Not this time, I thought. I knew that getting angry was the wrong thing to do with these people; yet against my better judgment I blurted out, "You people have taken away the only day off I have had in over two weeks. I do not appreciate it, and I feel that you have imposed an embarrassing situation upon a resident's son who is trying to have a nice visit." I handed back the paper with the fine on it and told Mr. Southerly I refused to accept it.

"Mrs. Connelly, you will have to argue that out with someone else. I feel that the man is a resident here," he said.

I looked around for the nurse. She fortunately had not gone. I asked her to please come to the table. She said, "I have heard everything. Are they nuts, or what?"

She told Mr. Southerly that she had called Roberto to come down here because his mother's condition was deteriorating rapidly. She then asked Mr. Southerly if he would step outside with her. I, of course, went with them as I never let anyone from HRS out of my sight.

When we were on the porch she plowed into him with vengeance. "I have never witnessed such a display of ignorance in my life. I do not know where you got your complaint or the nature of it. However, you have made a bad situation worse, and I find it incomprehensible that a person representing the public could humiliate a person as badly as you have Rosalie's son."

I wished I had stayed inside because I knew he could really make trouble for me if he chose to do so.

He turned on his heels and went inside. By the time I came in the door, he was asking Roberto for his driver's license, which he promptly produced. Mr. Southerly apologized for any inconvenience he and his team might have caused, picked up his books, and turned to leave. I picked up the fine notice and said, "Haven't you forgotten something? I don't want this." One of the ladies took the paper and they went out the door.

In days to come, I would have many unpleasant experiences with the HRS surveyors. I would have to bite the bullet and fight with all my might frequently just to stay in business. They would not soon forget that a fine had been repealed.

Chapter Ten
The Cruise

With all their faults, HRS did occasionally have the residents' best interests in mind. Activities for residents were high on the list. That residents should perform certain activities was even a law, and I agreed that residents should stay active. They needed to keep their bodies moving. But realistically, the goals HRS set were unreasonable. The residents could perform the prescribed and necessary steps to get to the dinner table or the television set, but that was about it. We were all accused of parking them in front of the set and ignoring their rights; however, the truth was they just didn't care enough at this stage to exert themselves.

Sure, I was bothered by the residents' relative inactivity. I wanted desperately to keep them busy and try to improve their mental capacity, but it was not to be. I couldn't even get them to fold the dish towels. The majority were bitter souls with little to no interest in life. Life for most had become just too hard.

I could never resign myself to such indifference. To my children I was elderly. To their children, they were elderly. Age is only a way of obtaining, increasing, and exchanging knowledge. I did not feel residents deserved special privileges just because they were twenty or thirty years older than I was. They complained of being tired, but I and my staff got tired, also. There were even times when I felt that I wanted someone to take care of me.

The people I took care of had maid service, a laundress, a cook, a grocery shopper, a chauffeur, a secretary, a private valet, a dishwasher, and someone to dress them and keep them clean. They did nothing to even exercise their fingers except to hold a fork or spoon and bend their elbows at mealtime.

Frustration became my constant companion because I came to realize that those of us who took care of the elderly lost all of our rights. HRS could do anything to us and we were at the mercy of this agency and others. It was against the law to say anything derogatory to HRS, to fight back, to refuse a surveyor the use of the phone if he or she wanted to call the police. It was against the law to lock the door to keep residents inside if they wanted to run away or to violate their rights in any way, and they had more rights than my employees or I did. So I really went out of my way to provide them with extracurricular activity. I honestly tried to get them to play cards, play checkers, to help out with small chores. There were few activities I could get them to take part in. One would listen to music, and Ilga would dance. Occasionally, she would dance with James. The others either watched or fell asleep.

I knew another ALF owner, a friend of mine, who endured similar difficulties. One time, when she was expecting HRS to do an inspection, she made a calendar, which took all awards. She presented an activity sheet to the HRS that could put the rest of us out of business if HRS believed the residents were doing these activities. The activity sheet said her crew took residents water skiing, boating, swimming, bicycling, jogging, overnight camping, canoeing, and engaging in other activities for the vigorous person. Of course her residents did none of these activities. Unbelievably, the HRS team stated that they wished the other homes would try to do these activities, too. What a laugh! I could not believe they actually thought residents were so active. I guess I did do the ultimate activity for the area though. I took three of them on a day cruise. It was for fifteen hours in the bay.

All of us carefully selected the ones we felt could withstand the ship and the water, and took into consideration which ones had the money to go. I insisted that the guardians pay my fare as well as that of two staff members. We had to have a stateroom for the residents to rest in if need be, and that cost extra money. The stateroom would accommodate four persons.

Finally, we chose Ilga, Prudence, and Marie. Ilga and Marie would be fine as long as James wasn't along. I did want to take him along, but his daughter wouldn't pay for it. Besides, Ilga and Marie fought constantly over James. Ilga loved life. She was vivacious and always doing something, mostly dancing to keep her body in good shape. I felt she would enjoy dressing up for the evening music, and maybe even do a little dancing. She was tall and slim and looked very nice when appropriately attired.

Marie always looked well-dressed and was a lady, except for fighting with Ilga over James. Her hair was professionally done once a week, her nails were long and beautiful, her hands were untouched by water or work, and her clothes were always immaculate and neat. We felt she needed something to add to her memoirs.

Like Ilga, Prudence was 91 years old. Marie was their junior by four years. Prudence had been a schoolteacher and was thoroughly disciplined when lucid. She could walk, but I took her wheelchair along. She was tall, but not as tall as Ilga, and always looked nice when we made her up. She was pleasant and had some decent clothes to wear. Also, she played the piano. She only remembered one song, a school pep song, but it was fun to listen to it. The funny thing was she played wherever her hands landed on the keyboard. We could all tell what she was playing regardless of the key signature, and, more importantly, it was obvious she received much joy out of playing. She would applaud as much as we did.

The women packed a bag, mostly a change of clothing for each and some necessary items such as diapers if needed, pads for the beds, and a few other items.

I carefully chose the staff members to accompany me. Maxcine was my trusted friend who worked nights and Matilda was one of my day shift workers. She was good to the residents and took good care of them.

The big day arrived. This trip was sure to be a treat for Maxcine and Matilda, who had never been on a ship. We took a bus to the port. Even though the ship was large, it was used only for short cruises. There were good reasons for not taking longer ones. It caught fire frequently, there were outbreaks of food poisoning, it employed a staff who could not speak or understand English, and, at one time, the ship almost turned over in the Gulf of Mexico during a New Year's Eve cruise. Also, it was somewhat shabby and had obviously seen better days. The County Health Department monitored the ship closely now, and its staff had been thoroughly indoctrinated on how to fight fires. I didn't feel unsafe because the ship would never leave the immediate area, and I'm sure the Coast Guard was never far away.

We boarded the bus and got the ladies situated. At least they seemed interested. I don't know how long it had been since they had been on a bus, if ever; the bus ride was an activity in itself.

We were crossing my favorite of the three bridges over the bay. Ilga was singing, Marie was laughing, and I heard Maxcine say, "Oh shit!"

No! Prudence was bus sick. What in hell was she going to do on that ship? I had Dramamine and tried to get the scopolamine patches, but they were ill advised for the elderly. If I gave her Dramamine, she would fall asleep. She puked her guts out. Thank God she had not eaten all of her dinner the night before. The poor thing had dry heaves. I decided to give her the anti-motion pill. All we could do was wait to see if she fell asleep. She did. It was a disaster getting her off the bus and into her wheelchair because she didn't want to wake up, and she was still a little bit sick. I was already regretting this escapade.

As Maxcine wheeled Prudence up the ramp to the ship, I saw her head slump off to the right. That pill had whooped her. Ilga and Marie were walking with Matilda, and I was handling the tickets. I thought how glad I was to have reserved a cabin. On board we took the bags and Prudence to the cabin. I told Maxcine and Matilda I would watch Ilga and Marie, but they had to take turns watching Prudence until she woke up.

I took Marie and Ilga upstairs to the big lounge. Music was playing and Bingo would be starting soon. I ordered a soda for the two women and sat there with them for a while. Ilga enjoyed the music, and Marie took in everything, acting as if she had never been anywhere before. Across the room were the slot machines. They called to me, so I had to check them out and, in doing so, discovered I had an unobstructed view of the women from the machines. This was great! I ordered them another soda before I left to go lose my fortune. It would be a few more minutes until they announced the call for breakfast buffet. I played a few dollars and, of course, lost it before I heard the call.

Of course, before going to breakfast both Marie and Ilga had to go to the bathroom. I took them before we went downstairs to check on Prudence. Prudence was asleep. Maxcine and Matilda were nowhere to be found. Man, I was going to have their hides. I couldn't leave these two women in the cabin, and there was no place to put them while I went searching for those two scalawags. I took them to the dining area where I sat them down in a chair. I couldn't go through that line three times and still watch them while they ate. I explained to them I was going to look for Maxcine and Matilda. I found them in the disco, and, of course, half the crew was there with them.

Did I mention that Matilda was young and had a great figure, including a great set of knockers?

"Is Prudence OK?" Maxcine asked.

"How should I know? That was your job! I need help in the dining room with the other two until I get them served. Could at least one of you help me?" Both of them were willing to help. Matilda went to check on Prudence, and Maxcine came with me.

Naturally, when we entered the dining room, Marie and Ilga were not where I had left them. But thank goodness they were at a table eating. One of the waiters had filled plates for them and had given them juice and coffee. I thanked them and made a mental note to tip well. I filled my plate with food and sat down with the women. The atmosphere had changed those two: they were acting like ladies. I saw no sign of mental confusion.

The food was surprisingly good. Matilda came back from checking on Prudence and said that she was still sleeping. Then she filled a plate for herself and went downstairs to eat. When she came back, I told both Matilda and Maxcine they could leave Prudence as long as they checked on her frequently. Both of them were pleased with this decision. When we finished eating, we went back to the lounge. Marie asked me if she could have a Bloody Mary.

Ilga said, "Me, too."

I ordered them but told the waiter to hold the booze. They were thrilled and apparently did not know the difference. I smiled at their genuine pleasure.

I went back to the slots but made sure I could see both of them. People were mingling around them, and there was no telling what they were telling their newfound friends. Every time a machine drained me, I would go check on them. They were fine. Soon I stayed with them while they played Bingo, and later I tried to take them outside, but they wanted no part of watching the scenery. The lounge was dark and the sun was glaring outside. I suppose seeing all that water could be frightening to someone who had not been on a ship before, although Ilga might have taken a ship on her several trips to Europe. However, now she certainly gave no indication of remembering going by ship.

Surprisingly, it was almost lunchtime. I would drop a few more bucks and take them to the dining room. I was gone about an hour this time. I had found a machine giving me back some of my money and I was not paying attention to the time. The waiter came up and asked me if I was responsible for their bill, pointing to the two of them.

I nodded and he said, "That will be seventeen dollars, please." I opened my purse for the money before I realized what he had said.

I noticed he had a sly little smile on his face. And then it dawned on me. I asked him, "What did they have?"

He replied, "Four double vodkas on the rocks and three scotch and waters."

Damn! I paid him and gave him a good tip and went to see what damage had been done. They were both shit-faced with their heads on the table. I needed help, but I couldn't spend an hour looking for Maxcine and Matilda. I was finally able to stand Ilga up. She could barely walk! Somehow I managed to walk her to the cabin and put her down on the other lower bed. Of course, Maxcine and Matilda were nowhere to be found. Prudence was still asleep.

With both of them out, I went back to get Marie. I had to ask one of the waiters to help me walk her to the cabin. He did so without reservation. When we arrived there with Marie, I sat her down in a chair and asked him if he would go find Maxcine and Matilda for me. He smiled as if he knew who they were. I attempted to describe them, but his gestures of extending his arms out at chest level told me he knew where they were. He came back with Maxcine. She looked at all three of them and burst out laughing. We somehow got Ilga in the top bunk and tied her in with a top sheet. Marie was placed on the bottom. I told Maxcine to go eat and bring back one plate for Prudence and something for her to drink. She wasn't hungry, so I went.

I brought back enough food and drink for all three of them and sent Maxcine to go get Matilda so both of them could go eat. I would take the first shift with them. I was getting tired and could use a short nap. They were to be back at the cabin in two hours.

Prudence started moving about. God, I hoped she was over her vomiting! She sat up in the bed and announced she was hungry. I fed her and gave her a glass of milk. Thankfully, the food stayed down. I took her to the bathroom and washed her face and combed her hair. She was ready to go back to sleep for an hour or so, and then she was going to get some air and at least listen to some music.

Ilga and Marie slept until Maxcine and Matilda came back. I helped Prudence get up and put her in her wheelchair and then put Ilga down in the lower bunk. I left Matilda with instructions to start waking them up and feeding them. No more disco for a while.

As I went out the door to the cabin, a string of Bahamians met me, not just cabin boys and waiters, but officers as well. I tried to tell them that Matilda was on duty now, but they didn't understand me. I opened the door and asked her to explain to them that she couldn't see them until evening. She could speak their language. She looked funny but started talking to them. I would have to make a run down here in a few minutes. I wanted my employees to have a good time, but they had also agreed to take care of the women.

I caught up with Maxcine who was pushing Prudence around in the lounge. Music was playing, and preparations for faux horse racing were beginning. It all would be a lot of fun. Maxcine was buying tickets, and she said she would help Prudence participate in the activities. By now Prudence was strumming her fingers on the table keeping time to the music. I told Maxcine I would be back in an hour to take over. She smiled. I went back to the slot machines. So far, I was out about $150. I had to do better than that!

However, luck was not on my side. When I dropped another hundred without one quarter returning in a half hour, I quit. I went to the bar and ordered a plain soda. I sat there relaxing and people watching, and there were many interesting people to watch. Many of them came up to talk to me. They did not praise me for doing something for the elderly; they wondered why I endured such a chore. I tried to explain that it was what I liked doing, but I don't think they understood. Then I ambled over to Maxcine and Prudence, who were actually having a good time. Prudence had won $30 and, although she didn't have any concept of money, she knew she had accomplished a feat. I left to go down to the cabin. Ilga and Marie were awake, but Matilda was not there. I washed them up, took them to the bathroom and gave them a sandwich and milk. They seemed to be sober now, or a t least they were standing. We walked back to the lounge. I told Maxcine she could go wherever she wanted. I would take care of all three ladies. She looked at me kind of funny and then, with a nervous sort of voice, said, "Where is Matilda?"

"She chose to leave the two of them alone while she took off with half the crew," I answered.

I knew the crew was not supposed to socialize with the passengers unless they were officers and then only with the captain's approval. It was time to look for the captain. Matilda had no intentions of helping me care for these ladies, and I had no intentions of taking her on a cruise and paying her wages for taking on the crew.

I ordered sodas for the ladies and asked the waiter where I might find the captain. He pointed at a gentleman at the bar.

I walked over, introduced myself, and told him that my employees were cavorting with his on duty crew. He thanked me and left. I knew the crew would lose their jobs. I had watched crewmembers get fired in the middle of the ocean and be confined to their cabins until land was reached unless they wanted to pay for a fare. The captain would be very strict even on this bucket. The only fair thing I could do was to fire Matilda when we got back.

On the other hand, even though Maxcine had had a good time she had been faithful in returning to help. I felt good about telling Maxcine to go and have a good time. I was content staying with the three ladies and could probably get them through dinner on my own.

We sat and listened to the music. People were starting to dance and Ilga was warming up. She so loved to dance and have a good time! There were a lot of older men there. Surely one of them would ask her to dance, but it was not to be. She waited as long as she could and hit the dance floor by herself. She could really dance but solo acts were not appreciated. She moved out to take up most of the floor, and people were giving her dirty looks. Finally an elderly gentleman asked her to dance. She swung right to his step all the way. He had a smile on his face and winked at me. When he brought her back to the table, he thanked her and told her she was a good dancer. Ilga smiled from ear to ear, and pure joy shone in her eyes—it warmed my heart. She hadn't the vaguest idea of what he had said, but she knew she had been with a man on the dance floor. Her joy made the trip worthwhile.

I wanted to go outside. These people needed to see the sunlight, and there was a calypso band playing on deck. I pushed Prudence's wheelchair and instructed the other two to hang on and follow me. We made it outside, but no one was interested in the sunlight after being in that dark lounge. Fortunately, I had sunglasses for all of them, which we put on immediately. I walked them over to the rail to see the water. Prudence was terrified, Ilga wanted to jump in, and Marie just stood there and stared at the water. I found some shadier spots and sat them down in lounge chairs. Prudence had on the broad-rimmed hat I had been carrying around. They began to enjoy the music and settled down to listen.

As I watched the water, it became rough. I didn't remember anything in the weather report about a storm, but that didn't mean much. The water grew dark, and the waves started to pound the ship. I could feel the motion. I doubted if this ship had been baffled for easing motion, for it was rocking now. My memory clicked that this very ship nearly turned over last year. The conditions were so bad that the Coast Guard had to evacuate everyone.

We had been anchored for some time now, but now the ship was starting to move. Perhaps we could still outrun the storm. The sky was cloudy but not threatening. Sunbeams still appeared between clouds that were starting to turn dark. My watch showed it was 5:30 p.m., almost time to take my group down to dinner.

I hoped the ship would settle down before we ate. All I needed was for them all to get sick. I looked around to see Maxcine coming through the door. She sat down after asking the ladies if they were having a good time. They smiled, thus indicating they were.

It was now 5:45 p.m. I told Maxcine we might as well eat dinner. There would be a line, but sometimes the waiters would help us to a table ahead of the others. We ambled inside and toward the dining room, forgetting to remove our sunglasses until the ladies complained they couldn't see.

Neither Maxcine nor I mentioned Matilda. We got in line, but this time no one helped us. Word had spread that I had finked on the crew. OK, I thought, I wouldn't tip either. When the line shortened, I found a table large enough for all of us and seated the ladies. I went through the buffet and filled up two plates. The food looked as if they had mixed it up in one giant bowl and then distributed it to various large containers. I took them pasta, salad, and bread. Maxcine picked up milk and coffee for them. I asked, "Have you ever seen anything so disgusting?" She shook her head. The meatloaf they had served for lunch was floating around in some tomato broth and was called soup de jour. Gross!

When I went back for my food, I saw a table with cold roast beef, and ham and cheese sandwiches. I took the ham and cheese and hoped I had made the right decision. I found the mustard, coffee, and water. While we ate, Maxcine and I chatted, but Maxcine did not mention Matilda. She knew me well enough to keep quiet until I cooled down.

Marie and Ilga were hauling it in, but their taste buds were probably dead. When I had eaten a sandwich, I went back to look for something else. There were some pastries left over from breakfast. I picked up several and returned to the table. When we were finished, I took the three ladies down to the cabin for a short nap. They were no trouble and appeared eager to lie down. I told Maxcine to go and enjoy herself. I was certainly through with the slot machines and had nothing better to do than to draw up a chair, sit down, and wait until the ship docked. It was now nearly 7:00 p.m. and the ship was supposed to dock around 10:00 p.m.

I remembered being on some beautiful ships and had been treated like royalty, but I had been young and in my right mind. Why would I even ponder whether I would take another cruise with the elderly? Was I nuts? I don't think my ladies even knew they were on a ship, let alone have a good time. Well, I thought, at least the ship didn't turn over, and the sea had settled down considerably.

Maxcine came in about 9:00 p.m. She told me to go upstairs and enjoy myself for a while. She still didn't mention Matilda. I went out on deck to get some air. The air was cool and a nice breeze was blowing. I stood at the rail listening to the calypso band. I could see some of the landmarks as the ship went through the channel. Several passengers asked me where the ladies were. I was even complimented for being so daring as to bring them along. Well! There was some notice of my efforts on board after all.

I stayed on deck until the tugboats started pushing us in. This was my favorite part of the cruise. There was something truly remarkable about those little boats pushing and pulling around these great big ocean liners.

Soon I went down to get the ladies and Maxcine. Maxcine had them ready and everything packed. I gave Prudence another Dramamine for the bus. We were on the bus when Maxcine asked me if I was going to wait for Matilda.

My response was short and sweet: "No."

I figured she knew when the ship stopped and surely must know that the bus would be waiting. Besides, I'm sure she wouldn't have any problem getting home. She didn't! She wandered into the home the next morning, asking me if I would take two cabin boys back to town. I handed her the money she had earned to date with a termination slip stating that she was not eligible for rehire. She and her friends left.

A new ship berthed a short time later. We could see it sail in and out every Sunday, but I wasn't about to introduce any other residents to a day cruise or any other type of cruise for that matter. I had had my fill of cruises.

Chapter Eleven
The Grand

I was still intrigued with that big old building down by the bay that was for lease. One day I drove by and wrote down the name of the owner and his phone number. I wanted to see the inside and get some details on the building. Finally, I called for an appointment.

The owner was a prominent person in the community and intimidating from the start. The building was about to be placed in the Historical Society's Hall of Fame, which required restoration, and, since my knowledge of restoration was minimal, I was a less-than-perfect candidate in his eyes. He did, however, agree to let me view the property.

We left his office and drove over. It was even more massive than I had imagined. I recognized immediately that at least two of the huge rooms would have to be made into several bedrooms. I could easily place 40 people in there with the existing floor space. It would serve no purpose to lease it with only the use of the five bedrooms.

Had I known what was going to happen to me, I would have left the rooms as they were and concentrated only on the fire protection and whatever else had to be done to license.

My assessment of the work was completely unrealistic. All I saw was a dream. Money would be my biggest problem. I would have to get the existing rooms ready and prepare the kitchen without spending much money before I could proceed further. Thank God, the kitchen was already commercial and could be ready for inspection with minimal work. There would be costly things to do such as putting in a fire-protection system, but they would not drain me financially. Once the kitchen was organized, the rest would be easy, or so I thought.

We went back to the owner's office and discussed what had to be done. The monthly lease would be within my means financially, but I asked him for some time to formulate a renovation plan before making a final decision. He agreed. I stayed away from everything and everybody until I could fully comprehend all that this enormous venture entailed. Unfortunately, my excitement and enthusiasm blinded my reason, as I reveled in the light of possibilities. I felt ready to tackle the complete job, rather than to simply comply with HRS rules and laws. If only someone would have stopped this manic obsession of mine…

I formulated the temporary plans and addressed them on paper for my next appointment with the owner. Immediately, he realized that my enthusiasm didn't translate to reality. He was, however, impressed with my knowledge of HRS requirements.

"How do you plan to do all of this, Carolyn?" he asked.

"Well, a step at a time, I guess." I replied.

"Do you have a lawyer?"

When I mentioned my lawyer's name, he looked away as if to avoid eye contact with me. I wish my guardian angel had forewarned me at that time, but as with everything in my life, I had to be tested and learn how to climb over the rocks. We set up a date to sign the lease. I left the office and went home to try to call in some markers and find some financial backing.

Most thought I was crazy. A few thought it could be done if I could keep twelve to fourteen residents hidden away someplace until I could get it opened. My family just thought I had turned on the lights, but there was nobody home. If I listened to everyone, surely my dream would go up in smoke. With confidence and perseverance, anything is possible, right?

I signed the lease. I was given six months to complete the HRS requirements. If I failed, the lease could be revoked.

My first trip to city hall was a nightmare. I came out of there berating bureaucracy again. It took me a half hour to get five words out of the people at the windows.

Those words were, one at a time, "Go To The Last Window."

By the time I got to the last window there was NOBODY HOME. The woman behind the window hadn't the vaguest idea what I was trying to find out. All I wanted to know was where I should start to obtain an occupational license. I was fostered out to zoning, permits, hazardous waste, downtown development, fire department, planning and development, EPA, rezoning variances, permits, and on and on…even to animal control!!!

When I finally arrived at animal control and the person behind the window asked me how she could help me, I replied, "Everyone in this building needs to be in a cage!"

I left there and went to the mayor's office. This was my last resort. I hoped they could at least advise me as to where I should begin. When I got there, one of the secretaries looked at me with knowing sympathy and mumbled, "Was it that bad at city hall?" I just nodded, too numb to speak.

She listed the places where I had to go, the people I had to see, and in what order. I leaned over and kissed her on the cheek and expressed my gratitude. I left, determined to achieve my goal for that day, which was to find out what I had to do first.

By the time I arrived back at city hall, suddenly everyone wanted to help me at once. I was in trouble and knew it. That secretary at the mayor's office had called to warn them I was coming with my gun cocked. I found out that zoning was first. I got lucky! The home was properly zoned, which meant I could go to step two. In step two I had to fill out an application for a license. Easy enough. However, I had a list of projects to complete before they would issue the license.

I had noticed a man following me around ever since I walked back into the place. He had a folder with him and was writing in it. As I went through the door, I turned around in time to see him close the folder and walk away. I went directly to the office of my lawyer, Barnaby. I told him what I had observed, asked him if he could find out about the man following me, and whether he could help me get through the list I had to complete. He quoted an exorbitant fee. My desperation led to easy agreement.

After hiring several people, I put two in charge of the kitchen and told them exactly what had to be done. They did the work over and over again until they got it right. Others were assigned to housework. Hardwood floors had to be scrubbed and waxed, thousands of windows washed, blinds taken outside and scrubbed, closets and store rooms cleaned and painted, and bathrooms scrubbed, painted, and wall-papered.

While the house was whipped into shape, I purchased food and thousands of dollars worth of linens. I also worked on the HRS regulations. I asked for an early inspection so that I could bring in the fourteen people I had stashed away. I was approved, but with a list of deficiencies to correct before I could bring them in…no problem, what with all my spare time!

With the staff cleaning around me, I sat down to formulate the placement plan for residents. I still had Nancy, Peggy and Walter in my private home. They could be moved to The Grand, and then I would have my home back.

Ilga and Marie could be moved here from The Inn. After the families were called, we moved them and got everything settled with job descriptions for the staff in both places. That everyone knew his or her job pleased me because it freed me to concentrate on the administration of the new place.

My waiting list consisted of Mattie, William, Norman, Solomon, James, my grandmother, the three from my home (Nancy, Peggy, and Walter), and the two from Shoreline, Marie and Ilga. Now I could safely operate. The others were not yet ready to bring in.

Mattie was the first new one I brought in. I liked her daughter, who was terribly nervous about placing Mattie in a home, but her family had insisted. Mattie was a sweet person, who waddled when she walked and entertained the others with many funny tall tales. She also liked to eat and wasn't a bit fussy. She started gaining weight almost immediately. Keeping these people away from food was not my idea of fun, but Mattie was just eating entirely too much. She ate double portions at almost every meal. I would definitely need to control her eating, as well as Peggy's and my grandmother's.

Yes, my grandmother, Mimmy, had decided she wanted to live with me instead of with my mother. She did not want to go to a nursing home, and my mother could not take care of her anymore. She didn't like the smell of the bedside commode in the mornings when it had to be emptied. No, my mother was no different from any of the other daughters. They simply did not want the responsibility and would look for any and every excuse to get out of caring for their mother. However, I had chosen this path; it was my life. I welcomed my grandmother to travel along with me. According to her, I had been the only grandchild she had, although altogether she had six. Unfortunately, something had happened a few years before, and afterwards she withdrew from me, and turned to the rest of her grandchildren. She didn't approve of me, was sharp-tongued, and mean to me. I accepted her abuse, attributing it to the aging process. She never did adjust to being there with me, but the others liked her, as she could be very friendly.

The breakfast menu varied from morning to morning, but weekly it consisted of fruit or juice, cold or hot cereal, a main course of French toast, scrambled eggs, fried eggs, pancakes or Danish, and doughnuts, bacon, sausage patties or links, or ham. Sometimes we served gravy and home made biscuits.

The days that scrambled eggs were on the menu, Mimmy refused to eat. She was convinced they were powdered. She would scream at the cook or me until we fixed her fried eggs. On occasion she would throw her food on the floor. Needless to say, when her fried eggs arrived, Peggy and Mattie would insist on having fried eggs, also. I wasn't trying to mean to Mimmy and her friends, but I needed them to quit asking for special favors. After all, I was providing balanced menus and good portions, and not because theHRS regulations were particular in this area of care but because I was committed to providing excellent nutrition. A lot of caregivers were not providing balanced meals and adequate portions. When residents lost weight, the HRS was quick to target menus and portions.

When all of us had endured enough of her tantrums, I put my foot down and told her she could just eat around the scrambled egg. The menu would no longer be changed. The three of them had no breakfast for three days. I put out leftovers, such as toast or donuts on the table, and later the food would be gone, so they didn't go hungry. However, Mimmy continued to use and abuse me, all the while causing an atmosphere of chaos.

I moved Peggy, Nancy, and Walter from my home to The Grand. Nancy went upstairs next to where I would place Marie. I knew she would watch after Nancy when we were not in the room. She had always been good about coming to tell me when she thought Nancy was uncomfortable from lying in the same position for too long. As I had anticipated, Marie was thrilled to be close to Nancy. She was like a mother hen around her.

Peggy stayed downstairs. She could not be trusted to climb steps. I put her in a four-bed room, but it was huge. Also, my grandmother and Mattie were there. A round alcove on one side of the room was 14 by 20 feet. It was perfect for Walter. He would be away from the ladies and in a place where I could watch him.

Next I brought over Marie and Ilga from The Inn. We were all prepared to carefully watch Ilga while scared to death she would run again. However, when she saw James, she sat close to him as possible, and I honestly do not think for one minute she thought about running. What a laugh!

All jets cooled down when I brought in 102-year-old Norman. Once he had been a baseball player. Norman was a gentleman, and we learned to love him and his family. I also got some good publicity by having him. He had been on national TV several times, and the local media knew where he was. He took a liking to my grandmother, and the two of them quickly formed a friendship. Now Mimmy's attention was on Norman instead of on me. Whew! That surely took a load off me. Since Mimmy was in a wheelchair, he pushed her everywhere and was constantly at her side. They ate together, much to Peggy and Mattie's disgust, and he would even push her around the neighborhood. This much activity was surprising, considering his age!

Norman still chewed tobacco and had his private stash brought in from North Carolina. He kept it under his bed and had beer in the small refrigerator in his room. Mostly, the beer was reserved for my staff after work hours. But I knew that sometimes a beer or two disappeared during shifts. I guess they thought they could get away with taking a beer and not being caught. I wasn't too harsh with them because, frankly, there were days when I would go get them beer, for it was difficult to maintain sanity sometimes.

Marty, my three-year-old granddaughter, was living with me for awhile, along with her mother and little brother while dad played war on a big aircraft carrier. Marty was extremely observant and had no fear of the elderly. On the contrary she was unusually open with the residents. She loved them, especially Nancy. She would sit on the arm of her chair or the side of her bed for hours talking to her. She was gentle with Nancy and observed everything I did for her.

Nancy was incontinent, and needed a catheter. The catheter was attached to a drainage tube, which carried the urine to a collection bag. Marty would watch the urine run down the tube into the plastic container used for storage, and watch attentively as the bag was emptied. A home health nurse came in to change it when it was necessary and to fix it when something went wrong with it. Whatever the problem, Marty sat at the head of the bed holding Nancy's hand and always spoke softly to her. "It's OK, Nancy," she would say. "It won't take them long, just a few more minutes."

These words were sincere and were often accompanied by tears. Her caring nature and her words were comforting to Nancy. Nancy's face was always relaxed as well as her bladder. Unless the bladder was relaxed, it would be difficult to insert a catheter when a change had to be made.

On one of these occasions, the nurse failed to hook up the end of the catheter to the drainage bag, and, of course some urine ran onto the bed Marty yelled at the nurse: "If you can't do it right, don't do it!" She actually grabbed the end of the catheter and pinched it to cut down the flow. The flabbergasted nurse quickly attached the end, and then helped me change the bed. For a three-year-old, her keen observations and knowledge were remarkable, but she needed reprimanded for the way she spoke to the nurse.

Later on, I caught her emptying the drainage bag into a bedpan and carrying it to the toilet to dump it. She did not spill a drop and had covered the floor with a plastic bed pad before she put the pan down to drain the urine bag. Gently, I stopped her from doing this procedure because I did not want her exposed to the germs in the urine. She did not understand but accepted the fact that it was the nurse's responsibility and that she should let the nurse do her job.

Residents don't always display their true feelings when placed in a home. Some are resentful and act out their feelings but most keep them inside and gradually become either hostile or start to deteriorate physically or mentally.

I wasn't sure about what was happening with Mattie, but she was beginning to show signs of change. She was not eating well, she was sleeping a lot, and she seemed to be withdrawing from my grandmother and Peggy.

I called the daughter and suggested she take her to the doctor. Usually I would take a resident to the doctor, but this family wanted to handle Mattie's appointments. I told the daughter that Mattie had some bleeding from the rectum and asked her to mention this to the doctor. When they returned, there were no specific instructions from the doctor, and the daughter just sort of shrugged off the trip to the doctor as needless. I didn't like her attitude. Did she think it was fine to trust me to take care of her mother but not okay for me to know what was wrong with her? I instructed the staff to watch the bleeding, to keep bed pads under her at night, and to start using diapers.

Later that evening, the doctor phoned me at home. He asked questions about the home, about me and my education, and explained that he had just set up practice here and knew nothing about the care provided by homes for the elderly. He also wanted to know about the different types of homes and what could legally be done in each of them. I described every type of home and the licensed capability of nursing care. I was licensed for a Type 3, which meant I could perform certain procedures with a doctor's order and could keep people who could not walk. My homes had fewer restrictions because as owner I was a registered nurse. Some other types of homes were restricted to residents who could walk

After listening for a while, he asked me a hypothetical question. He wanted to know if I could let a person bleed to death from a GI hemorrhage without doing anything about it. He then inquired if this was something I would handle, and did I think I could possibly do it legally and morally. I realized the question was more than hypothetical, so I could not answer him right away. I had never been subjected to a proposal such as this and was deeply concerned about the ramifications of such an action.

Apparently the daughter had arranged for her mother to sign papers stating that Mattie would refuse all operations and tests or procedures.

The doctor explained that he thought Mattie had a bleeder inside, but to confirm this he would have to go in or at least perform an upper and lower GI test, both of which were refused by the daughter. If he hospitalized Mattie, the Utilization Review Committee would require him to do the tests because of the bleeding, regardless of the paper the daughter held, which had been signed by her mother. The doctor's back was up against the wall. What he was asking me to do was to allow her to stay at the home until she expired. I reluctantly agreed to comply.

After I told the staff what the doctor said—and I can assure you they had plenty to say about the daughter—they agreed to take care of her. This decision was one I did not feel good about. How could I honestly ask these men and women, whom I trusted to provide as normal a life as possible for the residents, to clean up Mattie's blood until there was none left? I knew they felt doing so was immoral, if not unlawful. They would be deviating from the path of virtue. I felt so bad for them and for Mattie. After all, what did I really know about that piece of paper?

I was told in the beginning that Mattie did not have any money, so I only charged her $700 a month. I later found out that she had been a very wealthy woman until the daughter stepped in. What family members will do in the name of greed never ceased to amaze me. I knew in my heart that Mattie hadn't signed the paper willingly but had no way to prove it. Mattie was semi-comatose, thus unable to carry on a conversation.

She sank lower and lower into oblivion, rarely moving or making a sound, a pathetic sight to behold.

It took only three days—quicker than I had anticipated—for all the blood to drain out. My faithful employees changed the blood-soaked pads every hour. They tried to get them to the dumpster in a plastic bag as quickly as possible, but the odor was offensive. The residents did not complain, but we did. Someone was always gagging. It was the most horrible odor I have ever smelled.

When Maxcine changed a pad during the third night and found barely a trace of blood, she called me. I went over right away. Mattie was close to death. We reviewed the procedure, and I called the doctor. He expressed his appreciation and said that he had not thought death would come this rapidly. All I had to do was tell the paramedics to call him and he would sign the death certificate. I had been unable to call hospice in because I was in the gray area of the law.

She died within an hour. I called the daughter and the paramedics. The paramedics were puzzled because of her color, which was chalk white, but didn't inquire further when I told them she had a bleeder that was irreparable. The police came and talked to me, and, afterwards, when they talked to the doctor, I was allowed to call the mortician.

The family came and said very little until one of Mattie's sons asked me why I didn't send her to the hospital. He was irate and focusing on me. I started to remind him of the papers refusing treatment because I assumed he knew about the arrangement, but then the daughter stared at me with widened eyes, so I knew she didn't want me to tell. Whatever she was trying to pull, she was not going to take me down.

I asked her in front of the family if she had told the rest of her family about the paper for no treatment. Obviously she had not. To cover myself, I told the angry son I would call Mattie's doctor. I walked off to the kitchen, called him, and informed him of the angry son so that he could prepare himself for the son's phone call. When I came out of the kitchen, the daughter asked for her deposit. What a thing to say at a time like this!

I said, "You will receive what is left of it within 30 days as per contract." This was about all I could muster. My license could be in jeopardy because I did what she wanted, and she was insisting on a few measly dollars!

The next morning one of the hospitals phoned with an admission. I was wary because this hospital rarely called. The caller must have had a major problem placing this particular patient, or she wouldn't be calling me. The patient was a gentleman, alert and somewhat oriented, pleasant, and "cute".

"Does he have any money?" I asked her, for there had to be something wrong.

"Yes, as a matter of fact, he has a substantial bank account," she replied. I agreed to take him, but when I asked if there was someone to sign the papers, the answer was no. He had a wife but the hospital had been unable to locate her. She did give me the name of his bank and account number. I decided I would take this gentleman to the bank and have him withdraw the first month's rent. I couldn't afford another freebie!

When Sam and I visited him, we saw immediately that this sweet little old man was anything but sweet. He was a fighting Irishman who was about as stingy as they came. He made it clear that I would not have any of his money. His name was James O'Leary and he was confused as to time and place and was about as oriented as a turkey. He did not trust me but took a shine to Sam. We asked him if we could go to his bank to withdraw the rent money. He refused. I tried to explain to him that I couldn't take him unless he paid me. This was precisely what he wanted me to say because what he really wanted was to go to his own home and take care of himself.

Finally, I decided to accept him and hope the rent would somehow appear later. The next morning Sam and James left for the bank. They came back a few hours later with money and some tall tales. The teller knew James very well. He was known as the town drunk. The teller hadn't seen the wife in a while.

James's savings account was rather large, and the teller said James had full access to it. Sam withdrew three month's rent plus deposit and allowed James to put the money in his wallet, thinking he would forget about it by the time they got home. Wrong! He took the money and hid it! The next morning while James was eating breakfast, Sam went snooping and, after a three-hour search, found it on top of a ceiling tile.

The teller had also told Sam that James had been hit by a car in the middle of Main Street, and that was what had put him in the hospital. A priest who happened to overhear some of the conversation joined in because he was interested in where James was staying. Sam told the teller and the priest where James was now going to live. He gave them my business cards. The priest told Sam that he sometimes would find James in the church passed out.

I knew enough to keep him away from the cocktails and beer. It was funny! He did not remember that he drank. One of the girls offered him a beer, and he turned it down.

As a passing thought, I wondered if James could withdraw some of the money and put it into another account in his name only. The bank teller said the wife had resurfaced and was trying to get all the money. Because I wanted to be sure I was protected, I called the bank and asked for the teller who had helped Sam. I explained what I wanted James to do so that there would always be money for me each month. She talked to her supervisor and the two agreed that it could be done.

Sam and James went back to the bank. I also sent a contract with the three months credited to show that I was charging him $900 a month. They transferred $50,000 into a new account with only James's name on it.

With that over with, I could at least relax about getting paid.

The wife finally answered the phone after I called several times. I told her I had James and asked her if she would like to visit him and meet me. What she had to say clearly indicated she wanted nothing to do with him or me and that she would not pay me a dime. This time I had used my head. There was the second account when the three months ran out.

Also, I called Barnaby to tell him what had happened. He didn't see anything wrong but wanted a copy of the contract. I sent one.

After a few days, the teller at the bank called me to let me know that James's wife had been to the bank to close out the account. She was somewhat irate when she found out about the money that had been transferred. She was James' second wife; the money was from his first wife—the money wasn't even hers! I called Barnaby and alerted the police. I had no way of knowing what she would try to do. What she did was declare war!

When she arrived at the home, she mentioned that James had a daughter whom she thought lived up north somewhere. She accused the daughter of cleaning out her bank account. She hadn't a clue as to what had really happened. I didn't know then that she was not James's first wife and the daughter was not hers.

She ranted and raved at me and stated, amongst other things, that she would not pay me, and James could rot as far as she was concerned. She created such a scene that I finally had to ask her to leave. After her departure James threw a temper tantrum, which eventually became frightening. He was worse than a banshee. No wonder they lived apart!

I put up with James's tantrums because I truly liked him. He was stubborn and instigated a lot of quarrels, but they were always interesting and delivered in an eccentric fashion. The strangest thing was that he seemed to have forgotten that he was an alcoholic. This probably accounted for his delirious behavior at times.

He wore a watch but never looked at it and constantly asked what time it was, especially what time dinner was. His internal clock was right on track He would sit at the dinner table precisely at 8:00 a.m., noon, and 5:00 p.m. every day. If food were not served immediately, he would glare at the staff, mumble under his breath, and start pacing until it was ready. He never knew what time it was, but it was always time for him to eat.

One day, he demanded that I hem a pair of his pants. James never asked, he demanded. He badgered me every fifteen minutes until it was done. He would not wait for anything. This pants episode was something new and exciting. I looked at the pants and, realizing how old they were, was afraid the fabric would crumble if I ran a sewing machine over them. I attempted to hem them while James stood next to me in only his underwear, glaring a hole right through me. As I sewed, the fabric fell off from the power of the needle. I tried to explain to him that the pants could not be hemmed. . Those were his trousers and they would be hemmed, he insisted.

I finished up the other leg and let the bottom of the leg fall to the floor with the other piece and handed them to him. He saw the raw edge and told me he was leaving my house right there and then. I was so angry, I told him to leave.

He picked up a paper bag and left, walking down the street with those pants on. They ended up about four or five inches too short.

I called Sam for I knew James would listen to him. He came right over and drove away to look for him. James got in the car without even remembering where he was going or why. When he walked into the house with Sam, he asked, "How are you, Missy?"

When I managed to find the daughter, her voice dripped with honey. "Oh, you do not have to worry about getting paid," she said, "I'll see that you get a check every month."

She came to town, not to see her father or me, but to see an attorney to get legal guardianship. She also wanted to get her father a divorce from his second wife, who was not her mother. Which should have come first? I sent her to Barnaby, my lawyer, to let him decide, and he screwed up royally. He got the guardianship first and then could not file for a divorce because James was now legally incompetent, according to the law. What major perplexities this was sure to bring! Even though his daughter was his guardian, he was still legally married to his wife. James was about to collect a large settlement from the driver of the car that had hit him. Fireworks would surely be happening soon.

The daughter had papers drawn up and served on me to prohibit me from letting his wife see him for any reason. She also signed all of my papers required for him to stay with me. I reminded her that she was now responsible for all the rent money and any expenses incurred by James. I clearly explained when the rent was due and that I would charge a $10 a day late charge. She turned a deaf ear to me. I never got the rent on time and would have to yell at her every month about it. It was more that I wanted to endure; it was difficult enough to endure his temper outbreaks. On one occasion, Barnaby was able to secure rent money or three months in advance, but other than that one instance, the rent continued to be late, and she had an apathetic attitude when I called her. I was expected to keep him hidden from his wife, but, in her eyes, I didn't deserve to get paid. Of course, she had taken control of the separate bank account at the bank by now.

The only good times were when he actually acted like a gentleman and entertained Marie and Ilga. They both thought he was a spotted rooster. It was funny to watch them. However, Marie and Ilga were so jealous of each other for his attention they sometimes actually fought. Once Marie tore into Ilga and pushed her down on the floor before we could separate them. Marie had found her a man and she was not going to turn him loose. However, the story ended differently from what she wanted. It ended up with James and Ilga becoming a social pair. I even let them sleep in the same room together. This was, of course, with the guardian's permission.

James would laugh and cut up with Sam about having sex with Ilga. None of us ever really saw anything happening, but that doesn't mean they weren't having some sort of sex. My mother did observe them making out from my condo window one afternoon while she was visiting. We could see across into the third floor where James's room was. He had Ilga on the bed, but she quietly moved away from him. Her mind was too shallow to realize what he was trying to do.

James and Ilga were to have a long-term friendship while living with me. They became part of our family, sharing our special moments and holidays. They were accepted by my married children and their children; Ilga and James even participated in the marriage of John.

The day Solomon came to live with us all our lives were forever changed, for this was a turning point in our education and understanding of Alzheimer's disease. Solomon came through the door and made his way to the room I had chosen for him. This would be his asylum for the duration of his stay.

His son gave me little information about his father. He wanted to leave quickly, but I delayed his departure long enough to get the papers signed and to gain a little information. Solomon had been a mercantile owner and was up very early every morning to get the chores done before he left for work. Apparently, his wife was spoiled and seldom did any housework. He made the coffee, the breakfast, did the dishes, ran the vacuum, and whatever else had to be done before he went off to work. Doing these tasks was a habit of many years.

On the first night he woke up at 4:00 a.m., got out of bed, pulled out the bed, pissed on the floor behind the bed, and scooted the bed back. Next he walked into the huge living room where he turned on all of the overhead lights and all of the lamps. Next, the kitchen. He turned on, plugged in, or started everything that was run by electricity or gas. Then he climbed the stairs and went from room to room, turning on all the lights. The radios and televisions were last.

When he completed his rounds, he went back to bed, pulled it out, drank a glass of water that was on his night stand, pissed on the floor again, pushed the bed back and crawled in to sleep until breakfast was ready. This would be his routine for awhile.

Maxcine about lost it. For a lack of knowing what else to do, she followed him, turning off everything he turned on. Also, she made him get out of bed so she could mop the floor. In the morning at breakfast, he was a totally different person, completely unaware of what he had done during the night.

Since I had been told that Solomon had Alzheimer's, meaning he could not control his thoughts or actions, I asked the staff to be more lenient with him. In fact, I had guidelines for dealing with mentally impaired residents. For one, we treated them as if they were normal. I made sure that the staff related to these people as though their minds were competent. We spoke to them in a rational tone of voice, put them at the table for meals with the other residents, took them to scheduled appointments, structured their environment to be as close to their home as possible, and most important, we never talked down to them. Every word was spoken as if they could understand what was said. Some responded to this, some were incapable, but at least they were treated with the dignity they deserved.

I always wished I could do more for people with Alzheimer's. These people were essentially stranded by society, by their own families, and literally dumped somewhere—anywhere—that would just take the burden away. Every minute I could, I spent reading and doing research on what made these people tick but was constantly frustrated by the lack of resources. From what I could comprehend, however, losing one's mind is not always a disease, and is not always a natural part of the aging process. In fact, a slight forgetfulness is normal, but only 10% of the elderly suffer from severe mental impairments; nearly 85% test normal.

All of the mental symptoms of the elderly can be categorized into one word, DEMENTIA, which is defined as "a loss or impairment of mental power." Dementia describes a group of symptoms and is not the name of a disease.

There are two major conditions that produce symptoms of mental confusion, memory loss, disorientation, or intellectual impairment. They are delirium and dementia. Delirium may cause drowsiness or a fluctuation between drowsiness and restlessness, confusion, forgetfulness, or disorientation. It can be caused by illnesses such as pneumonia or kidney disease.

The second condition, dementia, impairs the intellectual function in a person who is clearly awake. The symptoms could point to a treatable disease such as thyroid disease or, more likely, Alzheimer's disease, the most frequent cause of irreversible dementia in adults. Multi-infarct dementia is believed to be the second most frequent cause of irreversible dementia and is caused by a series of strokes within the brain.

With this in mind, and it is only the tip of the iceberg, caregivers take note. A lot of the problems with your so-called crazy relatives and friends could be eliminated with simple changes to their lifestyle. Both malnutrition and negative effects from medications can cause the same symptoms as dementia does.

Almost everyone I admit comes to me in a malnourished state. They do not eat because they are unable to prepare meals at home, and, in many instances, there are no family members to assist them. If they are able to get to a grocery store or can make someone a list of items to purchase for them, you can bet cinnamon rolls, canned Spam, cookies, and raisin bread will be on the list—not an altogether nutritious diet.

Medications are also high on the danger list. Just about every one of my residents suffers negative effects from their medications. They do not know what they are taking, for what ailment, and Lord knows, how much to take. Too often, they are given medications to keep them under control, mentally and physically. Is it any wonder their intellectual functions are impaired?

Chapter Twelve
The Hurricane

Hurricane Elena threatened the west coast of Florida on Labor Day weekend, 1985. More than half a million residents left their homes in the largest regional evacuation in U. S. history. Two hundred thousand people went to Red Cross shelters for three to four days as the storm stalled in the Gulf of Mexico. When the storm passed, the damage totaled more than $150,000,000. The damage resulted from a storm that never came ashore. It remained 50 miles out in the Gulf. Elena was a category 3 hurricane that would have been capable of ten times the damage had it moved inland.

It had been 65 years since a major hurricane hit our area. The last one in 1919 had no name. Very few people even knew it was going to hit. There were 287 deaths and over 500 casualties and ships lost at sea.

I was proud to be a part of the regional planning and disaster team for Elena. We put a plan into effect that had to work. Of course there was much more to learn, but this hurricane would clearly demonstrate to the public, to me, and 57 elderly persons how much damage hurricanes could cause and what people were capable of withstanding and, hopefully, keep people from being complacent about approaching hurricanes in the future.

The population in 1985 was fifteen times what it had been in 1919 and hundreds of people lived in high rises and expensive homes so close to the bay that the locals called these domiciles temporary housing. Despite warnings from environmentalists, building permits had been approved for every inch of sand. There were no sea walls, sand dunes, sea oats, nor any other vegetation. There was the sea, a beach, the brick and concrete buildings, the two-lane road, a small tract of land, and the bay. It didn't take a weatherman to predict total destruction from one good storm surge.

The forecasters were predicting the storm would come ashore at the mouth of the bay. This meant that the bay would be sucked dry and all the water thrown back in a fury with the next high tide. The entire Gulf Coast would be under water. The bridges would be thrown from their pilings. No one could evacuate quickly enough if this happened. All of this had been the biggest fear of the planners. The only way out was one highway if the bridges collapsed. There were nearly half a million residents, and a quarter of them lived at the beaches, which were attached to the mainland by four bridges. This area covered about 35 miles. I knew the damage would be extensive as we watched the TV for progress reports.

I lived next door to The Grand in a condominium with a lot of glass. My son-in-law placed mattresses and box springs in front of the sliding doors. This would offer some protection, but The Grand was my big problem.

About this time while I was at The Grand, I heard a loud knock on the door. When I opened the door, in came several persons, two of whom I recognized as HRS inspectors. I knew they were due to see if I had corrected my deficiencies, but surely they knew that the entire town was preparing for the storm. I led them to the dining room and wondered how I would bluff my way through this inspection. I hadn't expected them for another week or so. Thank goodness the paperwork was prepared, and as far as they were concerned, having the paperwork done gave me the power to operate. We chatted for a few minutes, mainly about the hurricane, and I thought that this would be a good time to announce that I was evacuating Shoreline and bringing residents here. They weren't interested in my plans.

The dietitian asked to see the kitchen, so while the others were involved in the policy and procedure manual, I took her to inspect. What a wonderful time for an inspection! It couldn't have been better. All needed food was in, everything was spotless, and all the appliances were in good operating condition. The open food was sealed and contained, procedures were posted, and thermometers were in place in the freezer and the refrigerator. They could look for days and be hard pressed to cite me with a deficiency. However, they never left a facility without finding a page full. I answered the dietician's questions and made correction notes, knowing they usually didn't write you up if they thought you would comply with their requests.

We rejoined the others, and I was pleased to hear compliments on my policy and procedure manual. Even the fire inspector surprised me. He could see that the fire prevention was not finished, but he granted me a two months' extension. During the exit interview, they permitted me to keep the eleven residents already there until everything was finished. I couldn't believe my good fortune! Maybe the hurricane was a blessing, distracting them from their usual nitpicking.

With the inspection completed, I could now concentrate on the problem at hand—elderly residents in the path of the hurricane. I could use The Grand as a shelter, but since Shoreline was directly on the bay, it would have to be evacuated. The only other choice I had was to take them to a public shelter where they would have to sleep on hardwood floors and eat whatever food shelters provide. A public shelter wasn't really a choice as I was not prepared to change diapers or control these people in an unfamiliar environment with no conveniences. So, to The Grand they would come.

I mentally recorded the steps to take to protect The Grand. With plywood placed on the huge lobby windows and the main doors, I could accommodate 20 or so residents in the lobby areas. The beds could be split up, half of the people on a mattress and half on a box spring. Linens that I had recently ordered had just been delivered, so there was an ample supply. Emergency supplies were ready, and over $3000 worth of food was stacked in the supply room. A lot of it was frozen, but we could begin cooking it as soon as we were sure the storm was going to hit us. I had a commercial kitchen with a gas stove, but part of the disaster plan was to shut off everyone's gas.

God! I was scared. Too much to do, too many people to protect and take care of, and such a short time to prepare. I checked out the latest predictions. We were still one big target.

"Shouldn't we start on this food?" one of the cooks asked.

I thought about it and decided he was right. We could always eat it and if we were hit badly, I wouldn't lose all that meat. I watched the cooks go into action and start assessing the situation. These people had it all together. They respected me and were truly devoted to their work. In return I respected them and was grateful for their service and expertise. When I was sure they could handle this bigger-than-usual chore, I left the building. I had to get away and think. I had the emergency plan firmly in my mind; now I had to implement it.

The sun was shining. It was unusually hot and the air was steamy hot, making it difficult to breath. I started walking and decided I wanted to see the bay. There were some beautiful trees, a lot of grass, blooming oleanders and other flowers along the way. It surely didn't look as if a storm was coming. On Beach Boulevard there were lots of shops and galleries. Some of the windows were being taped and others were covered with plywood. The owners weren't taking chances.

The Grand was slightly elevated from where I was standing. It was built in the early 1900s and was in good condition. The last bad hurricane apparently had not damaged the building much. I felt that it would be safe.

As I looked out over the bay, I expected to see a great deal of turbulence and high waves. Instead it was slightly choppy and there were a few white caps. However, the water looked almost black with the sun shining on it, not its usual greenish color. I sat for a few minutes and listened to the sea gulls and watched the people strolling by. On the way back, I took my time, knowing that it would be a while before I could relax again.

When I opened the door, I saw Sam nailing plywood over the windows in the lobby. He was drunk, more so than usual, but he was working on his own time. I couldn't say anything unless he became a safety hazard. I thanked him for the help and paid him for the materials he had brought. An alcoholic for sure, but he never missed a day's work and did not drink on the job unless I told him and the others to have a beer. I put up with trying to keep him sober because of his relationship with the residents. I liked his kind and considerate approach, and he had a calming effect on those whose minds had gone astray. Being able to manage situations with the elderly was a definite gift of his. The day he was hired is a lasting memory…

When I came in the back door, I saw a strange man on a ladder taking down the blinds and washing the windows in the dining room. I wondered where he came from, for I had not hired him, and people didn't usually work for free.

Bill, the person I had hired to do cleaning, including the windows and the blinds, was standing in the kitchen.

He called me aside when he saw the puzzled look on my face and said, "I hired him. He is a bum off the streets and I got him for two dollars an hour. He is only temporary. He wanted food, but I told him he could clean for money."

Bill was on probation for ninety days and certainly was not in a position to be hiring anyone. His references were evasive, giving me hire and termination dates only. The people I knew with the city would tell me if there was anything wrong about him, but I had not had time to call them. Ordinarily I would not put anyone to work prior to checking on them fully, but Bill was a paramedic and could be extremely valuable to me.

I introduced myself to Sam.

Being polite, he shook my hand, and said, "I do appreciate the job and I will prove worthy." He didn't look like a street person. His clothes were good quality and he had recently shaved and showered. The only car in the parking lot I didn't recognize was a new model that had to be his.

I went to my desk and made out a list of chores for Bill to complete. Sam was told to finish the windows.

I gave Bill a typed procedure for the tasks he was to do and he said to me, "Why can't Sam do these when he is finished?" Right away this boy was in trouble.

I told him, "You will do well to complete this list today." Why I didn't fire him right then is still a mystery.

The noise of the front door slamming brought my wandering thoughts back to the present. My son-in-law, Tom, had returned and was ready to help Sam with the windows. I told him about the day Sam was hired. We laughed about him being called a street person, for he was not one but had turned out to be the best employee I ever had. I even raised his salary to a level equal to what the others were making.

I watched the weather on TV. Things were sounding bad, and they were calling for voluntary evacuation of Zone #1, which included the low areas along the shore. Shoreline was located in one of these areas as was my own house.

I should have gone ahead and brought the residents up to The Grand because the weather wouldn't be improving, although the sun was still shining and it was hot! I asked Sam and Tom to make up the beds and get the disaster supplies ready. Glancing at the TV again, I saw just how monstrously large this thing was. Suddenly, I was frightened. Damn. This thing covered the entire Gulf of Mexico.

Knowing that I had an agency (contract labor) person at Shoreline taking care of the seven residents, there would have to be ample time for her to get the residents, their clothes and medication, and supplies together. The disaster supplies were all easily accessible because they were in one closet. It was the clothing and medication I was worried about. I called her. The phone rang forever. Sometimes when I was busy with a resident, I would let it ring. The person calling would call back if the matter was important. She answered finally, sounding very sleepy. It was 10:00 in the morning.

"Were you busy with a resident?"

"No, I was asleep," she replied.

Assuming that she had finished all of the morning work and was taking a nap, I let it go. When I asked her about the water and if it was rising, she replied, "It's OK." I asked her if she had read the disaster plan and she told me she had.

"Well then, we are going to evacuate the home and bring the residents to The Grand. Is there anything you want me to go over while we are on the phone?"

"No," she replied, "I know what to do." The last thing I wanted to do was alarm her and start a panic, but I had the feeling that she didn't have the foggiest idea of what to do or how.

Anyone would be hard pressed to find a procedure or policy that was not operational in my homes. I had just completed the disaster plans for Shoreline and for The Grand. I had reviewed them the evening before to be sure they were workable. My only deviation from the plan was the evacuation site. I was taking a chance, but the safest place to bring them would be The Grand, not the designated church site.

I took a few minutes to call the staff. I needed to know if they were going to be able to help me, and if so, whether they were bringing their families. Most of them agreed to come in. I was pleased. Their help would be valuable. The cooks were doing fine. The aromas coming from the kitchen were mouth watering. They were not gourmet chefs, but the meals coming out of there would please any palate. I was assured that there was ample food there for a week and we would be able to feed 50 people.

My friend Dee called. She had a home with seven residents, or so I thought. She wanted to know if she could bring her residents to The Grand instead of to the church that had been designated. I said, "Yes, but please bring your own supplies and food. She showed up with 14 people. Then I knew she was hiding people at various places.

Carefully counting, I came up with eleven people from The Grand, seven from Shoreline, and fourteen from Dee's. Thirty-two elderly people in a hurricane! I could almost feel the barometer dropping. At least, mine was. A full moon, especially now, would mean trouble. Full moons generate higher than normal tides, which meant higher flooding, but also it meant that people's own barometers dropped, making them act crazy.

I asked Sam and Tom to let me know when they were finished so we could get the residents from Shoreline. I had sent Bill home. By then the people in the building were starting to get real squirrelly. My grandmother was asking too many questions and was doing her usual thing—kicking the doors open to the kitchen. I tried to keep the residents out of there, but she was family and damn well let me know it. She didn't understand why there was so much food being cooked when she only wanted a sandwich. She would never adjust to a structured environment.

When Mimmy was around, she would try to find out when the food would be ready in answer and then sneak it to residents who complained of hunger. When I discovered what she was doing, I told the residents it was not mealtime, and we would feed them when meals were ready.

Kris came in with her three girls. Her husband Robert would come after work. She was about finished with the morning care, and the men had the beds in place in the lobby. It really didn't look so bad. God knows we had room enough in the dining room to feed an army.

My policy called for notifying families of my evacuation intentions in the event it became necessary. I sincerely hoped some of the families would come after their loved ones but doubted they would. When Kris began bringing in residents for lunch, I was free to start placing calls. I went into the office and dialed the first number. Although I knew that Naomi's guardian had no way of caring for her, I still talked to him. He wished me luck! It was much the same with all the families. What they said in sum was "Just do the best you can and keep us posted!"

Nancy's family offered to help. I gratefully accepted this genuine offer. They were such a loving, caring family. I started making calls to the families of the ones at The Grand to let them know I would not evacuate residents from The Grand. Some were pleased and some were concerned. I suggested to the concerned ones that they come for their relatives, but suddenly concern magically changed to acceptance of my plan.

After making the calls, I turned on the TV again for news of the hurricane. It still was bad. This storm was heading directly toward us. Voluntary evacuation was being urged, except for Zone #1, which was to change to mandatory evacuation by nightfall. I asked Sam to go with me to Shoreline to bring back the seven residents. Kris and Tom would down the fort at The Grand. When we arrived there, I was stunned to see the residents still in their nightclothes, even though it was nearly noon. I had hired an agency nurse's aide to give my regular staff the day off. I asked the employee in charge why they were not dressed.

"I had to get some sleep!" she replied. The residents had been left alone all morning.

"Did they have any breakfast?" I asked her. She nodded. I went into the kitchen, and what a mess I found! She hadn't done the dishes or cleaned up. The table was full of dirty dishes, left over food—and now it was lunchtime. I looked at Sam.

"Carolyn, can we get this mess cleaned up and get them over there by ourselves?"

"That's exactly what we're gonna do because we have no other choice. Now let's get started." Sam knew from my tone of voice that I was upset. He had that right.

I called the hiring agency that recommended my Shoreline employee and explained about the mess I had found. I requested that her lack of care be taken into consideration when the bill for her pay was sent to me. I told the employee to pack her bags and hit the trail. Sam had already started dressing the men and packing their clothes to take to The Grand. I cleaned off the table and put the dishes in the dishwasher and finished up the kitchen. They could eat lunch at The Grand. I phoned Kris to tell her to have lunch ready for them. She said that Maxcine had come over to help. Bless her heart!

I started the dishwasher and went in to help Sam. We had all of them dressed and ready to go in less than an hour. I loaded one of the cars with all the blankets, pillows, and the emergency supplies. Naomi started screaming as soon as she saw me. I was not one of her favorite persons.

"If you keep screaming, I will dump your skinny butt into the bay!" With that, I got one of her other voices, the deep throaty one with raspy sounds, which said, "You do and the others will get you." By now, her multiple personalities were driving *me* crazy, and there were times when I wondered what she could do if she convinced herself she could destroy. No matter what, she had to be put into one of the cars.

Sam took three residents, and I took four, including Naomi. I put Bea in the front seat with me, Hannah, Mac, and Naomi in the back with

Naomi in the middle. I probably should have put her in the front, but I was afraid she would cause me to wreck the car. I rationalized that by putting her in the middle of the back seat, she could not get out of the car doors. The screaming continued and it was as bad as it had ever been. The neighbors had long since realized that I was not killing her and had been gracious enough to stop complaining. When I was assured that the house was secured and everything turned off, we left.

We started up the road with Naomi screaming at the top of her lungs and using every profanity known to man. I just had to ignore her. It started to rain, Naomi kept screaming, and Bea was leaning on me. I kept pushing her over, but she didn't understand I had to be able to turn the steering wheel. My nerves were starting to fray.

Suddenly, the screaming stopped and inside the car it became very quiet and still. Then I heard a murmuring sound that sounded like a tiny kitten meowing. I turned around when I came to a stop sign to see Naomi not long for this world. She was black in the face and Mac had his cane across her throat. I flung open the car door and jumped out in traffic. I opened Mac's door and tried to get the cane away from him. He was determined he was going to kill her, and I couldn't overcome his strength. Thank God Sam had stayed behind me and had pulled up when I stopped. It took both of us to get that cane away from her throat. I wanted to collapse right there in the street. My first thought was to take Naomi to the hospital, but, when she started screaming again, I knew she was all right.

I started the car and moved along smoothly until we were almost there. This time Bea kicked up her heels. She tried to get the door open. I had to yell at her, or we would have never made it. Finally! I blew the horn for whoever was in The Grand to come out to the car. Maxcine and Kris came running as well as Jim, who had come over to help. I walked in, fixed a cup of coffee and took time to have a small nervous breakdown. I cried and shook so badly I couldn't hold the cup of coffee. How much longer would I last?

The ones from Shoreline, all except Naomi, were placed in the dining room for lunch. They were hungry. We made sure they had plenty to eat, in hopes they would take a nap so that we could get better organized.

First I turned on the TV to see if there were any changes. The storm had estimated winds of 115 miles per hour, and they were becoming stronger. The barometer had fallen to 28.6. The storm was 350 miles southwest of the mouth of the bay and movement was 15 miles per hour. It was located at 85 longitudes and 25.6 latitude. If the hurricane continued in this course, it was predicted to come ashore by noon Saturday and this was Thursday. A surge of seven to ten feet was also predicted. A reconnaissance plane had just come back in, and the pilot reported that this had been one of the roughest rides he ever experienced. According to the Saffir-Simpson Hurricane scale, Elena was a category three hurricane. The scale went from one to five with five being the strongest.

Naomi was still screaming her bloody mouth off. I called her doctor, who then prescribed 75 mgm. of Thorazine and 10 mgm. of Valium, both by injection. I injected her. We had to move her to a back storeroom before someone tried to kill her, but her screams were still audible. Sometimes I wondered what God had in store for me. Was my destiny to be forever a caretaker for His poor lost sheep in the waiting room to heaven or hell?

Family members started to come in, some mine, some others. All of them started helping with mealtime, and they waited to eat until the residents had been served. Also, they brought their own blankets, pillows and personal care items.

We were concentrating on keeping the residents in the large lobby because it was boarded up and would be safe. Doing this was difficult. They were restless and needed to be entertained. I asked Jim if he would turn on some music and try to get them to dance or sing or talk to one another—anything to keep them occupied.

My grandmother was being my worst nightmare. She would not go into the big room and refused to have her bed moved. I don't know if she didn't understand what was happening, if a defense mechanism was kicking in blocking out the hurricane, or if she was just being stubborn. In any event, the residents began straying out of the big room, wanting to know where Mimmy was. I had to close off the large, ceiling-to-floor, heavy vinyl door to keep them out of the dining room.

I didn't like the sound of the wind, which had increased and was now howling. The sky was black and the rain was coming down in torrents. I didn't want Mimmy by those windows. I went to fetch her. She was in her room near a window. "Mimmy, you cannot stay here. It is just too dangerous."

She did not stutter as she said, "I just wish I could die. Let the damn hurricane take me."

I told her that if this was the way she felt, she could stay where she was, and I would somehow find her body and bury her when the storm was over. . "Yes, I will send you to Tennessee for burial," I said and left, closing the doors to that room and went about my business. Later Maxcine talked to her, but to no avail.

Peggy was acting up, and I knew it was because Mimmy was being allowed to do as she pleased. She was really using that walker today and getting into everything. When she had to go to the bathroom, she called someone to take her as if she were incapable of going by herself.

Mattie, Nancy, and William had been left in hospital beds because they were bedfast. None were any trouble. They just needed to be changed every two hours or so. Their bowel movements created bad odors that were not welcomed by others in that small space, so all disposable diapers and pads were put in plastic bags and taken to the dumpster quickly, and the room was sprayed to kill the bad odors as soon as possible. There was little if any air circulating in the lobby. I asked Jim to find some of the box fans, place them in the corners. Turned on low they increased the flow of air somewhat.

Gig and Hannah had been on the sofa most of the morning. Hannah was in her own little world and certainly didn't know that a hurricane was about to clobber us. Gig was usually visiting, going from neighbor to neighbor, but, surprisingly, he had not made an effort to visit with anyone since the hurricane threatened to hit us.

Even though I had told the residents of Shoreline why I was moving them to The Grand, I thought that maybe it was time for me to talk to the residents again and at least try to explain why their lives were being turned upside down. Some would comprehend, and the rest would be able to recognize that something was wrong and that I was trying to keep them safe. They trusted me for I was all they had.

Mac was rambling about and still mumbling about Naomi. She was still screaming. I really did have to do something with her, but what?

Suddenly, several people ran to the back door, and, being the curious one that I was, I followed. Apparently Dee had finally arrived. When the door was opened, the rain poured in, driven by a ferocious wind. Why had she waited until now to evacuate elderly persons? She brought in 14 people. I knew she was hiding out several, but here were six more than she was licensed for. They got drenched coming from the car and were all upset. Some were crying, some were stupefied, some were curious, and others seemed unruffled by the disruption to their lives. Her staff didn't look like happy campers either. Knowing Dee (a dictator-type), I'm sure they were there because of Dee's iron fast rules rather than because of the emergency conditions.

We all pitched in to get them dry and settled. One of Dee's employees insisted I remove Nancy from her hospital bed in order to have a bed for one of Dee's residents. I had to get tough on this one. Dee could have had her hospital beds moved here if she had done so the day before. I felt sorry for the resident, but the staff would just have to be inconvenienced. A bed was made on the floor for the resident, and if the caregivers had to kneel to care for her, so be it.

What confusion was everywhere! To organize I told the staff to take care of the residents while I concentrated on making sure meals were prepared and that everyone would eat. The cooks had long since gone but not before cooking several roasts, a hen house full of chicken, a large ham, several meatloaves and even some Swiss steak. It was all in the refrigerator and so far we had not lost power and were able to warm up the food. I found a large bowl of potato salad and another of coleslaw. Today, it would be ham sandwiches with lettuce and tomato, potato salad, and coleslaw. Also, there were large cakes in the freezer, one of which I took out to thaw. I found out later that people in the shelters were lucky if they got bologna during the storm, so we were lucky.

Robert, Kris's husband, came in to help me get dinner ready. He was a butcher and knew just what to do with the ham I had chosen. It was sure beautiful. No visible fat. Noticing the meat's good quality was a small pleasure in the midst of chaos.

We made over 100 sandwiches. Instead of dressing them, we placed small containers of mustard and mayonnaise on the tables. Most of my residents would tear off the lettuce and tomatoes but at least I had served it to them. I had to prepare some soft or pureed food for about seven people. For these people, junior baby food substituted for foods like potato salad and coleslaw.

I asked one of Dee's employees to help me with Dee's residents' plates, since I didn't know what size portions they would eat. "Can't you do that?" she asked. I didn't bother to respond. I just put half a sandwich on each plate and small servings of the salad and slaw.

When I announced that dinner was ready, those who could walk were there in a flash, those who had to be pushed were impatient, and those in bed or in geriatric chairs with trays attached were squirmy. Everyone was hungry.

I had always been a friend to Dee and helped her when I could. She passed herself off as a nurse (R.N.), but she wasn't one. I had to study hard for the privilege of being an R.N., and, frankly, I resented her falsehood. Nonetheless, I overlooked this fantasy of hers and tried to teach her what I could. She paid her help a lot more than I did, and now I knew how and why. She housed many more residents than she was licensed for, probably at all her properties.

Naomi was still screaming. I could hear her better when I was in the kitchen since it was close to the storeroom, and the storeroom was near Naomi's bedroom. I had been in several times to offer her something to eat and drink, but she refused everything and spit the juice and milkshake all over herself. Of course she had to be cleaned up, which made me angry. When I took her to the bathroom, she screamed over and over again in her raspy voice, "You goddamn son of a bitch!"

She had changed personalities at least three times since the move. I know the people in front heard her, but they were not saying much about it. Mac didn't use his cane on her again, but I could see him gritting his teeth. I guess he could really kill someone if he so desired.

Dee was trying to take over, telling my staff what they should be doing. I didn't want her to do this. All four of them were in on their own time, which made me extremely proud to be associated with them. They were all good people. I would have to tell Dee to take care of her own and let me handle mine.

I counted 57 elderly people at the dinner table and there were four in bed. Where did they all come from? I could have sworn they were coming in off the streets.

Then I heard noise coming from the front of the house. As I approached the lobby, I saw several firemen. One of them asked who was in charge. I answered that I was. He ordered me to take all of these people to the church a block and a half up the street. I tried stating my case, but he wouldn't listen.

"If you remain in this building, we will have to fill up the body bags when it is over." What a cruel thing to say in front of these people. Any hope they had been able to grab onto was shattered now. I stood by my original decision. It would be tragic to try to move these people a block and a half up the street. The firemen shook their heads and left.

Soon it was time to give Naomi another injection. I couldn't stand any more screaming, and I was sure the others felt the same way. I knew the medication would not help but drew it up in the syringe. It always amazed me that she could scream for so long. She had been screaming for nearly six hours, and I had known her to scream for two days. The look on her face told me that she had no intentions of stopping. I had to get her out of here before someone did try to kill her. As a matter of fact, I had seen Ilga walking around with a pillow in her hands. I called the administration of the fire department. I didn't want to dial 911, for I was sure that the paramedics and police had their hands full.

I explained what was happening and the lady said, "We have assigned our units to certain areas. Let me see what the ones close to you are doing." She came back on the phone to tell me they would be right out. Thank God! At least we could have a few days rest from her.

When they arrived and heard the screams, they immediately walked to the back room. Granted, it didn't look the best, but I had made her comfortable. She was terrified of strangers. When Marc, a paramedic I knew, walked into the room every voice came out and he got the "Goddamn son of a bitch" in about three voices. Marc backed off and asked me why she was not in a state mental institution.

"She has been there many times, but they just keep discharging her," I said.

"What medications has she had?" asked the paramedic I knew.

"I gave her 150mgm Thorazine and 20mgm Valium in six hours, IM. The last injection was given just a few minutes ago," I said.

"You've got to be kidding, Carolyn. "How can you give her that large a dose without…?"

"Here, see for yourself." I said, handing him the doctor's orders. Kris had brought the orders the minute Naomi started screaming. He shook his head and told the EMT's to load her up.

I asked him how it was outside. "Are you running your tail off?" To my surprise, he said that they were not even that busy but were prepared for the worst, as the storm got closer.

I watched them haul her off to a local hospital, the only one in town with a locked ward. I felt as if a thousand pounds had been lifted off me. Sam, Jim, Maxcine, and Kris all hugged me and thanked me for taking action. Under their breaths, Dee's help said, "It's about time."

I went over and asked to talk to them. I politely told them that they would probably be under water if they had stayed at home and most assuredly would be on a hardwood floor if they had gone to a shelter. If they wanted to stay here, there would have to be a change in attitude and some teamwork put into play. Apparently, Dee had left. I gave them assignments which included cleaning, helping prepare meals, cleaning up afterwards, and entertaining the residents. These tasks were in addition to taking care of their own residents. They looked relieved. Maybe they just needed some direction.

I was tired. I sat down in front of the TV to watch the latest news about the storm. It seemed to be stalled. That meant trouble. When these storms stall in warm waters, they built up intensity. The hurricane was a little more northerly than when I had last watched. Coordinates were now 92 longitudes and 26 latitude. Winds were estimated to be 135 mph. It was about 50 miles closer but could change directions now with the slow down. I needed a nap. Tomorrow would be a hellacious day no matter what the storm did. I stretched out in the chair and closed my eyes.

When I awoke, residents were being placed in beds. I looked at my watch and couldn't believe I had slept for nearly two hours through all the confusion of dinnertime. Everyone seemed okay except for my grandmother. She woke me up saying, "I ain't going to eat that tough ol' roast beef. Fix me something else." I told Sam to ignore her for I knew the beef would fall apart with a fork.

Peggy had to get her two cents in and said, "I'll have whatever Mimmy has." I shook my head and went back to sleep. At evening snack time I woke up again. Norman helped Bea sit down and then joined me at the table for an extra cup of coffee. Gig had been unusually quiet. I dreaded the time when he decided to make up for lost time. Mac hobbled in and took his seat. The employees were getting the bedtime snack ready for them. Ilga, James, and Maria ambled in with Maria making sure James assisted her with her chair. Poor Ilga's mind was so shallow she didn't realize Maria was trying to steal James away from her. Maria was very obsessed with James but had cooled her jets a little after the fight she and Ilga had had. Most of Dee's residents had to be fed, but I watched with pride when Maxcine and Kris started feeding some of them custard and milk.

When snack time was over and everything cleaned up, we helped them get ready for bed and then sat down to eat something. There was a case of beer and several bottles of good wine locked up in the storeroom. I got them out. The beer was warm, so I put it in a bucket of ice. I laughed when I heard Sam say, "It's about time." It was surprisingly quiet that evening. We relaxed and took turns sleeping.

I wanted so desperately to go home, take a shower, and change clothes, but the condominium had closed off all the doors to the inside. I could look out from the third floor of The Grand and see directly into my condo except where Tom had placed the mattresses and box springs. Resigned, I grabbed a couple of blankets and a pillow and went up to the second floor when it was my turn to sleep. There was a place outside the ballroom where there were no windows. I spread out on the floor and slept.

A noise woke me. Thinking my husband was there, I patted the floor and said, "It's OK, come lie down with me." To my surprise it was Jim with his boom box. He must have thought I was nuts. We laughed and I fell back to sleep.

Saturday. When I awoke the next morning, there was nothing to wash my mouth out with except toothpaste. I had new toothbrushes but could not remember where they were. My appearance must have been rumpled at best. Oh well, everyone else would look rumpled, too.

The staff was busy getting breakfast ready, and the residents were washed and had on clean clothes. The TV was on and I sat down to watch. The storm was still stalled. Were we going to be sitting here forever? It had been three days since we heard about the approaching storm.

At breakfast I realized that people were walking in off the street to eat. I didn't recognize several of the women sitting at the dining room tables. Sam was asking one of them who she was when I walked over. She gave him a name and stated that she was staying at the church shelter up the street. She didn't like their food. I told her she couldn't eat here and suggested that she go back to the shelter. We could not feed any more people. She was highly indignant but went out in that ferocious rain and wind. All the new people were approached and asked to leave while they could get back to the shelter. Was I being cruel? The staff didn't think so.

I went back to the TV. The announcer was saying that the Saturday morning traffic was light compared to the usual rush, but the roads were beginning to clog up as people prepared to evacuate. News reports had frightened people, even though a voluntary evacuation order was all that had been issued. Also, sheriff's deputies and local police were gearing up for the possible massive surge of maniacs hogging the roads and not obeying traffic laws because they were in a hurry to get out. Then a new bulletin came on about the probability of the hurricane striking the coast. It ranged from 10% to 100% around the Gulf Coast. Our county had the highest probability of a strike.

According to the anchorman, it was time to issue the emergency evacuation order by zones, starting with Zone #1, which included the beaches and all low-lying areas. Thank goodness we had already evacuated Shoreline. I prayed for the people who lived in these areas. Could 700,000 people leave their homes and go to a shelter or get out of town in time to escape the storm?

Now people would try to get the supplies they should have gotten days before. Hostility would prevail in the form of a lot of grumbling and growling at grocery stores and gas stations. The natives were so complacent about hurricanes that they made no preparations, thinking that they could just ride them out. This time they were scared. The media had finally managed to put the fear of God into the population.

There were preparations to be made besides buying groceries and gas. Boats had to be secured, lawns freed of anything that could blow away, pools taken care of, animals taken to a shelter or veterinarian, and windows taped or boarded. Important papers had to be packed along with any medications, and prescriptions had to be filled. Leaving a home behind and knowing that there probably wouldn't be one when and if you returned, wasn't easy to do. I couldn't understand why most people had an apathetic attitude and did nothing until it was almost too late.

The Disaster Planning Commission had set up a plan that would prove workable. They had been notifying the public by instructions placed in the newspapers for weeks. They were honest and the plans seemed well laid down. If the choice was to go to a shelter, chances of survival were greater than trying to evacuate at this point in time because of the many rushing to leave.

I heard that the phone lines were starting to become jammed with frantic callers, mostly from the elderly who were becoming frightened and disoriented. Arrangements had been made with the ones who had called Civil Defense to be picked up by busses and taken to the shelters.

They also said that the Sheriff was evacuating the county jail. The maximum-security prisoners would be moved to the old jail downtown. Patrol cars were placed at all intersections and traffic had been stopped to allow the transfer. Force would be used if necessary to control the irate drivers who were trying to evacuate.

Sunday. News of the storm and its impact on the county was almost continuous now and seldom was anything repeated. There was something new and important with every breath. The storm had grown in intensity. The barometer was now down to 27.6. Lowering barometer readings had been the Disaster Planning Commission's greatest fear when Elena slowed down and eventually stopped because they indicated growing intensity of the storm. There would be nothing left of the town if this storm came ashore here.

I needed a break and decided to walk to the bay. It had already been a long and tiring day, and I had slept for only a couple hours the night before. It was awfully dark and ominous looking but the rain had stopped, and there was enough light to walk. It took me longer than usual to walk the two short blocks because of the wind. The rain started again when I got to Beach Blvd. The water was over the seawall and the white caps were huge. The water was black and murky. It had churned up the sand on the bottom of the bay and would, of course, wash it all out to sea. The same thing was taking place on the gulf side except the sand it took from the beach would be gone forever. I wasn't sure when high tide would be, but it would do a lot more damage than what I saw now.

The sky had a greenish cast, and the clouds were getting thicker. It was time to go back. It didn't take me as long to get home, for the rain was coming down heavily. By the time I ran in the door, there was lightening and thunder. The newsmen said we were getting the feeder bands—the outer borders of the hurricane. When this happens, the hurricane just sits there, swirls in a clockwise direction, pushes in the storm bands, and sucks out the tides and sand. From what was being said on TV, this action would obliterate quite a few pieces of property.

Someone ran in the back door for refuge. This could be a potentially dangerous thing, and by now it had happened several times. He said that the bay had come ashore a mile up Beach Boulevard and everything was underwater. I gave him a cup of coffee and informed him there was a shelter a block and a half up the street.

I walked into the dining room and couldn't believe my eyes. It was full of people I had never seen before. I told Sam and Tom to ask them to leave for the shelter, but they were afraid to send them out. I didn't know what to do because my insurance would not cover them if they were injured or killed. Most of them were moochers in ordinary conditions and, during a storm, they could take full advantage of my hospitality. Finally, I told them they were welcome to sleep on the floor. Later on we were able to give them a few blankets and pillows.

A bulletin flashed on TV. The storm would be a direct hit. I had seen pictures and heard tales about what happened with the last storm to hit in 1919. It had sucked the water out of the bay so that a person could actually walk on the bottom and sent it spiraling back with such fury it swallowed up whole neighborhoods, and no one had survived in the low lying areas. I could not imagine anything as horrible as that.

The howling wind and pounding rain were constant companions now. The residents calmed down in an eerie, frightened way. The tension rose, the barometer fell, and we settled in for a long night.

I decided to take night duty along with one of Dee's girls. She wasn't happy about getting the duty, but I reminded her of where she was and that I was calling the shots. I asked where Dee was and I got all kinds of answers. It was obvious she was taking care of other residents she had hidden out. We changed diapers and positions every two hours. Then, again the storm quieted. We watched a movie that was on cable when we were not busy. It amazed me that we still had cable and electricity.

I fell asleep after the last round at 5 a.m. but woke up two hours later. Sam called me to come into the kitchen. The news reported that the storm was moving slightly to the north. Maybe it would move away from us. Could we be so fortunate?

The news showed pictures of the beaches. The backsides of homes were gone and many other buildings were gone. A few of the concrete condos were partially standing, but there was no beach. The water was over Gulf Boulevard. God! It was awful. Shore View, a beautiful community, was under six feet of water. It always flooded there, but I had never seen anything like that flood.

Suddenly Peggy's brother, Jim, appeared at the kitchen door. I was shocked to see him out in this mess, but he said he wanted to be sure Peggy was safe. I assured him that all my residents were safe. He sat down for coffee, and we persuaded him to eat. He had been staying at a mall, which was being used as a shelter. I couldn't believe what he told us. It seemed the people at the mall were actually having fun all the while wondering if they had homes left to go to. The local theaters had opened up to the people in there, and popcorn was on the house. The newspaper had unloaded tons of newspapers and one of the paper company suppliers had unloaded a truck full of large plastic bags. Someone had the sense to put the children to work stuffing these bags with the crushed newspaper to make beds. It worked. No one had to lie on the concrete floors. Another truck had delivered a load of hot dogs and canned hams. A bakery brought bread and buns. The grocery stores had donated canned sodas. He said people were getting along and singing. The music store had someone playing the piano and guitar. As far as he knew the same thing had happened at another mall. Oh, things were looking good now, but this storm had not even hit!

I hoped people would be this happy afterwards. Jim had lost everything. It was painful, but he told us the TV showed the street his house was on. It was under four or five feet of water. He acknowledged our condolences and then said he had to return to the shelter because his wife was still there. I hugged him and offered both he and his wife prayers for safety.

Just then Ilga started to scream. It was probably Maria going after her again. Sam and Jim separated them, but the screaming continued. Poor Ilga. She just would not fight back. Maria had clawed her face with her long nails and had pulled out chunks of hair. What was I to do? James really wasn't worth the effort, but all they saw was a man. One thing was for sure. Maria's fingernails were going to be cut off today! It was done with her squealing all the while. I figured that if I put on some music, Ilga would forget the ruckus. I turned on the stereo and played some of her favorite music. She didn't need a partner; she danced all day by herself.

Lunch was a breeze. I guess my residents and Dee's had adjusted to their new surroundings and were satisfied to just eat. All afternoon was spent watching the storm. Then it temporarily stopped again. When was this ever going to end? We were all exhausted. The TV news showed the damage over and over again. The news media really wanted everyone to see what had been done, even before it had come ashore. After our charges were in bed, we played cards until bedtime. It was Maxcine's turn to work the night shift.

Monday. The next morning came quickly; it was Labor Day. The entire crew at The Grand was weary. It had been four days of hell. The natives were restless, starting to pick at each other, not eating well and doing all of the crazy things one might expect them to be doing. Sometimes I would just stare into space, not knowing what to do next.

Finally, the weatherman predicted a change. It looked like the storm was moving north. If only it would hold that direction and not turn around, we would be free of it. It was still mammoth in size, with 150 mph wind and higher gusts. The beaches had been pounded with 80 mile-an-hour, sustained winds from the feeder bands.

I made coffee, started the sausage frying, made biscuits, put on a pan of water for oatmeal, and started setting the table. Kris went outside. When she came in, she was smiling. The rain had let up, and she said that the boards at the entrance to the condo I lived in had been taken down. Oh God! I could take a shower and change clothes. All of us could.

I finished making breakfast and announced to the residents that it was ready. They responded quickly. Even my grandmother was anxious to eat. Sausage, gravy, biscuits, coffee, juice, and milk—comfort food meant to calm the soul. They stuffed themselves. After they left the table, I put on a fresh spread of food for the staff. We deserved it.

When I was sure that the storm was moving out, I took Sam and went to Shoreline to see if the residents who lived there could go back. The only problem we found was the stinking refrigerator I had unplugged. The water had risen to the back door but had not gone in. We turned the power back on, cleaned the refrigerator, and went down to check out my home. It was the most amazing thing. The water had gone into my neighbors condos on both sides and had done severe damage. Miraculously, my home wasn't flooded. The pool was overflowing, but there was no damage. The neighbors across the street had extensive flooding. The water rose and went down both sides of my house but did not enter it. All the neighbors' homes had been damaged, and they were amazed mine was spared. My husband had stayed there because he couldn't stand the noise and confusion at The Grand. He said he was scared a few times, especially when the water came over the seawall but just hung on.

John and Alyssa had missed it all. John was out at sea, and Alyssa had gone across the bay with Tom, and they stayed there throughout the storm.

Thankful for being spared damage, I went back to The Grand to take seven lost souls home, but, on the way, I realized there was no one to watch over them. I had fired the agency lady. I couldn't take on this added burden. I was stressed out, way beyond burn—out stage.

I asked Sam, who had gone with me, what he thought. "I would do it but I am as tired as you are, and sooner or later Naomi will be sent back there, and then what?"

We turned around and headed back. When we pulled into the parking lot at The Grand, I saw Tom getting into his car. He stopped and came to talk to us. He asked very excitedly, "How bad was the damage?" Sam told him and he was shocked. "I expected worse, and there was no damage?"

I don't know what I was thinking, but I knew that maybe my problem was solved. I asked Tom, "How would you like a job?"

"Doing what?" he asked.

"Running Shoreline."

He was genuinely surprised, but I knew he needed a job, and so did my daughter. I offered him $1200 a month with room and board and one day a week off. I further explained that it would be tax free and under the table. I thought I saw a glimmer of hope in his eyes.

I quickly said, "It starts today."

He got into the car and yelled, "Let me go see if I can persuade Alyssa. I'll be back soon."

With that problem almost solved, I was feeling pretty good, even smiling when I opened the door. Quickly, my smile faded with the news report. Elena was almost on shore close to New Orleans when she backed up, turned around, and headed southeast as if she had forgotten something in our area. No! It couldn't be. That storm could not come back!

It was still huge with 150 mph winds. Most of the day, it stayed on course toward us; then, late in the afternoon, as suddenly as it had turned back, it stopped. I decided it was time for the Shoreline residents to go back, and I would have to stay with them until I heard from Tom. In the meantime, I would need to hire a live-in caregiver, so I called the agency, for I knew I would not be able to do that job and work at and oversee The Grand simultaneously. Jim said he would help me take them back while I was getting their clothes ready. We would need food. Kris packed fresh vegetables and meats. I had plenty of non-perishables down there.

As we were putting the food in the car, Tom and Alyssa drove up. I had caught them at an opportune time. They were broke and had no jobs. He got out of the car, walked over to me and said, "You've got a deal." What a relief!

We moved everyone down to Shoreline, and I drove back, not to The Grand, but to the condo. I wanted a bath and some clean clothes. Kris had already beaten me to it, but I had two bathrooms. I kept the condo for purposes such as this. Close to The Grand, it was a convenient refuge from the world of pandemonium.

Elena turned northerly again, almost went ashore at Apalachicola, did a lot of damage, backed up again, and played around in the Gulf before coming ashore near Panama City. It crossed the lower end of the country, went out to sea in the Atlantic, and eventually fizzled

Chapter Thirteen
The Motel

I continued to work to bring The Grand up to code. Now I was trying to get permits for installing the fire protection systems and dividing the large rooms into smaller units.

Even though I had hired a contractor, I was told by an employee at City Hall that I still had to have an architect to draw up the plans. I didn't have a clue where the money was going to come from, but I hired one, and architect named Harold. When Harold went to the building department to pull the permit, he came back empty-handed with a perplexed look on his face.

"Carolyn, what in hell did you do to aggravate those people? I have never had a problem getting a permit, but, when I mentioned your name, I suddenly received some very cold shoulders."

I was speechless! I had hired this particular architect because of his good reputation, thinking he could accomplish anything. Now this. I was an unknown but I had certainly pissed off a lot of peopl

He asked me to repeat everything I had done in that building and to whom I had spoken. As I answered I watched his brow crease more with every word. He was especially concerned about the man following me, but I assured him that my lawyer would handle the problem. He shook his head in dismay and said, "Boy, you have ruffled some feathers and damned if I know why. Let me check around and see what I can come up with. Hell, I know your landlord well, and believe me, he wants something going in this building, and you are the best offer he's had." We said goodbye, and I called Barnaby to tell him about the architect's experience and to get an update. He had none to give.

I had to find out why that man followed me every time I went into City Hall and why he was keeping notes on me. I might add that he was not even inconspicuous about it, which made one or both of us stupid.

Out of sheer desperation and because I was beginning to feel like a savage ready to attack, I got into the car and drove the short distance to my lawyer's office.

"Barnaby, you have got to try to find out what is going on. The building department employees are driving me and Harold nuts and I do not know why." He was his usual apathetic self but admitted that there might be some harassment. He agreed to meet me at City Hall the next morning at 9:00 a.m.

Now those bastards would know that I meant to get those permits one way or another. We met as planned. When Barnaby opened the front door to City Hall, the first thing I saw was the snoop. He saw me and walked fast to an office, returning with that mysterious folder. I nudged Barnaby and pointed. The snoop tried to hide, but Barnaby did see him.

"I'll be damned," he said and told me to wait there until he came back. When he returned, he ushered me into the city attorney's office. The city attorney had the man and his folder brought to his office, but it was the wrong man. The city attorney made another phone call. We waited a few minutes before the right one made a rather embarrassed appearance. I was agitated by then and, at the suggestion of my attorney, I left. He assured me he could handle this.

Apparently there were city council members who did not want me to open a home. They owned hotels where they were illegally warehousing the elderly and getting away with it by hiring home health aides to come in and take care of them. They were charging these people $2000 a month, an outrageous fee at the time. The hotels were old, dilapidated buildings that hadn't been updated in years, including their fire protection systems. They were obviously not up to code but had been grandfathered in.

A copy of the file of notes the snoop had written was given to my attorney and the original destroyed in the city attorney's office. There had been an entry every time I came to City Hall, which noted what I said and to whom. Why? I was raising so much hell that the city council members were trying to protect themselves. I wanted to raise even more hell about this illegal breach of my privacy, but Barnaby convinced me of the futility of fighting, so I let it go.

At least a deal was cut, and I could move forward. I was told that when I supplied the building department with plans for remodeling and a separate plan for the fire protection, the permits would be issued, probably within thirty days.

However, the fighting wasn't over. Soon afterwards I discovered that my attorney and the owner of the building were bitter enemies over some ancient dispute. I immediately notified the owner of my plans for The Grand, but, since four months had already gone by, he did not appear to be thrilled. It seemed he really didn't care if I succeeded or not. I was determined to follow through with my plans, but the odds against me were stacking up. When he asked me if I would be willing to discharge my attorney, I was flabbergasted.

When I asked him why, his response was, "I don't need a reason but if you do not have that place approved by HRS by the end of the sixth month, I will have to take back the building."

"Talk about difficult!" I muttered as I walked away.

From there I went to my attorney and informed him that the work had to be finished within thirty days, one way or the other. As I left the room, I heard him say that the owner was "a mean son of a bitch." On my way home I thought that maybe it was Barnaby who was my real enemy. It was possible that he was the one stirring up the problems to get back at the owner…

As I went out into the bright sunshine and horrible humidity and heat, I wondered if I had gotten myself in too deeply. A lot of people were behind me and were giving all they could to help the cause, but did I have the stamina to weather the storm of obstacles that always seemed to lie in the way of success? I called the architect and told him the plans had to be at City Hall within one week. Thank God he had completed them, so I sent the filing fees over to his office.

Work at The Grand was continuing. The sprinkling system was almost finished, although it had been put in without a permit. The owner of the company assured me that once the permits were in hand, the whole project could be finished in two days.

The room division could wait. Only what the government required for licensure was being done. Since all the paperwork was complete and the kitchen was ready, I should be able to let HRS know I would be ready for inspection in a week.

In the meantime, I had residents to care for, some of them needing a lot of care. Since I had been unavoidably away from them, I needed to check them individually, monitor their progress, and notify the families of the progress in bringing The Grand up to code. I had kept a good record of Walter's feedings until lately. A certain amount of liquid was delivered into his NG (Naso-Gastric) tube every four hours, and I always wanted to be assured he was receiving enough nutrition. While checking the refrigerator one morning, I thought there were too many cans of liquid food. When I checked the count and looked at the flow sheet, I realized there were eleven cans too many. Each employee had to initial the flow sheet when Walter was fed. There had been no initials for five days. I questioned the staff, but no one admitted to feeding him. I checked the schedule. Lonnie was responsible for the past week. I approached him to find out why he had not fed Walter. He denied that he hadn't fed Walter. When I confronted him about the number of cans of formula left, he turned away from me and mumbled, "He ought to be dead anyway." I was furious. No one would starve to death in my home.

I grabbed his arm, swung him around, and asked him what he had said.

He came back with, "I don't care what you say, he was fed."

I pulled a disciplinary form out of the drawer and prepared to write him up. He smarted off that I couldn't fire him. He said he had influence. At that point, I didn't bother to write up anything. I stood up and asked him to leave. He refused. I called the police to escort him out. He laughed in my face. He wasn't a large man, but he was more than I should have taken on. At the time I had enough energy generated by my anger to grab him by the arm and start him toward the back door. When I got close, I threw him down the steps with him screaming what he was going to do to me.

I was exhausted. Someone had taken a can of formula and fed Walter. Sam came to see if I was okay. He told me I was justified but that I would probably regret throwing Lonnie out. I found out later that Lonnie had been fired from the fire department for mental problems.

Walter failed quickly after that episode. I notified his family that death was imminent. They wished to be called when he died, so they could see him before the crematory picked him up. Of course, I agreed. He died early the next morning before the day shift came to work. I went in to help Maxcine clean him, remove the tubes, and pull the sheet up to his neck. I did not like to cover anyone's head when there was a death. The sheet pulled up only to the neck gave the appearance the person resting. When the staff came in, I told them of the family's request and asked that he not be disturbed until they arrived.

After breakfast we sat down for coffee and a cigarette to unwind. When the nurse who usually visited William came in, all of us wondered what reaction she would have, but never in my wildest dreams did I imagine she would do what she did. Although William was her patient, she always checked on Walter, too. As usual she went to Walter and looked him over. She didn't touch him, but she was looking at him closely. She couldn't help but notice that the NG tube was gone, but she said nothing.

After she took care of her own patient, she asked to use the phone. I directed her to the kitchen. We weren't paying much attention to her until we heard her raised voice. She was saying to her supervisor, "But, he's dead and they are just cutting up and ignoring him. He feels like he has been dead for some time." I knew for certain she had not touched him.

I went into the kitchen and asked her if I could speak with her supervisor. She reluctantly handed me the phone. Before I could speak into the phone, she said in an angry tone: "You think it is some kind of a joke. That man has been dead for a long time and you people are not even aware of it."

Instead of responding, I explained to the supervisor that I knew he had been dead for several hours, but the family requested I keep him where he was until they arrived. She apologized. I requested that the nurse not come back, that I would prefer another nurse to see William. When I gave the phone back to the nurse, her supervisor apparently asked her to leave, for she did so, quickly. The staff had scattered when I got on the phone, but now they came back, bursting their guts laughing.

That nurse's nose had gotten her into trouble this time, and all I needed was someone like her spreading vicious rumors all over town. Some nurses did not have any scruples and were certainly brainless. It was not always this traumatic with home health nurses. I usually appreciated the assistance they gave, and there was something to learn from them with their every visit. My staff was good, but they were not nurses. Consequently, they often had difficulty communicating medical disease terminology.

After the family made their final visit to see William, I called the police and the paramedics to come.

Early the next morning one of the fire inspectors paid a visit and asked to see me in private. He apologized as he said I had twenty-four hours to move the residents until I got the fire protection finished. It was then that Sam told me that Lonnie was the fire chief's stepson. I knew that bastard would come back to haunt me.

I begged the fire inspector for another week. He told me he had to take his orders from above. HRS agreed with me, but in this business, city, county, and state can each supersede the other.

I left the building and walked down to the bay. It was stinking hot, but here, finally, there was a breeze. I sat down on one of the famous green benches, hoping I would not be mistaken for a lady looking for a man. I sat there for an hour or so, wrestling with the situation and trying to come up with a solution. Suddenly, what I had to do became obvious.

A friend of mine owned a house that was empty close by The Grand, and he would probably rent it to me for a small fee. I went back to the home, called him, and arranged to meet with him. I took Sam with me. It wasn't long before I had a handshake and a deal.

This place already had a fire protection system. The only major thing I had to do was put in a bathroom downstairs. The room was there as was the plumbing. I called Jim, one of my employees and asked him if he would take the responsibility of putting in a bathroom. He said he would because his father was a plumber. I sure as hell would not ask for a permit to install the bathroom. I wasn't ready to face City Hall so soon again.

With that taken care of, Sam and I set out to clean the place. We could do it in two or three days if I could come up with some more help, but, no, the job had to be done that day.

I called HRS and asked them if they could inspect this place and explained what had happened. They agreed to be there by 5 p.m. I simply couldn't imagine that the agency would comply with my request as they had never been cooperative before now. I guess they didn't want these elderly people out on the street.

I went downtown and picked up several street people on the corner to clean and haul trash. If HRS gave us an emergency clearance, these men would be hauling furniture from The Grand. Then I rustled up all family members I could find, for I knew it would be an all-nighter. I had until 8:30 the next morning. I was reasonably certain that the fire department would be on time.

While one street man cleaned windows, another swept and mopped floors, and the third cleaned the stove and refrigerator. Sam and Jim helped Jim's father put in a bathtub and a sink. The toilet was already working. He had been fortunate enough to find the exact-sized fixtures. Soon the place looked good enough to actually wax the hardwood floors. It was amazing what this team could do.

The monitoring company for the alarm system was already there and hooked up everything and tested the electric fire and smoke detectors. Right on time, as impossible as it may seem, HRS arrived. The representatives wanted to know how it happened that we had moved out of The Grand. They said it wouldn't be possible for Lonnie to work at any nursing facility again because HRS had to clear him to work with the elderly.

They looked around and asked where the food was and when I would be placing the residents there. I told them I did not want to bring food or furniture until they gave me the go ahead.

I was pleasantly surprised when they said, "Go for it." I found myself wanting to hug them.

The one important thing I had not been able to have installed was a telephone. It was 4:30 p.m. when HRS left. At 5:05 p.m. Mike came down to say that HRS had called at The Grand to say that the residents could not be brought to the new place. I was to return the call. I ran all the way up to The Grand. Apparently one of the HRS representatives had reported back to the agency that she was not pleased with the building. This nurse wanted a new and larger venting system installed in the kitchen before approval be given. I knew that the adequacy of the ventilation system was rightly the purview of fire inspector, though she could cause delay by ordering a new inspection. Furthermore, she had not mentioned the venting system when she was there previously, and she knew this was an emergency. I argued, but it was obvious she was determined to throw the proverbial wrench into my time schedule, and there was nothing I could do.

Legally, I could put three in the new home and take three back to my home, but I had fourteen to place. I couldn't take any more to Shoreline because it was full. Also, after paying everyone for their work and paying for the new bathroom, I couldn't afford to pay additional help, which I would need, if I split up the residents into different places.

I called a few of the family members together, and we discussed possibilities. The only solution we were able to come up with was to rent rooms at the city-run motel where the rooms were cheap. Then, with a little luck, I could have The Grand finished in a day or so and move residents back in. I was so angry at HRS I wanted to fight them, but I still needed that permanent license at The Grand. It would serve no purpose to ruffle their feathers.

Suddenly, all my plans and my work were interrupted by severe pain below the ribs. On examination, my doctor said my gall bladder had to be removed. How could I just stop and have an operation in the midst of chaos. How lucky I was to have a great staff, who simply took over while I went to the hospital. I left Sam in charge.

John and Sam went to the motel and rented rooms. Then after dinner they packed everything the residents would need and moved it down there. Two of the motel rooms had a kitchenette, and that is where they set up the supplies needed to manage the care. Sam stocked linens, food for snacks, bedpans, clothing, soap, shampoo, lotions and creams, and, of course, medications. Meals would have to be prepared at The Grand and brought to the motel, but it could be managed. Hadn't we already proven ourselves to be super human? But this would prove to be the worst ordeal we had been through, and it turned out to be a turning point in my life.

After the operation and while I was still in the hospital, I made plans for my staff to move residents the next morning after breakfast. I came home from the hospital in time for the move but soon realized I would be supervising more than working. Some of the families came to help. It was good of them, but I really wanted them to take home their relatives. That would have been the best of all possible worlds—at least for me and also for their loved ones. However, I had found out long ago that once families were rid of their elderly relatives, they were not going to chance having to care for them again. I was even offered money to keep them. I accepted it.

As I expected, the move was disastrous. I finally called wheelchair transport to take several of the residents, Nancy, Peggy, my grandmother. The others were taken by car. They were miserable, unhappy, and babbling incessantly. For such a short drive, they acted as if it was the end of the world. Mimmy and Peggy were the worst. They plotted to get even with me when they arrived at their destination. Nancy just moaned, justifiably so, for she had not been in a car or out of her normal position in a long time. The others just bitched about everything. James kept asking how much farther to Waycross.

After three short blocks, we arrived and began to get them settled in. I tried to get Nancy out first for she had been the last one in, but Mimmy shoved her chair forward to the door and would have wheeled herself out the door if the driver had not intervened. Damn, she was being nasty as hell. Peggy tried to follow her until I asked her to stop and wait until I got Nancy out. She didn't dare to push me like Mimmy was doing.

I had planned where each person would be put tentatively, but mind you I said "tentatively". Nothing seemed to go as planned. I wanted to separate Mimmy and Peggy because of space. Those wheelchairs took up so much space there could only be one per room. I knew there would be a fight, but I was not prepared for what occurred.

I planned to place Nancy, Peggy and Ilga in the largest room, which would also be our headquarters. I wanted Ilga in that room so that she could be watched constantly. Mimmy was going in with Maria.

My grandmother started yelling at me in front of everyone: "I took care of you all of your life. I gave up everything for you, and this is how you treat me. I want to go to Sharon's house. (Sharon was my mother.) She treats me like a human being. I wish I had never laid eyes on you." There was much more, but I just tried to ignore her and to hide the hurt, but her tirade ended up being the last straw for me.

By now, I was only a few days post operative. I should have called the families and demanded that they come after these people until I was well. I should have been resting, not working, and I certainly did not need any more of this abuse. I sat down in the car and cried. The rest of my crew took over and finished the move. After a few minutes I went in to use the phone. I called my son and asked him to come to get Mimmy. He must have called my mother, for she was the one who came for her. She asked what had happened. Before I could say anything, my grandmother yelled that I was not fit to take care of these people. I just ignored what she said and, thankfully, both she and my mother shut up. Then   as I bent down to pick up some clothing that had fallen to the floor, I put my hand on Mimmy's wheel chair to keep her from plowing backwards into me. She felt she had to watch everything I was doing because she didn't trust me, and, in trying to see my actions, she put her feet against the bed and pushed with all her might backwards with the handles going into my fresh incision.

As she yelled, "Get out of my way!" I fell to the floor. She saw me on the floor but ignored me. I called out and someone came in to help me before I passed out. When I awoke, I never felt such intense hatred for anyone as I did for her.

It was hell having to go to the hospital while the move was going on, but I had the greatest people working for me, and I knew that Sam would take charge and get the job finished.

I had to have a few sutures put in where the wheelchair handle had gone into my fresh incision. The surgeon was none too happy to see me in this condition. He threatened to put me in the hospital if I didn't go home and rest.

Mimmy was moved to a nursing home. Finally, I lost all respect for my grandmother, realizing how selfish and mean she had become. Believe it or not, Mimmy had been my favorite grandmother. She and I were very close most of my life; she had been very kind. However, old age and differences of opinion had taken their toll, and our relationship suffered greatly for it. Her dislike of me hurt so bad that I actually felt a physical ache every day when she turned on me. But, even though she now lived away from me, her attacks weren't over. She would return at a later date, and I would again endure unending abuse.

Tom came to the hospital and took me home where I lay down and slept for a few hours. After I woke up I felt better in spite of the pain, but it would pass.

Thank God I am an organizer by nature. I had procedures for everything. Menus were made up, and all the food was left at The Grand to be cooked and taken to the motel to serve. Snacks were at the motel as well as ice chests, bottled water, juices, sodas and even beer. I had purchased disposable dishware and glasses to make things easier and had done all I could think of to smooth out the wrinkles, even giving Sam and Maxcine money for whatever they might need.

HRS had forgotten about me for the moment, thank goodness, so we could concentrate on the immediate needs of the residents, which were many during this traumatic time.

There had been times when I could not meet payroll. Some family members chose to pay me long after the monthly rent was due. I didn't suffer financially, just emotionally for my employees. Many of them would say, "Just give me what you can." Others would say, "Skip me.

I can wait. Pay the ones with families." And then there were the ones who would write letters to the newspaper, complaining that I didn't pay my employees. Others complained by calling the labor board. These last two groups were the ones I would pay last.

It was about this time when the theft started at The Grand. If items weren't nailed down, they were stolen. I knew whom I could trust, and I just got rid of the rest of them. My dream was coming to a close, and there was no point in dwelling on those people who had chosen to go against me.

I stayed at the condo in the afternoons to rest. One such afternoon the phone from the security entrance rang. Mike was away on business, and I didn't want to stay at home alone, so Tom kept an eye on me since Shoreline was just up the street.

Sam was at the door. He had been about to start lunch for the residents but first wanted to see if I was OK. I buzzed him up. I really did feel better and decided to go over and help him. He argued with me, but I went anyway. Flossie was coming in everyday to help me at the condo, and she was not happy that I went to work at the motel even for a little while. I promised her I'd be back in a few minutes.

I knew Sam wanted to talk to me. That was why he didn't argue too much about my going to the motel to help him prepare lunch. We made sandwiches and warmed some homemade soup I had in the freezer.

Sam told me he thought I should get rid of three more people. They were stealing me blind. They were taking whatever they could from The Grand, mainly food. I quickly agreed to fire them and asked him to have a locksmith change all the locks on the doors. Only he and I would have a key. I phoned these employees to let them go, using the excuse I would be closing The Grand. They had little to say. Then I told Sam to tell the employees at the motel what had happened and to call the police or me if the employees I let go came around.

In three days, Ilga had run away six times. She had a rap sheet a mile long now. The police kept a picture on file and all of her vital information they needed. It would usually take us three or four hours to find her. She looked normal when she was out walking, and therefore didn't create suspicion except when she went out bare foot. Finally, we made a laminated identification card and hung it around her neck. At the insistence of her guardian, I had to have an extra person who did nothing but watch Ilga. I'm sure my employees took turns watching her, but at least they could keep up with her this way. At night, they tied bells on her legs and arms and on the doors.

Another resident who greatly challenged our patience and endurance was Soloman. We had set up stations in the rooms, each of them having equal amounts of supplies, snacks, and disposable dinnerware. A large ice chest was filled twice a day at The Grand and taken to the motel. Soloman quickly made a change in his routine. He would walk to the kitchenette, lift the lid to the ice chest, piss in it, scoop up urinated ice with a plastic glass, fill the glass with water, drink a sip, and throw the remainder into the ice chest. Then he would walk out the door, around the building, in the front door and repeat the process. The staff let him continue doing this—though, of course, they didn't use the ice in the chest after he did—until I saw what he was doing. I bought three new ice chests and went to the trouble of hiding them, but to no avail, for he sniffed them out. I called his son and asked him to come to get his father immediately. He became indignant but not nearly as indignant as I was. I wrote him a check for the rest of the month, including his security deposit, and took a financial beating. Sometimes this was the way things had to be done.

While all of this was going on, I hired a contractor to complete the job in the kitchen at the other home, which I affectionately named "The Inn." I knew we would end up moving the residents there. Jim was painting and papering the rooms. I stripped the floors and refinished them, bought new blinds, bedspreads, and new furniture for the living room and the dining room. It was really an adorable place. I didn't know what else to do for HRS as they had said that I only had to put in the new venting system and nothing else. I had already written all of the policies and procedures and had complied with everything else I knew to do before the improvements were done. Jim's father had done a wonderful job on the bathroom downstairs. Both baths had new ceramic tile, and they looked shiny and new.

The place really looked sharp now. I called HRS to do a repeat inspection. They were not required to let me know when they were coming this time, so it was a wait and see game. How much longer we could hold up in the motel remained to be seen. Life was a bit easier with Soloman gone. The staff didn't complain. The residents seemed to be adjusting to their new surroundings. Peggy still tried to be a pain in the ass, but no one put up with her shenanigans now that Mimmy was gone. Somehow I would come to terms with Mimmy, but the hurt was still a hard rock in my gut.

When I was sure that The Inn was ready for inspection, I called the fire protection people to finish the job at The Grand. They started that night. I had no permit, so the work would be done on the Q.T. They had it installed in two days. Also, the vent system in the kitchen at The Inn was being finished and would be operable the next day. Everything else was done except for the room divisions. I would license for whatever HRS would allow as it was.

I phoned HRS and asked for a follow up survey, to which they agreed. I was surprised, as I had really raised hell about the surveyor saying the venting didn't fit regulations. I guess they had to come out to be sure the place fit legal parameters.

I asked Barnaby to be present at both surveys. I was not going to take any more chances of a repeat performance. With notes on both doors to call me when and if they showed up, I settled down to wait.

They came to The Grand first. It really looked good. I had wanted to finish more renovations before they arrived, but the cosmetics could wait. They approved everything for licensure but wanted to see a city license. The explanation that the city would not license without HRS license flew over their heads. Finally, one of them called the city for verification. They were convinced, shook my hand, and left.

I sent my lawyer's assistant, Charley, to City Hall to get my license. They had to send out an inspector to check the fire protection system. Who came to inspect? The same fire inspector who had shut me down. He looked around, tested the system, and gave me a piece of paper that stated the system was tested and approved. He didn't ask me for the permit. I took the paper he gave me to the landlord and the copies of the

HRS approval to the landlord. He stated he would have a lease drawn up for me to sign and would call me.

I still had a week to go on my temporary lease, but the calendar was closing in on me. When I only had two days to sign the permanent lease, I discovered that Barnaby had not produced the city license, I called him. "We'll get it for you today," he said.

I called the landlord. I could tell something was wrong. Maybe it was the tone of his secretary's voice, but I didn't think she was being honest. I felt that my next phone call would result in disaster. I simply couldn't get to the office to sign the lease on the day appointed or didn't think I could. Looking back, I know I would have dropped everything to go and sign. But I thought that no one would put a person through what I had been through and not allow for an extra day. That kind of thinking was my big mistake. When I phoned the landlord's office the next day I wasn't able to talk to anyone who knew anything about my case. My faith in human nature was destroyed that day. It was over.

The next day I received a certified letter from the landlord stating that the time had lapsed for a new lease to be signed. I could have been beaten up and not felt the pain I was feeling. It felt as if the blood was draining out of my body. I really do not know how long I lay on the floor before Mike found me. He read the letter I still held in my hand. I looked around and saw what I would have to do. The landlord did give me 15 days to get my belongings out.

I went to the motel and told the staff. They felt as bad as I did but were optimistic. After all, we still had The Inn.

I went into Barnaby's office the next day to tell him to forget about the license. He kind of smiled and said that he knew I wouldn't be given the lease, and that was why he had not gone to City Hall. I asked him how he knew that. He reminded me that he had told me how he and the landlord despised each other and that that was why he would not let me sign the lease. Since he handles my finances, I asked him how deeply I was in debt.

He abruptly said, "A little over $150,000."

I sat there in a daze. How could this have happened? I had been giving him money all along to pay for the work that was being done on

The Grand. Where had the money gone? His flippant shrugs let me know what I should have known long ago. My long-time corporate attorney, whom I had trusted, had royally screwed me.

Chapter Fourteen
The Inn

When I walked out of Barnaby's office, the day was gloomy with black rain clouds and streak lightning in the distance, but the storm inside me was raging just as badly. I was losing control. I felt violated. I craved revenge.

I sensed another storm brewing when I walked into the motel. The staff was edgy and the residents were wild. It seemed that today everyone had a low barometer reading just like I did.

One of my staff said there was a note on the door at The Inn that said to call HRS. I did. The representative said surveyors could re-inspect the next day. "I'll be there," I said. Then I called Charley, my lawyer's assistant, and asked him if he could be present for the inspection. He asked me to call him when they arrived.

I arrived at The Inn early the next morning, and HRS surveyors came about 10:00 a.m. They commented that they had driven past the house, as they did not recognize it. Yes, I had hired a company to paint the outside. Charley arrived soon after I called him. When I introduced him, one of the men representing HRS commented that he did not see the necessity of having a lawyer present. I resisted comment.

They found a few nitty-gritty things to correct, but everything else looked fine until one of the women pulled out a newspaper clipping about me not meeting a payroll.

Suddenly, they all had strange expressions, and then I could almost see the handwriting on the wall until Charley stood up and said, "This is why Carolyn needed me here. The subject of that newspaper article has no bearing on whether or not she can license. Her financial status is strong and you have already inspected the books and accounts. The newspaper article is not open for conversation and is considered conjecture on your part by even bringing it up."

She folded it carefully and placed it in her purse.

Charley asked her if it should be in her purse, which was personal, or in my file which was a matter of record. She was furious.

Since it was the fire inspector who had stopped me from opening earlier because of the vent system, he was the one who said, "As far as I am concerned, you are cleared to open." The others agreed. I thanked them and wished them a pleasant day.

Hello, The Inn, good-bye motel!

My friend, a private investigator, happened to be in town, so I called him. I said that I wanted a background search on one of the HRS surveyors, the woman who brought out the newspaper article. He said, "Say no more."

Two weeks later, he brought me a file complete with pictures and a tape recording. Unbelievably, he had purchased the woman's body for $50 on the street. I was amazed that this was the same female HRS employee who tried to use the newspaper article against me. He also brought me a signed and notarized statement that certified I had hired him to do the background search on this woman for a fee of $500. When the time was right, I would have my ammunition. Nobody surveying the public in a state job should moonlight as a prostitute.

I wanted to have everything set up before I moved any of the residents into The Inn. The food and the kitchen utensils went first, then the linens and incontinent supplies. We didn't need the furniture from The Grand so I sold what I could and gave the rest to the employees. Amazing as it may seem, the building was emptied out in one day.

First we moved James, Ilga, and Marie from the motel to The Inn and settled them in. Norman's family took him out because I could not keep him for free any longer, and I did not want to accept the $400 offered to me. My budget was limited now that I had found out how much I owed. I would have to accept a resident who could pay the going price. Nancy was taken to Shoreline and I moved Naomi and Vera to The Inn. I was licensed for eleven residents there.

As I cleaned out the motel, I happened to look around. There were no fire or smoke detectors and no fire extinguishers. This trap was run by the city. They could get away with not complying with regulations, but I couldn't, even if I was inclined to try, which I was not.

Life went back to normal, as normal as it would get—at least for a while. Tom and Alyssa were doing quite nicely as directors of Shoreline since I had moved Naomi moved to The Inn.

Tom said, "I can at least sleep through the night without having to wonder which of her personalities will try to attack me."

Since I had been away from her, I had forgotten just how bad she really was. Just moving her to The Inn was traumatic. Over time we had learned just to pick her up quickly and do what had to be done, rather than try to pacify her, for she wouldn't mellow out under the best of circumstances.

She was now into her fourth or fifth voice. I couldn't keep up with them. They would get into shouting matches, and she would swing out to try to hit various people. She was nastier and meaner than ever. At mealtime we never knew whom we were feeding. She would raise her voice to a high pitch and tell us to "feed the rice to her; she's a goddamn bitch anyway. Here, you reprobate, shove this food down your slutty throat." The voices used slang words and phrases, some of which we never heard before. There were languages we could not identify, and several of the persons listening were familiar with other languages. Now there were five clear and distinct voices with other indistinct ones coming in.

Ilga and James were placed upstairs at The Inn. I don't know why, but some of us believed it would be more difficult for Ilga to get away from us if she were upstairs. After breakfast was finished, I bathed Ilga and dried and curled her hair. She went into her room to lie down about

10:00 a.m. I called her and James for lunch at 11:45 a.m. James came down and asked me where Ilga was.

"You don't know?" I asked him.

His mental failings usually took me by surprise because he looked sharp on the surface. At first I thought he was capable of bathing himself, but he wasn't. Sam caught him running the water and getting out of the tub. Only his legs and feet were wet. Upon inspection Sam found some ground-in dirt. From that moment on, he was bathed by staff. We were going to have to give James more attention because he obviously needed it.

Ilga was gone again. There was no point in looking for her because she might have been gone for several hours. I called the police and reported her missing. The desk sergeant laughed when he recognized her name. I didn't think it was so darned funny, but he surely did.

As soon as the rest of residents were down for lunch, I drove around looking for her. This was the first time she had left from this house, so there was no telling where she had headed.

We were still looking for her at 11:00 p.m. The police came by every hour or so, but this time she had really escaped. Then, while they were at the house, a call came in that a taxi driver had seen her on the other side of town. They went to talk to him and, ultimately, took him to jail. Apparently he had known about her since the first broadcast at noon, had her in his cab and continued to drive her around, milking the meter. He thought he would get a big fare out of her by playing innocent.

When the police found the taxi driver, he had already let Ilga out of the cab, and she had taken off. A man and woman found her several blocks away. They knew she did not belong out on the street late at night. They took her home with them and called the police. She still had the card around her neck when they brought her home. The card was in full view for the taxi driver to see, and yet he had taken advantage of poor Ilga. He belonged in jail as far as I was concerned.

When the cabby knocked on my door at six the next morning and wanted $300 for fare, I sent him to Ilga's lawyer. He never got there.

Later in the day, I had a visit from a police detective. He reminded me of the seriousness of her escapades. I told him what we had done, and he agreed that there was not a lot I could do on top of my efforts already in effect. He strongly suggested a locked place and said he would talk with her guardian to see if he had any suggestions.

I knew one thing. The front door would remain locked and chained, and I would have a very loud alarm placed on the door. HRS could just go fly a kite if having a lock on the door wasn't in the code. I was not going to allow an accident to happen.

Sam and I went over to close up The Grand for good. We looked around and made sure all of the closets were cleaned out and all of my belongings had been moved. We both cried when we locked the door and took the keys to the landlord. I handed them to his secretary and left. There was nothing more to say.

When we got back to The Inn, there were a couple of messages for possible admissions. I was glad because without more residents, I hadn't the foggiest notion of how I was going to get out of debt. The first call was from a lady who had been referred to me by a lawyer. I asked her to come over to visit. I would show her both Shoreline and The Inn.

When I answered the knock on the door at The Inn the next morning, I thought the two ladies standing there were looking for someplace else. Certainly they did not look like they belonged here. Then one of them introduced herself and her mother to me. They were both good looking, elegantly dressed, and southern bred. They were originally from Alabama. I could see either of them commanding a plantation during an earlier era. The older one, Roma, was the one who was looking for a place to live. She was so alert and coherent that I couldn't imagine her living here. As usual, I counseled them on what was available and what services was available in each type of home in the area. Roma's daughter asked all of the questions while Roma looked around.

She went into a room and sat down on the sofa and then a chair. She smiled at me as she said, "I'm just testing out the furniture."

I asked if she wanted to lie down on one of the empty beds. The look on her face indicated she was pleased. We discussed the rental fee and what it covered. That was not a problem for them. I said I would drive them over to Shoreline, but they were quite pleased with what they had seen already and wished to sign the papers. I kept a file on myself to allow any prospective residents and/or their family to see my references and resume. These always made a good impression.

I charged $1200 a month now. They signed all of the papers, filled out what was necessary, and wrote me a check. Roma would move in the next day. Her cousin had requested permission to take her out to lunch and dinner occasionally. I believe I finally had a cream puff. Roma was someone I could talk to, and she would be able to answer back—heaven!

The other call was from a nursing home. Minnie was a sweet little lady who was wheelchair bound but could feed herself. That was about all she could do alone, though. She was alert, but she had a speech problem. I said I would be down to see her that afternoon.

Shriveled up in a wheelchair, she had a big smile on her face when she saw me. As I introduced myself, she reached out to hug me. I returned the embrace. There would be a lot of lifting, but she was light as a feather.

The social worker had little to say when I asked about her finances. There would only be one reason for them putting her out. She had been on Medicare, which paid 100%, but which had just been disallowed. According to the social worker, Minnie was in the unlucky lower middle class! Too much income to qualify for Medicaid, not enough for private pay, but enough to pay me. She did not have a legal guardian and there was no family.

"Might I ask who is going to pay me each month?" I asked her.

"We'll have her social security and her VA checks sent to your address. She can sign the checks. You will just have to keep an accounting." I preferred not to do this, but I guess it was the only way to take her.

I pulled out papers in front of the social worker, had her explain to Minnie what they were, and asked her to sign them. Her checks would come the second month after she moved in because social security was always one month behind in payments. Of course, that meant I would not get paid for the first month. The social worker called in a change of address before we left. Yes, we. I took her home that very day.

I loved Minnie from the very beginning. Her speech was difficult to understand, though, according to her records, she had not suffered a stroke. My guess was that she was deaf and had been so for years, which caused the speech defect. Regardless, she could make her needs known. Everyone loved her and enjoyed spending time with her, though she tired easily and when she had had enough activity, she would ask to go to bed for a "little nap."

My little family was happy at The Inn. They all got along nicely with one another, usually trying to do things together. Their handicaps prevented too much in the way of activities, but we could get them involved in a card game occasionally, and for the most part they would sit and talk to each other. During mealtimes, they ate well and didn't like to be interrupted unless it was to have more food placed on their plates.

Maxcine called me early one morning to come over to The Inn before she left. She was anxious and wanted me to see something. That morning when she was dressing Minnie, she noticed a rather large mass on her right breast. It was warm and red. I suspected it was mastitis but, nonetheless, I would take her to the doctor. I made an appointment and off we went the next day.

I could never be sure of exactly how the federal hospital grants worked, but hospitals were paid a certain amount from the federal government to perform surgeries of various types on certain people. Minnie was qualified for the mastectomy program. She might not have needed a mastectomy—her cyst might have been benign—but a mastectomy was what she got because the doctors would be paid for doing surgery if malignancy was suspected. She came home in three days with orders to "keep the dressing clean and see a doctor in a week."

Maxcine called me the morning after she came home and asked me if she had had a mastectomy.

"I didn't look at the incision, but the orders indicated that they did do one," I said. "Why?"

"Well, you had better get over here and take a look. I think her breast is still there."

Just when I thought I'd heard everything…

When I arrived, I went into her room. Minnie was naked from the waist up, and there was a breast on each side. The dressing had come off and Maxcine noticed the problem while trying to replace the dressing.

I put on a pair of sterile gloves with the intention of cleaning the wound and placing a dry sterile dressing on it again. I reached for the peroxide to wipe it off before placing the dressing on. Maxcine asked if she could clean the wound because she already had on her gloves. I handed her a pile of sterile 4 x 4's gauze bandages and the peroxide. As I turned away for a second, I heard a scream and spun around. A flood of putrid, gray pus was pouring out of Minnie's false breast. The doctor had done a mastectomy after all, but there was so much infection in the chest that it looked as if the breast had been left on.

We cleaned Minnie up and called the doctor. The doctor saw her right away and prescribed antibiotics. The sack of pus drained several times more and finally started to clear up after a week or so.

Sometimes residents changed overnight. Roma was one of them. When she first came to live at The Inn, Roma was amazing to watch. She fussed over her clothes like a mother hen and remained immaculate at all times. Her cousin came every day to take her out, either to lunch, dinner, or shopping. She insisted on going to the beauty shop almost every day, and her room looked like a room out of *Better Homes and Gardens*. I always encouraged residents to bring their favorite things, including any small pieces of furniture they wanted. We even unfurnished rooms if residents wanted to bring in their own furniture and accessories. Roma's room had all of her own furnishings. She had twin beds with spreads of a white Heritage type and the dresser matched the bed. All were white wicker. Every day Roma would putter around on her beautiful mauve carpet most of the morning. If doing that made Roma happy, great! The rest of our clientele knew Roma was around, but I don't think they realized she was one of them, though they would in time.

Breakfast was in the making one morning when James came running into the kitchen.

"Carolyn, Carolyn, Carolyn, come quick. There's a woman in the bathtub."

He dragged me toward the bathroom by my arm. I called out to Kris, but she couldn't stop what she was doing. After deciding that nothing could be as bad as he was making it out to be, I shook off James's hand from my arm and went back to the kitchen because the biscuits in the oven were turning a light golden brown and needed to come out. After taking them out, I turned everything else off, and went with James, who was terribly frustrated by now. As we approached the bathroom, he became hysterical.

"See, see, Carolyn, look at that."

I saw what he saw, a naked lady lying in the bathtub with her head under the faucet, the water slowly dripping on her face and into her mouth. How hilarious! I started laughing as Kris entered the room. She burst out laughing so much she cried. Roma was lying there totally oblivious to anyone watching her and obviously out of her mind. James wanted her out of there so he could use the toilet. He was frantic. We picked her up, and I made sure there were no injuries before Kris and I took her to her bed. James literally pushed us out the door, his need was so urgent.

When we got to her door, I realized why she had gone to the tub. Her rear end was covered with feces, both dried and recent. I had it on my apron as well. There was discoloration all over the mauve carpet, and the odor was offensive. Roma would have died of embarrassment and shame if she had been in her right mind.

Kris, who had gone to the kitchen to finish preparing breakfast, yelled, "Breakfast is ready!"

James came out of that bathroom and took the steps two at a time. Thank goodness he was quick, for Roma was about to get her first bath from us. She had been bathing herself but not today. Something drastic had happened to this woman. Her mind was fine earlier in the morning, but now it was lost. At breakfast she just picked at her food as if she did not know what to do with it. I tried to feed her. She wouldn't open her mouth.

This was her habit the rest of her stay unless I told her she was going out to lunch with her cousin, and then she would resort back to her true self.

As time went on, we would find her in the closet sitting in a corner, under the bed, or hiding wherever she could find a place. In just two weeks, Roma changed from an immaculate granddame to a deranged stranger scooting around on her buttocks, spreading her own feces.

Losing one's mind is bad enough, but then she would revert to perfect lucidity at times, with no recollection of her bizarre behavior. We never knew what to expect.

In one way or another, the elderly all eventually change. Some lose their minds, while others change personalities. Most of them show signs of depression and despair, which causes rapid deterioration. They expect family members to take them in and provide the care they need. When they become totally confused or viciously angry, families literally dump them in a home like unwanted animals.

I wanted to cry when I thought of the total neglect too many of my residents suffered. Most were burdens to their families. More often than not, a family would place an elderly relative with me, then, within a short time, cease to visit. It broke my heart watching a resident stare out a window for hours, obviously hoping a loved one would appear. It seemed that families saw their elder relatives as burdens they couldn't wait to get rid of.

Poor Roma went through months of deterioration. I never knew who she would be from time to time and rarely was able to help her in any way except to keep her clean, dry, and fed. Even when she dressed up to go out, she showed signs of failure. Her color was gone, her face sallow, and her body mere skin and bones.

Her cousin questioned me about taking her for outings anymore. I felt that Roma seemed to rally a bit when she did go out, so I told her cousin to continue taking her out as long as she could. After a while it got to be too much of a chore, for Roma just didn't comprehend what was happening. Then the outings stopped, stripping Roma of her one last hold on reality. She deteriorated rapidly after that.

When I took her to her doctor, he was appalled at her appearance. Lab work later revealed pernicious anemia. Roma was physically ill as well as mentally imbalanced.

Roma could no longer eat, so her cousin insisted she be given a gastronomy tube for feedings. I agreed, for I had some deep-rooted feelings about not allowing people to starve to death. I taught the staff how to do the feedings, and we kept her in excellent condition until her demise.

No matter what crisis occurred with the residents, HRS inspections were always at the back of our minds. The inspectors were due back any day to re-inspect and to judge if the deficiencies they listed on their last visit were corrected. If corrected, they wouldn't return for a year or so. They could, of course, pop in at any time, especially if they had a complaint, but their caseload was so heavy they didn't have time to visit unexpectedly.

Most of my time was being spent at Shoreline now. The Inn was running smoothly, and it was not that Shoreline was having problems, for they weren't. It was just spruce-up time. We needed to review the policies and procedures and be sure everything was going to be okay with the survey coming up in a few months.

Although Tom and Alyssa did well at first, they were now pulling their hair out what with the overwhelming responsibilities they had in running a home. The realities of elderly care were becoming too much for them to handle. They did a great job, however, because all the residents were surprisingly healthy. They agreed to stay long enough for me to hire new caretakers.

I pulled up the carpeting and had it replaced. Also, I bought a new dishwasher. The rooms needed paint and the yard needed landscaping. Our location on the bay made annual maintenance necessary. The salt air and spray killed anything that grew.

The renovations took a couple of months, and an additional $1000. I knew I would have to eventually concern myself with the mounting debt, but keeping busy was a wonderful form of denial.

When my excuses for delaying finally ran out, I called my lawyer to get the bad news I'd been dreading. As usual he avoided me; he didn't return my phone calls. Why hadn't I seen this problem coming? Next I called all of the creditors I was aware of to get a final billing statement. They were anxious and willing to send me bills.

After receiving a week's worth of mail, I went into shock. I had no idea there was so much money involved. I always paid upon job completion. How on earth did these amounts build up? It seemed as if Barnaby hadn't paid any of the bills with the money I had given him.

I had been advised in the beginning to hire a financial advisor. It would impress HRS and save me a lot of time and energy. Barnaby advertised himself as one and as a corporate attorney. I put all my trust in him. This blind trust would now cost me over $100,000, and more bills were on the way. I had to take action and fast.

A friend of mine had recently completed her degree in accounting. I begged her for financial advice and assistance. When she looked at what I had, she lit up like a neon sign and shrieked, "BANKRUPTCY!" We both laughed, but I knew how real this could turn out to be.

Several days later, she called me for more information. The first thing she wanted was the receipts for every penny I had given my lawyer. Next she wanted my accounts receivable and payable. Rather than putting figures together over the phone, she said she would pick up my records. Before she hung up, she suggested that we might consider selling The Inn.

With thoughts of this monstrous debt, I fixed a cup of tea and sat down in a daze. The phone rang, startling me. It was Sam. The Inn was on fire. I raced down the street, and my heart stopped when I saw the flames shooting up into the sky. Black smoke billowed out of the windows. Firemen fought the flames, and barked at everyone to stay back. I ran to the front of the house just in time to see a fireman bringing out James and Ilga. Sam came out and told me the rest were in the front and that no one was hurt. Thank God. The firemen praised Sam and Jim for following proper procedures for a fast evacuation, crediting them for saving everyone's life. Jim told one of them that it was the boss who drilled evacuation procedures into their heads and how glad he was that I had.

The residents were scared to death. Bless their hearts! I couldn't imagine what was going through their minds. It probably seemed like hell on earth to them. I called Allysa at Shoreline to let her know she would have six more people for dinner and to stay over night. The next day I would take two of these six to my condo. That would leave four new residents at Shoreline to add to the eight already living there. Next

I called other family and a few close friends who all agreed to take the remaining eight residents temporarily. Now all fourteen would be taken care of. Sam and the others guided the residents to the cars that would take them to safety. I made a mental note to call my condo manager to let him know about the two temporary residents coming to my condo the next day.

Now that the residents were safe, I turned my attention to The Inn. I started up the back steps but was stopped in my tracks.

"Too hot, Ma'am," the fireman said.

But I was able to see into what was left of the kitchen. Not much. The dining room also looked demolished. I walked around to the front. The damage seemed slight, but there was a lot of smoke pouring out, obscuring the view. Because I wasn't allowed to go in, I sat on the porch, helplessly watching my dreams float away on the wind.

The same fire inspector who had put us out at The Grand pulled up in his car. I could only say, "Everything that was required and more was done here and look what it got me." I started crying at that point and walked away.

I called home. Johnny and Mike were there, and Mike called Tom to come help me. I called Alyssa to ask Kris to come in to help at Shoreline. By then the inspector said I could follow him in the burned out Inn. We went as far as the living room and had to stop. I could see that the dining room was about gone, and, as far as I could see of the kitchen, there was nothing left. Two bedrooms downstairs hadn't burned, but smoke damage had claimed about everything. I asked him if I could take some of their clothing out of the rooms. Sam and Tom came in and we were allowed to get what we could carry from downstairs. The steps were too hot to go up for the rest, but at least three of the residents would have clothing. The firemen told me to come back later on to secure the building. The back part was still too hot to do that.

I also called HRS and get permission to keep all these people at Shoreline and to report the fire. The chief concern was that I start finding more permanent homes for the eight persons who were not at Shoreline or my condo. The person I talked to at HRS didn't even ask how the residents were doing, whether they were upset, or if there were any injuries. How callous! However, he did tell me to do whatever I had to do, but to let him know who was where.

I finally left the Inn, tired and smelling of smoke. By the time I arrived at Shoreline, Sam and Tom had already arrived with the six residents and unloaded their belongings. Then Jim pulled in shortly with the truck loaded with clothing and three beds. We went in to find places for them and quickly determined that the Florida room was our only option.

Alyssa was talking to me a mile a minute while my poor head was trying to figure everything out.

"Ma, now we don't have any place to sleep." The Florida room had been Tom's and her room.

I asked, "Would the two of you like a break?" I thought I saw a big smile on her face. They didn't have to answer. It would be simple to just move the staff over to Shoreline from The Inn.

In my haste, I had not seen Naomi and had not heard her screaming. I asked Sam where she was.

"You did get her out, right?"

"Yes," he said. "In spite of everything, we would not let her burn. In fact, when Jim moved her out, she went with him willingly and didn't make a sound! I thought to myself but did not say aloud: Maybe this fire has placed her so close to hell that it scared the personality's right out of her.

Once everyone was settled, I had to go to my condo to check on my two residents. Maxcine had come in to handle things there. Then I had some serious thinking to do about the others who were just sitting at Shoreline. Shoreline was licensed for only eight, but now twelve were there, three in the newly moved beds and one on a couch. I had started out with residents in my private home and now, four years later, it looked as if I was back to where I started.

I called the insurance company, and then my accountant, and he had the worst news I could possibly hear. I was over $150,000 in debt. I had $13,000 coming in each month, and my expenditures were close to $10,000, and that didn't include any salary for me. I was in big-time trouble and there was no way out.

Back at the house I went for a swim and sat out doors for about an hour before dinner. It was amazing that there was always something new to see from my patio. One of my favorite scenes was the ships on the horizon. They slowly crept into the channel where I was able to get a better look at them.

This morning, after all the excitement, they were especially relaxing to watch. I saw a ship with red on it that I hadn't seen before. I watched until it was out of sight and then went in to look at my cruise ship brochures to see which one it was, but it wasn't there. Oh well, news of it would be in the paper the next day.

Calmer, I got up and walked into the kitchen, hoping to find dinner already made. Perhaps a little leprechaun had prepared it. The little leprechaun hadn't made dinner and neither would I! When Johnny and Mike got home, I called Alyssa and Tom at Shoreline to see if they wanted to go out for dinner because I was just too tired to cook. Shoreline would be covered because Kris was there and Maxcine was on her way.

We first drove to The Inn to secure everything. A couple of firemen were still there, and they showed us what had to be done. The back door was destroyed, so we needed a sheet of plywood to secure it, but the rest could wait until the next day. Tom and Mike went for the wood while we talked to the firemen. Their off-the-record speculation as to the cause of the fire was wrong wiring in the new vent system. The inspector would be able to tell me more tomorrow. I left him a key, and each of us wondered what would come next.

The Sea Bar was always the best place for seafood and beef tenderloin. We enjoyed the seafood, which was fresh and plentiful. When we were finishing our dinner, I dropped the bomb of the indebtedness.

"God, Ma, how did that happen?" Alyssa said.

"That damn lawyer has screwed you over," Johnny and Mike said simultaneously. The truth of their words would soon be clearly established.

Mike was quick to say, "I am not going to support those homes." There were two now, or at least the possibility of two. "They should be able to hold their own."

"Of course, you are not taking into consideration the fact that I was led into financial disaster at The Grand and that I have to get out of paying the debt somehow. What do you want me to do?" By now I was extremely frustrated.

"You will have to sell either Shoreline or The Inn in order to get out of debt at The Grand," he answered. Alyssa and Tom were quiet, but I knew they were nearly burned out and couldn't care less if either one stayed open.

I would have to meet with the accountant before I could figure a way out.

In the morning I called the insurance company. An appointment was set up for later in the day.

The man I spoke to said, "Are you sure you want to rebuild The Inn? The property is at a premium because of the new stadium going up nearby. You may want to consider just tearing it down." I explained that I did not own the property, only the interior and that I did not know what to do at this point.

I met with him and the fire inspector at the same time. They tentatively agreed that bad wiring had started the fire, and it was new wiring that had just been installed.

"Who is responsible for this now?" I asked the insurance adjuster.

"That will have to be decided," he said.

The fire inspector gave me a look that said, "Shut up," and I did. After the adjuster left, he said, "Let them pay you for the damage and rebuild. You'll come out better."

"I will have to take that under advisement." I said, and we both laughed.

HRS had not been come to see The Inn. I was really surprised, for they knew I had, in all probability, taken the residents to Shoreline.

Thankfully, all of the residents were doing exceptionally well. I made sure that two persons were on duty at all times. The residents all spoke to me when I went in and most of them understood what had happened. It was amazing that they had taken the bad experience so well. I swear that their diet made all the difference in the world. They ate high protein, low fat, and low sugar food, and the result was their brains came back to life.

Naomi shocked me one day, and actually asked, "Carolyn, I am so sorry about the fire. Was anyone hurt?" Sam caught me from behind as I buckled in amazement at her concern.

"Thank you for caring. Thank God no one was hurt, including you." I replied to Naomi.

"Was I there?" she asked. Her voice was different. It sounded normal. There was no squeaky shrill monologue coming out. She was talking to me as though I was a long, lost friend. She reached out to me and said, "Come here Carolyn. I want to give you a hug." In shock, I reached for her and gave her a big bear hug and a kiss on the cheek.

I had goose bumps on top of goose bumps.

My instinct told me to call Tom and Alyssa and have them come up and see her, but they were one up on me. They already knew about Naomi's change but had not mentioned it to me. She had been just as loving to them.

I went into the kitchen and sat down to have a cry. All of us had been through hell with her and now and angel spoke from her lips. I would need more time to observe her behavior, but for now, I just repeated over and over: "Thank you Lord!"

I had a meeting scheduled with Lisa, my accountant, at 2:00 p.m. With her help I hoped to be able to make a decision about how to proceed. On a hunch, because Lisa had expressed a desire to take over The Inn, I called Kris to see if she could attend the meeting because I had a feeling she might want to buy it, too. She could attend and did. Lisa laid it on the line. She said my debts at The Inn were $18,000.

"Since the fire was virtually the fault of the company who put in the system, the company would in all probability give you a fairly good price for repairs. The money saved there could be put into the walls, cabinets, and floors. In this way, some of the insurance money could go for debts," she said.

I understood what she was saying, but I asked, "If they were at fault, why do I owe them for installing the system in the first place?"

"You don't. They will be perfectly happy to let their insurance company pay them for the loss and then they will work with you," she said.

At that point, I asked Kris if she was interested in taking over the place for what was left owing.

She said she was, at $18,000, but asked Lisa, "Won't the balance be less after Carolyn pays off more of the debt with whatever is left from the insurance company?"

Lisa said, "Yes, but let's deal with $18,000, and, if repairs cost less than that, so much the better." Kris thought for a few minutes. I told her to go home and talk with her family and let me know. Besides, I didn't want to discuss the rest of my finances with her. After Kris left, Lisa asked, "Are you ready for the bomb?"

"As ready as I will ever be," I replied.

The total indebtedness at The Grand was $122,000. This included $58,000 for the architect I never wanted to hire in the first place. I was stunned.

Before I could react, Lisa said, "Carolyn, you can make arrangements to pay each debtor $50 a month, or file for bankruptcy.

A lot of the debts I didn't know about, for many of the companies involved had billed Barnaby directly, and he had never told me of them and certainly had not paid them. Lisa told me I had given Barnaby $38,000 to pay my bills and not a penny had been accounted for. He claimed the money went for his fees. When Barnaby needed money to pay an account or to pay his fees, he asked for the money, and I paid him. Sometimes he would not write out a receipt, saying, "I'll send it to you." Most of the time, I never received it. Let's face it: I had been screwed royally this time.

Chapter Fifteen
The Lawyer

I wasted no time confronting Barnaby. I asked him for receipts and statements of what I had paid him. I also asked him where the money had gone. He looked none too happy. I thought I was being emphatic, but apparently he didn't think so. He didn't answer the second question, and to the first, he said, "I'll get you the receipts when I get around to it."

I had a weapon I could use and fully intended to do so if I did not get satisfaction from him this time.

"Barnaby, I have to have the receipts by tomorrow morning." He smiled and started to work on something on his desk. His assistant came in, and I told him what I had asked for and explained the importance of getting the receipts and the figures on them.

Charley said, "Carolyn, Barnaby is very busy today, but I will try to have them ready by morning."

"Thank you, Charley," I said, almost in a whisper as I walked out the door. Barnaby never looked up. I would take him before the Bar Association if he didn't comply, and, if there was fraud involved, which I highly suspected, I would take the matter to the proper authorities.

My next stop was The Inn. I had called several people to give me estimates. When I got there, Kris was waiting. She had talked everything over with the family and decided that buying The Inn would be a good deal, that is, if I gave her three or four patients. Certainly, that could be arranged! Shoreline was over capacity now.

I was happy to discover that when the contractor's bids came in, they all showed figures under those of the insurance estimate.

After everything was tabulated, the total pay-off figure was only $10,647. Kris was thrilled and dancing out of her skin. She really was getting a deal. It included all furnishings that weren't burned, which only involved the dining room furniture because the insurance company was replacing the kitchen appliances. It also included a year's paid lease. It amounted to approximately $10,000 I would not have to pay.

We sat around for a few minutes talking. We decided who would come to The Inn from Shoreline. I also needed to find a new attorney to draw up the papers for Kris. I would do this as soon as possible. Kris left, smiling from ear to ear. I left feeling violated, yet relieved at the same time.

That night I told the family about the amount of debt Lisa told me I had. Tom and Alyssa announced they were moving out of town, and Johnny said he was, too. What a shock! I was dumbfounded, but then they explained their sudden decision.

Johnny said, "Ma, put this house up for sale. There will be enough to help pay off the bills, and you still have the condo."

"Is this why you guys have decided to leave? If that is so, I will never sell the house."

They beat around the bush, but finally said

"No, we were going to leave anyway."

I didn't believe them, but they were not going to discuss the matter any further because they changed the subject. Now they wanted to talk about what was going to happen with The Inn and Shoreline. I explained to them what had transpired from the time of my visit to Barnaby to the present. None of the family had ever liked him, but I had always given him the benefit of the doubt until now. All of my feelings toward him would change after I had seen his accounting.

I called a realtor and placed our home on the market. The ad read, "Easy Sale…by far the most beautiful house on the Island….a view that is unprecedented…." The proof would be in the sale, and I just hoped the realtor's ad would bring a buyer.

The reconstruction was going according to plan at The Inn. It was hard to fathom that it would no longer be mine. Sam was a great help with decisions about repair as he thought the same way I did, planned work the way I would do, and handled problems as I would do. Also, the rest of the staff respected him. I helped out when I could, but I was just too strung out to help much.

Finally, the work at The Inn was finished. The city inspectors came and found everything in order. Kris knew she could have three residents without a license, but we were going to try for four. It was good for the residents that Kris was now the owner because I was leaving the residents in good hands. She would be a good administrator and the residents liked her because she cared about their welfare.

We decided to move Naomi, Hannah, Gus, and Prudence to The Inn, thereby reducing the number of people to seven at Shoreline, a relief to me because I could let go several staff and cut my payroll.

I notified the families and guardians to let them know of the change in ownership. I tried to do the fair thing and keep the ones who needed the most care. James and Ilga were sort of my favorites and Minnie, Vera, and Nancy were definitely staying with me.

Saturday and Sunday came and went, and, thankfully, I was able to relax a little bit. I kept thinking about Barnaby and our impending meeting. Lord, I hoped he had been honest.

I stopped by Shoreline Monday morning to see if everything was okay. It was! Sam had introduced the residents to a new game. He had turned two walkers upside down and had them playing Toss the Ring, using embroidery hoops for the rings. It was gratifying to see them having such a good time.

From there I went on to the lawyer's office. I sat outside for a few minutes waiting for Lisa. She was prompt. I dreaded this meeting, and she knew it. She was calm, but then handling difficult financial situations and people was her profession. On the other hand, I was shaking, both inside and out.

Barnaby and Charley were in the big office waiting for us. Barnaby spoke first as we were escorted in by the secretary.

"Carolyn, I am appalled that you think I would mishandle your funds after all these years."

Lisa interrupted him by saying, "Barnaby, perhaps you do not understand the urgency of getting an accounting of what Carolyn owes and her assets. We are not here to accuse you; we are here to determine the exact figures and what they mean."

"Well, this is not what I have been hearing," he said.

"Charley, did you get together what I asked for?" I said. He replied that he had. I asked Lisa if she wanted to go over the accounting now or later.

"It really doesn't matter to me. It is whatever Barnaby has time for," she said.

He looked at his watch and muttered, "I do have an appointment in a few minutes. Why don't you go over everything, Lisa, and call for an appointment next week."

"Why not tomorrow?" she said in a sweet voice. Charley looked at his calendar and at Barnaby's and said that 10:00 a.m. would be fine.

As we left, I had a bad taste in my mouth. There are some things in life you just did not want to happen. This was one of them. I had been working with him for a long time; having built up what I believed was a good relationship early on. I wanted the math to be accurate, but I was afraid it would not be. Lisa was quiet.

I asked, "What are you thinking about?" She showed no emotion as if she didn't hear me. "Lisa, Earth calling Lisa!" She turned around suddenly and smiled.

"I'm sorry. I guess I was in another world."

"Well, what do you think?"

"I don't know Carolyn. I am not going to speculate because doing so cannot solve anything."

"Just do your thing and let me know," I said.

When Lisa arrived the next morning, the first thing she asked me was "Have you found another lawyer?"

"No, I really haven't had time."

"Then take time; there are some serious discrepancies."

"How bad is it?" I asked.

"Bad enough. There is a difference of $15,000. There is no accounting for this error, and we must take into consideration that there were times when he didn't give you a receipt for money you gave him and it would be entered into your books as having paid him to pay certain of your bills." $15,000! That was a lot of money!

When Lisa finished giving me a breakdown, I was officially $137,000 in debt. If we counted the $10,000 at The Inn, the debt was $147,000. I looked at her in disbelief.

"I cannot pay this off," I said.

"Carolyn, no one could," she replied.

Lisa told me to find another attorney, one who would file the bankruptcy and try to get the money from Barnaby. I did not want to file bankruptcy, but I did want the money from Barnaby if he owed it to me. I asked her if it would be better to wait and see what my house sold for and try to pay everyone off. I also asked her if my creditors would possibly accept a lesser amount if I offered them a set price to settle."

"That's a possibility, but you have to remember that these people are going to get vicious shortly. Can you handle all the stress involved?" She asked.

I didn't have an answer. "I'll tell you what I am going to do. I am going to call all of them and ask how they feel about waiting for the house to sell as opposed to bankruptcy."

Lisa responded, "Go for it."

After Lisa left, I called Sam to see if he could come down for a few minutes. Things were fairly slow there, and the employee on staff could handle Shoreline for a while. He came right over.

I told him what was happening and what I was facing.

His first reaction was, "How is this problem going to affect Shoreline?"

I told him it wouldn't affect Shoreline unless I had to file for bankruptcy. Shoreline was clear of liens and could hold its own financially as long as I kept seven residents there. I knew I was down to six at the time, but I didn't want to bring in anyone else until I saw what was going to happen. He, of course, understood this.

I had decided to wait for the house to sell rather than to declare bankruptcy. This was the honest way out. The money wouldn't pay all the debt, but it would make a big dent in the debt.

Finding another attorney was going to be tough, for they stuck by each other. They wouldn't talk to me or even take the time to listen. I would have to go either to another town or maybe even another state if I had any intentions of suing him because no lawyer in this town would help me. My final call regarding Barnaby was to the Florida Bar Association. They were interested in what I said, as the bar had received several other complaints about Barnaby. I didn't see any way to get the money back, but maybe the bar would have some answers.

The calls to the creditors were not much better. They had a genuine grievance with me, and I understood that, but I did not have any money until the house sold. Several of them threatened to sue, while others were sympathetic and would wait for the house to sell. I told the ones who were not agreeable that if they persisted in filing small claims or taking me to court, they would not get anything, for I would file for bankruptcy. They were not being cooperative, but I could see their point. On the other hand, if I had to declare bankruptcy, payment would be minimal if at all. My house with the pool had not been shown since it was put on the market the month before. I wanted to call the realtor, but I simply did not want to sound too anxious. I needed my asking price, and my agent would try for a lesser price if he thought I would be flexible.

We moved the residents from my house back to The Inn. I hated to move them again, but it had to be done. I knew Kris would be good to them and that made this move more acceptable. I walked out of The Inn, shaking my head in disbelief. If ever Naomi would kick up her heels, it was with a move. She didn't even open her mouth. I know I have been told to never look a gift horse in the mouth, but I could not accept that this normal behavior of hers would continue. When was the bomb going to drop? I wondered.

Bills started coming in two or three times a week from the same companies. They were calling me several times a week, and it was always the same question: "When may we expect payment from you?"

I answered them all in the same way: "Nothing has changed."

Sometimes I wished I had filed bankruptcy. I could change the phone number, but, if I did, the creditors would just call Shoreline. Kris had had her own phone installed at The Inn, so they couldn't call there.

After a few days of answering the phone, I put on an answering machine to screen the calls. Some of them still called Shoreline as I had suspected they would. The staff told them I wasn't in and offered to take a message.

In an attempt to hold them off, I made up a form letter and sent one to each creditor requesting that they hold the phone calls to a minimum and included a status report of finances. This was a waste of time on my part. The carpenters, the wholesale food company, the electrician, the architect, and mostly the employees who had been fired and were owed money were the ones most persistent.

Finally, prospective buyers started looking at the house. No one was questioning the price because it was in good condition and very tastefully decorated. I had already started moving some of the things to the condo, for that would be where we lived after we sold the house. I didn't want to give up my home, but selling it would be easier on us financially in the long run.

On several occasions, I thought I noticed a car following me, but I was not clever enough to be sure. The phone rang constantly, but there were never any messages, just hang ups. These things were frustrating, especially when I was always wondering what could be next.

Shortly, I would find out. I was definitely being followed. When I was able to get a license tag number, I called the police, who then took a report and called me back with the name of the owner of the vehicle. I did not recognize the name or the car or the person driving it. The investigator thought it was someone who was being paid, probably by one of my creditors. He promised to pick up the man for questioning. I called the police the day I saw him parked on my street a few houses away. They came and talked to him but never revealed to me what they discovered. I felt I had a right to know, but the police did not.

He continued to follow me every time I got into the car unless Mike was with me. Then he was nowhere to be seen. I continued to call the police whenever I had to leave the house. Sometimes they responded, sometimes not. He tried to run me off the road several times, at which point, I would just pull over to the side of the road and stop. Once I ran into a yard screaming for the person on the porch to call the police. This time they came. I told them I wanted to file charges because I had found out who the person was. I could not understand why he was allowed to follow and endanger me on the road.

I went to the station to fill out the paperwork to get a restraining order on him. While there, I ran into a friend who was a detective. When he heard what was happening, he got a funny look on his face and took me into his office to discuss the situation. He read all of the reports and said, "Carolyn, he didn't break the law as long as he just followed you, but now, by forcing you off the road, he has broken the law."

"Do you mean to tell me that there are no laws prohibiting someone following a person and harassing her?" I asked.

"Afraid not! He didn't do anything to indicate he intended to harm you."

"What in hell does he want, and why me?" I asked him.

"He's a bill collector who has been hired by an architect. Does that ring a bell?"

"Yes, I know who the architect is, but he is the last person I expected to do something like this." I explained my plight to him as he sat shaking his head.

"Carolyn, how in hell did you let this thing happen?"

"Oh, it was real easy. I overextended myself trying to do too much and did not pay attention to the cost or the bills because I handed them over to my lawyer and giving him the payments. Unfortunately, my trust in him was misplaced by a mile. But, I'll get through it, if you people can keep me alive long enough," I said.

They were holding the guy in the next room until the restraining order could be signed and served on him. I picked up the phone and called the architect in front of my friend. I very politely told him I would not tolerate this harassment, and he would not get a dime out of me if anything else happened. Of course, he denied involvement. I told him I was really quite disappointed that someone of his caliber would sink so low as to hire someone to harass me. After the restraining order was signed, I felt a little safer.

Finally, I had a prospective buyer for the house who was willing to meet my price. However, even when escrow closed and I received payment, I still would not have enough money to clear the debts, but they would be reduced to the level where I could make monthly payments. It was a wait-and-see game.

Now my grandson Timothy came to stay with me, and he live with me for awhile. He was only three years old, and I adored him. He went where I went and never whined or complained. Timothy never asked for much, except pizza. I swear he could eat it every night. I put him in a reliable daycare for about four hours a day, not because I wanted to get rid of him, for I enjoyed him very much, but I thought he should have some structured time with children his own age. This child was very special to me. His start in life had been difficult; he wasn't the typical big, bouncing, baby boy. Weighing less than two pounds at birth, he remained in the hospital for his first three months. He was by far the most curious child I'd ever seen. He did things as if in a hurry to catch up, but his body was not keeping up with his brain; thus he had had numerous injuries and accidents. He was into everything he could reach, and if he couldn't reach it, he would start climbing.

On a beautiful afternoon, I promised Timothy a picnic. I had packed a lunch and was on the way to pick him up when I noticed a car behind me. It kept following my car. I turned on to a side street and so did the car. I could not go through the pain of being followed again, especially with this child with me. I stopped the car and locked the doors. The other car stopped.

When he got out, I became very scared and started up my car and fled. I thought I recognized him but wasn't sure. I didn't know where to go. I sure was not going to lead him to the day care. All at once, I saw a police car. I stopped and sat down on my horn. The other car sped off around me, but not before I saw who it was. It was the milk man. The milk man! My God, why he was following me over a few lousy dollars!

I went to the police station after talking to the policeman and applied for another restraining order. The judge was not in, so the order couldn't be signed. When the order was finally signed, I was late to pick up Timothy, and I'm sure he waited for me instead of taking the afternoon nap. I left and drove to the daycare center.

He was standing there waiting and was about to cry. "I thought you were not coming, Nannie," he said.

"I was sure to come, especially after I promised you a picnic, now weren't I?"

He smiled and said, "Let's go!"

We went down to the water where he so enjoyed watching the boats. I found a nice place with a picnic table and spread out our food. Timothy was pleased with what I brought, for, of course, I brought his favorite foods.

After we ate, I spread a blanket on the grass and the two of us lay down. I needed a nap a lot worse than he did, but he fell asleep. I lay there and relaxed while he slept. After about an hour, he started to stir. I was singing lowly and partially humming when I noticed he had joined me. He didn't know the words but he was surely making a stab at them with his sweet little voice. What a joy he was to have around!

We left the park after awhile and headed for home. I was careful to watch in all directions for a car that might follow us. The way looked safe as we drove home.

When we arrived, there was a message on the answering machine from the realtor. He had a buyer for my house! Finances were sufficient for the mortgage company, and it looked as if the sale would go through. I called Lisa to tell her the good news, and she was thrilled. We decided to start by making each creditor an offer to settle. She would do that for me.

I would just sit back and wait.

Later that night, after I had put Timothy to bed, I heard a noise that sounded like a gunshot. Mike went outside and I flew up the steps. Timothy was screaming by the time I got to the top. My heart dropped, and I went in a state of panic. Dear God, don't tell me they shot my grandson! There was no blood on him but the window in the back of the room that faced the bay had been shot out. From the window I saw a boat speeding away into the distance. Mike called the police, and I tried to comfort Timothy. He was frightened and wanted his mommy. I couldn't give him his mommy. She was far away on vacation in Pennsylvania. With enough hugs and kisses, he settled down, but now we had a bigger problem.

The police were there when I went downstairs. Mike had already explained what happened, and they were on the radio to the Coast Guard. Chances were slim to none that they would find the boat, but at least they were trying.

I decided that we were going to move into the condo immediately. None of the creditors knew about the condo, so it was unlikely they would bother us there, and besides, the security there was strict. I would let the manager know what was going on so that, if any further attempt to disturb our privacy was made, security would be notified. I was beginning to wonder if we might be killed over my lousy debts. Mike had recently started working evenings, and that meant I would be alone with Timothy at the big house. Only two nights more in the house, and then we would be safe in the condo.

As luck would have it, the Air Force notified Mike that he was needed for active duty for a few weeks, just when I needed him to help with the move.

I kept busy by packing while Timothy was in school and then spent the afternoons with him. Thankfully there had not been any trouble at his school.

Lisa came over the day we were moving with news. Some of the creditors were accepting my offers and some refused to take any less than what was owed them. She had me sign a bunch of letters with the agreements, which would be mailed out for them to sign. I thumbed through to see who had been flexible and told her to mail them their payments.

We moved into the condo before late afternoon. Already, I felt safer. Of course, I could have been followed, but I didn't see anyone suspicious. The movers finished, and I hooked up a TV for Timothy. There was only a test pattern, which was actually a picture of a fish aquarium loaded with fish. I guess this stayed on when that particular station was not broadcasting. Instead of becoming bored, Timothy liked it and asked to see it when it was on.

I unpacked the kitchen and hoped that Flossie, my cleaning lady, who had not deserted me despite the fact I hadn't been able to pay her all I owed her, would show up the next day. Usually, when I really needed her the most, she didn't show up.

Dinner was pizza. What else?

The next morning I heard the security phone ringing, and it was Flossie. I let her in and as she got off the elevator, I could see she was panic stricken. She ran from the elevator to the door as I watched out the window. I could see that there was a man behind her as she rushed in the door and quickly closed it behind her.

"Miss Carolyn, don't open the door," she whispered.

She gestured for me to be quiet. The man stayed in the outer hallway. It was obvious he did not intend to leave, but it was also strange that he didn't knock on the door.

I called to him through the door: "Are you lost?" There was no response. I called out a second time: "You are not supposed to stay there in the hallway. Do you need directions?" Again there was no response. I looked out the window and he was still there. He couldn't see me, for I was peering through the blinds.

I asked Flossie if he had said anything to her and she said, "No, he just jumped through the outside door when you unlocked it to let me in and walked into the elevator with me."

I called the manager's office but no one was in yet. Then I called the police.

A policeman and a policewoman arrived and had him cornered when I looked out the window. I heard him say something about me, so I opened the door. As I did, he threw some papers in the doorway. The male policeman grabbed him and told him to pick up the papers and hand them to me.

"What is going on?" I asked.

He explained that the man was a process server with documents for me. I didn't understand. If he had papers for me, why hadn't he rung up on the security phone instead of breaking in? Flossie told the policemen what he had done, but he denied it. He told the police that he had rung up, and I let him in but wouldn't open the door when he knocked.

I tried to press charges, but the male policeman said to forget it. The female policewoman kept her hand on her gun the entire time they were there and said in a smart-assed tone of voice: "Ma'am, do as he says." What a jerk!

The process server handed me the papers and the police took him downstairs and outside. I opened the papers. The architect was suing me. Oh well!

By then Timothy was up and trying to find the fish aquarium on the TV.

Flossie went to the kitchen and put on a pot of coffee. She turned around and said, "By the way, Miss Carolyn, in the confusion I forgot to tell you that all four of the tires on your car are slit." My son went outside and came back to report that they had been knifed.

While Flossie fed Timothy, I called around to get some new tires. The car insurance would pay for them. All I had to do was to get the car towed in for the tires to be put on. After that was done, I poured a cup of coffee and sat down and called, and she agreed with me. However, there was no way to take him home now until Mike got back or until Timothy's father could fly down to get him.

Flossie started unpacking while I went to Shoreline to see how things were going. Everything was fine, but Kris had called for me to come to The Inn as soon as possible. Sam, with the help of Lilly and Janice, was handling the day shift, and Maxcine had nights under control. It just seemed unusual for the residents to be content and happy. Their appetites were exceptionally good, they were sleeping well, and their health checkups had been great. Their good condition certainly was a blessing.

Sam and Maxcine would get nice raises on their next checks. The others wouldn't yet because they were fairly new except for Jim, but he had been recalled to active duty with the Air Force along with Mike.

After escrow closed on my house, I sent out the checks to my creditors. Then my tires were slashed two more times, so we locked the car up in a garage at night and took a taxi back and forth to the store or to The Inn. We could have been followed, but the garage could not have been penetrated except by a bomb or a Sherman tank. I did feel safe about this hiding place.

Fortunately, I was able to pay off more than I had anticipated. The balances left owing were minimal to only a few persons. Surely, these last few creditors would leave me alone.

The Bar Association took care of Barnaby except for the money he owed me. They sent me a letter stating that he had had his license suspended for six months, had been put on probation for five years, and fined $1000 for each offense. Counting everyone, there were eleven offences, including mine. According to the bar, he did indeed owe me $14,056. It was suggested I might first request payment from him in installments; then if this was not satisfactory to him, I could take him to court. After what I had been through, I could not put another soul through the nightmare of having to pay the whole amount at once. I sent him a personal letter, agreeing to accept monthly payments after he was able to work again. He accepted in writing, but the future would tell that my life with Barnaby was not quite over.

Chapter Sixteen
Waterloo

Whether or not I would be spending the rest of my life taking care of the elderly remained to be seen. I had cared so much for the elderly and had accomplished so much for them, yet I couldn't help feeling the future was looking bleak.

I had just left Shoreline and remembered that Kris had called to invite me over. It wasn't lunchtime yet, so I ambled down the street to what was once The Inn. When Kris opened the door, she greeted me with a shrill, hysterical giggle.

"All right, what's happening?" I asked.

"Let's go upstairs and you can see for yourself," she said.

We walked up the steps and when almost at the top, I heard angry unfamiliar voices. Wow! Were they angry!

"Kris, who is that fighting?" She just put on a big smile.

At the landing I heard a shrill, squeaky voice, "You rotten bitch. You rotten son of a bitch. How much longer did you think I would stay gone?"

The other one said in a throaty raspy voice: "You go to hell you mother fucker. I got along very well without you."

As I started toward the voices, Kris stopped me and whispered, "There are a lot more."

"I'm hungry, you rotten bitch. Shut your damn mouth so I can eat."

"You can't have anything until I decide I have nothing else to say. You're such a prick anyway."

I whispered to Kris, "What in hell is going on here?" Then I knew what was going on when I followed Kris into Naomi's room. Oh, no! Naomi's multiple personalities were back! There she was, sitting in her chair with a tray of untouched food on the bed table. Several shrill voices suddenly greeted me, fighting for my attention.

"You slut! Where in hell have you been?"

"Come here sweetheart. I want a hug and a kiss, you bitch."

The voices were changing rapidly. Reluctantly, I approached her but wasn't sure I would let her touch me, for I did not know who she was. There were at least three distinct personalities taking part in this discussion, and all were different from the ones in the past. No wonder I thought someone else was in the room!

According to Sigmund Freud, multiple personalities evolve from the unconscious to the conscious. From the unconscious, the IQ gives birth to these variants, which split the conscious Ego into more than one encapsulated identity. Freud says that only one of these personalities would be on the conscious plane at a time.

However, Naomi was speaking as if there were many personalities talking at the same time. One sentence by one personality was followed by a sentence by another and then by another. This was a far cry from Freud's description. She was frightening me. I went closer to her but quickly backed away when it became apparent that she was not friendly, or at least part of her was not.

I looked at Kris and realized her previous giddiness was nervous tension. She now looked terrified. Even though I had an education in psychology, I felt unable to deal with Naomi, and Kris, who had no background in psychology, was being expected to take care of this woman. About then I realized that no amount of education would help in this situation. We had to turn somewhere else to get help for her. I hadn't the slightest idea of how I was going to do this since all previous attempts had failed, but I couldn't just dump Naomi on someone else and walk away.

I told Kris to do the best she could and to feed her when she was in one of her better personalities. I thought she had a good one who was usually hungry.

Kris confirmed this but said, "She has so many now, I can't keep up with them." I asked Kris if she had a tape recorder.

She said, "Yes. I don't know why I didn't think of that sooner." I went home and had lunch with Timothy and Flossie, during which I talked about the new Naomi. Suddenly Timothy spoke up and said, "Nannie, why does she sound like so many people?"

"I wish I could answer that, but I can't. Besides, it is time for your nap, little man."

He was such a good little boy. I went with him to the bathroom and then tucked him in. He asked me if he could sleep with my clown Bingo, who was dressed in a red, white, and blue outfit. Bingo was one of his favorite toys and his constant companion when he visited with me. Of course, I gave the toy to him.

The next morning I drove across the bay to the university to keep a 10:00 a.m. appointment with a psychology professor, Dr. Abraham. He looked somewhat shocked when I mentioned all of the voices Naomi had. He wasn't about to contradict me but seemed puzzled. "

"I too was in disbelief at first until I listened for longer periods of time," I said.

I told him she was 97 years old, and as far as I could find out, no one had ever documented her voices. I explained that she had been in Chattahoochee several times and several other local mental institutions but none had seen any evidence of her various personalities.

"I would like to visit Naomi," he said. "May I bring a colleague or at least collaborate with him?"

I replied, "Certainly. It will be interesting to see your reactions."

He took down my address, phone number, and directions. I was pleased with myself. Finally, I might be able to help Naomi or at least understand where all the poor souls were coming from.

I drove across the bridge and went home.

Suddenly, I was very tired and wanted a nap. I hadn't made any promises to Timothy today. Besides, it was his day to go to day care. He did love it there. I drove him to school and went home for a nap. I dozed for a few minutes but couldn't sleep. I kept thinking about my decision to free many residents from their drug dependencies and about all the warnings I received not to do that. I giggled to myself when I thought about how drugs probably wouldn't help Naomi anyway. At present she was on no drugs.

The only drugs prescribed for her were Thorazine IM and Valium, to be given only for temper tantrums, but it had been a long time since she had needed either medication. Neither of them had worked anyway. They had absolutely no effect on her behavior.

I also looked at the calendar and realized that two weeks had flown by and that Mike would be home the next day. It had been a difficult time for me, and though I had always been self-reliant, I knew I needed his help. I looked at my watch. It was time to go for Timothy.

He and I decided to have burgers instead of pizza for dinner. I stopped and picked them up on the way home and made a salad to go with them.

While we were eating, Sam called from Shoreline. He asked me where I had been all day. I told him about my journey and what was transpiring with Naomi. He wasn't surprised.

"Carolyn, look how good she has been. All that time these people were just sitting in her brain waiting to come out."

"I know Sam, but according to Freud, there is supposed to be only one distinct personality at a time. She has four or five now." He didn't have a lot more to say on the subject. It was obvious that he had something to tell me that didn't involve Naomi.

"Carolyn, there is something here you should read." I'll stop by and bring it to you if you want me to."

"Yes, please come over." I offered to get him a burger but he declined.

When Sam entered the door I noticed a look on his face I didn't like.

"Lay it on me, Sam, how much worse can it get?"

He produced a document that immediately looked threatening. As I read, I knew I would be in yet another position to lose all I had. It was an eviction notice. My lease was up at Shoreline in two months, and it would not be renewed because the house had been sold. I felt that I was going to pass out right then and there.

Timothy looked at me and said, "Nanny, are you OK?"

"Yes baby. Just fine." He gave me a hug and I started crying.

Timothy cried, too. I looked at his sweet, sad face and tried to smile. "Timothy, it is OK. I just have to move all those poor people again."

"Nannie, they don't want to move again. Can't you just put them in their rooms? They will behave if you do." I had to smile.

Sam asked, "What are you going to do?"

"I'll have to think about it."

"You know I will do anything I can to help you, so you just let me know."

"I have to get going, but I'll see you tomorrow." He left.

The next day came too soon for me. Mike would be back sometime in the afternoon. We would decide together about what we should do.

It was in late afternoon when he got home. After he settled in, I informed him he would be taking us to our favorite seafood restaurant for dinner. After the food came, I ate so much that Mike accused me of not eating the entire time he had been gone. I was really hungry and sick of pizza and burgers. Timothy put away a large order of crab legs and fries, so he must have been hungry, too.

As we left the restaurant, I started telling Mike about the devastating news about Shoreline. Either he wasn't surprised, or was so upset that he was speechless. When we got home, he poured a beer and turned the TV on. That was it? I asked him what he thought, and he mumbled something I couldn't understand. I asked him again and he said in a loud voice, "You are going to do whatever you want to do, so why are you asking me?" I certainly expected a more sympathetic reaction than this.

My heart dropped into my shoes, but I pursued the topic and asked for his ideas. He asked me what Sam thought I should do. I knew he had never liked Sam, but, lately, he was making a lot more out of Sam's and my relationship, which was a friendly, working one, than he should have been. Was he jealous of him? I told him that Sam had not voiced an opinion but had offered to help in whatever way he could.

"That figures," he said with a grunt.

"Did you know that Sam is gay?" I asked him.

I could tell he hadn't even thought of this. He was astonished. I had also been surprised when months earlier Sam confided that he had only recently acquired this sexual preference and had actually been married to a wonderful woman who had died a few years back.

"Mike, why are you being so defensive? You are making no effort to help me. You're just being sarcastic."

"Because you never want to hear what I have to say so why bother asking me?" I knew the discussion was closed when the ballgame came on, so I went about getting Timothy ready for bed. I sent him to my bedroom to watch some television while I found a book to read to him.

The next morning I went to Shoreline after taking Timothy to school. I needed to be close to those people while I was trying to figure out what I could do.

I loved watching Ilga and James. They were so devoted to each other. When they went for walks occasionally, James made sure Ilga came back with him, and when they sat on the couch, they held hands and smiled at each other. They would speak to each other occasionally, but mostly they sat quietly, enjoying each other's company.

Sweet little Minnie always had a smile and a pleasant mumble for me. I was never bothered by her speech impediment. I hugged her a few times and just held her in my arms.

Vera still babbled constantly and her arms and legs were in perpetual motion while she was in her chair. I often wondered why she was in that condition. She didn't bother anyone except me, and that was because I wanted to know more about how she came to be this person who could not function. I knew from prior experience, however, that it was fruitless to ask because most transferred residents are moved from place to place, usually with no one to keep track of their lives or their medical histories. More often than not, I had no idea what happened to them after they left my care. This was a constant source of frustration to me.

Now, what was I going to do with the residents in Shoreline? As I watched the residents go about their day, oblivious to this latest crisis, my heart sank, but my mind once again refused to give up.

I was down to five persons. I had already placed calls to all of the family members. They could, for the most part, care less what I did with them. Ilga's guardian wanted to be kept informed, Minnie had no one, Vera had no one who cared, and Roma still had a cousin but she wasn't in good shape. James's daughter never returned my call. I knew what the outcome would be. I would have to find a house large enough to accommodate the five of them as well as my family.

I did, but I would have to give up the condo, which had become a sanctuary to me. I would no longer have an escape hatch. Mike had always said we couldn't afford it anyway, at least not while we still had the house. But the house was sold now. It seemed that fate was playing a cruel joke on me. Now I could have used that home.

I found a house that would work, secured the lease, and we moved into it a month before the lease was up at Shoreline. The move was an ordeal, but chaos seemed to have ruled our lives lately. The house was split with three bedrooms on one side, and the master bedroom and bath on the other. The kitchen was the dividing point to the living room and the bedrooms and baths. The residents would have a full bath and the family room on their side.

Little did I know that the new house would be only a temporary resting place. It turned out that it didn't matter if I had privacy because we wouldn't be there long enough for me to need any. We were about to get the shock of our lives.

After we helped the residents get settled, Sam, Maxine, and another part-time lady took care of them while I left to rest. I had had enough mental and physical strain for the moment.

The doctors from the college were spending a great deal of time with Naomi, who was now living at The Inn. I was right there beside them because I was intrigued with what was going on and, quite frankly, a bit spooked. There were at least five distinct voices and personalities now, several of them coming out in sequence. She had truly broken the mold on multiple personalities. Because of Naomi's age, I was certain that the doctors were only conducting research rather than trying to help her. Actually they said little to me, conducting their experiments as if I wasn't there.

After four or five days, Dr. Abraham's pleasantly said, "Carolyn, as soon as we make a definite diagnosis and complete our findings, I will submit a written brief to you."

"Yes Doctor, I would appreciate that very much. Also, if you wouldn't mind, I am curious to hear your views on demon possession. Several ministers have left my home in a mad rush, saying Naomi was possessed. Is this a possibility?" He was so stunned that he was unable to answer for a few minutes, and I could almost see his academic logic fighting against Naomi's inexplicable behavior. With what I placed in his mind, he asked the other two if they were finished for the day. They nodded and thanked me as they left. He was thinking, almost out loud. But try as he might, he couldn't give me an answer that made logical sense, according to good science. Well, I guess the written report would be a good bedtime story!

I don't know why, but I started calling the new house Waterloo. The house was surrounded by water just as my other house was, and I could hear and see Napoleon fighting the battle of Waterloo every time I closed my eyes.

I thought Mike and I would have some privacy there, but I was wrong again. Ilga was proving to be an elderly version of Houdini. She could get any door unlocked. She interrupted our sleep almost every night. She would go through the kitchen, unlock the door between the kitchen and the living room and into our bedroom. I locked the door each night, but somehow she got it open. Mike bought a hook and eye, and put it on the inside. She broke it off. We bought a new lock for the kitchen door, thinking this would head her off at the pass. No! She just had to work harder. I think the last straw for me was when I woke up to find her dancing on my bed with one of those damn black dresses on.

This time I scolded her all the way to her bed, took her dress off, and put a nightgown on her. I thought that maybe the black dresses were triggering her dancing, and as long as they hung in the closet, she was bound to put them on. Solution! Remove the dresses. This worked to some degree, but the other problem was music. I could not let her hear music before bedtime. Believe it or not, taking these two things away from her actually allowed us to have a few nights' sleep.

Ilga was an innocent. She was straightforward and had a truthfulness that was refreshing, if not annoying. She just needed to move, to dance, to have fun…how could I be angry? Her vitality was a result of my anti-zombie policy. I created these results, and I always found creative ways of dealing with them.

On the other hand, Roma continued her troubling behavior. She was acting like a lady less frequently now, and her cousin was coming around fewer and fewer times. Her health was failing, and she still scooted on the floor through her own excrement.

In addition, within weeks of our move, Roma became despondent and depressed. When she quit eating, I suggested to the doctor that he order a gastronomy tube to be inserted into her stomach so that she could receive nourishment. She was alert most of the time, but I didn't think she knew that the tube was in place. She continued to dress herself when she had an opportunity to go out for lunch. We would just place the tube in an obscure position and tape it down. At the restaurant she would eat. It was when she didn't go out that we had to feed her via the tube.

One morning, after helping Sam get through breakfast and the morning care, I went in the car to run some errands. My first stop was to keep an appointment with a gentleman I had met a year or so ago. Jack Emerson had called and said he wanted to talk to me about something. He was an interesting person, and I was certainly curious as to what he wanted to talk about. He told me he owned property in the Keys, and wanted to open up a home for the elderly out of some condos he had built. To my amazement, HRS had recommended me for this project. He had been told that I was probably one of the most knowledgeable persons in the field.

He would be responsible for construction while I would be the consultant on HRS requirements, which would include writing the policies and procedures and ensuring that the condo designs and upgrades complied with regulations. These tasks in themselves would be a full time job. Additionally, I would be expected to supervise the care of five residents who would be housed in the first unit to be reconstructed. I would be allowed to set my own salary and would be given a generous employee budget. He wanted the people I trained to do the job right so that they could be trusted to function in my absence, which would be frequent. I wondered if I was destined to care for the elderly the rest of my life. Something seemed to be keeping me on this track.

When I arrived home, Mike handed me a letter from Dr. Abraham. He knew I was anxious to see what Dr. Abraham had to say about Naomi. I called Tom and Alyssa to come over because they had shown an interest in the findings. As I finished reading each page, I passed it on to the others. It said,

Dear Carolyn,

Thank you for contacting me, RE: Naomi. This was a first time experience for all of us and after our many and lengthy visits, our findings support our suspicions. This woman certainly fits the diagnosis of multiple personalities, as she does indeed have sudden temporary alterations in a normally integrated function of the conscious identity and motor behavior.

Contrary to beliefs, Naomi's personalities are fully integrated. Two or more are likely to appear at the same time. They do, however, have their own behavior patterns, memories, and relationships. They appear to be in control for a certain time period. Her multiple personalities are quite different, often talking to each other. In spite of Sigmund Freud's concepts, her personalities are frequently very much aware of each other, and she does not seem to have a dominant one.

In some instances, some of the personalities are aware of lost time, and others may sometimes wander into the conscious mind? They seldom know whom the other voices belong to.

They do have conversations with each other, although in different voices. For example, one might be hungry and want to eat. Another might interject by making a vile statement to the effect that she is not hungry. One might encourage the other to get up and walk, while one might not be able to walk.

We agree that there are often major mood changes and differences between personalities or among the several ego states of a person with multiple personalities. Similarly as in a fugue, a person escapes from

an emotionally charged situation into a calmer existence. The different emotional states may, in part, account for the selective memory loss that is supposed to occur.

We have no idea of how long this has been going on, but according to medical history, no one has ever reported any of the findings that are now displayed.

We would be hard pressed to try and determine which personality is the dominant one, and for that matter, to even distinguish exactly how many personalities are present.

We do concur that there are definitely two or more different distinctive voices talking to one another at a time, which is what makes this case so unusual.

At her age, we do not see any advantage to further exploring her condition except in a learning capacity. We remain interested and will assist you with any new mental developments in the future.

We appreciate the opportunity you have given us, and would, from time to time, like to visit her. Thank you for providing us with this exceptional learning experience.

Sincerely,
Dr. Ernest Abraham
Department of Psychiatry

Chapter Seventeen
The Keys

I awoke cold and reached for the bedspread. Unit air conditioners can nearly freeze a person. For a few minutes I forgot where I was and what I was doing there. I had accepted Emerson's offer and was in a little place near Plantation, Florida checking out his condos. We had driven down the day before, and it had been a miserable drive because it was hot as hell and took us eight hours of solid torture driving along Alligator Alley to get there. When we finally reached Homestead and Florida City, and drove onto US 1, it was smooth sailing and a beautiful drive. I was in heaven again as we pulled into our little hamlet around dusk. I wasn't looking for anything in particular, except for the streets that would take us to the condos. They were offshore on a cape, a magnificent spot, which would be safe until the first hurricane came along. Could this spot be safe for the elderly—for anybody?

We slept in one of the condos. In the morning after a shower, I threw on some shorts and a tee and went outside. It was a glorious and beautiful day. A light breeze was swaying the palm trees, and the ocean waves gently broke along the shoreline. It was refreshing to breathe fresh salt air after the stale air conditioning of the room. The condo units were all on the ocean side of the cape, set back several hundred yards from the shoreline. It was all quite magnificent. The landscaping was minimal, yet there was something marvelous about the way the sea oats danced in the wind against the background of the buildings. The gray clapboard units trimmed with white were built on stilts, with some of the units rising two stories high

I went inside to see if Mike was awake and he was. I thought I saw the same expression on his face that I'm sure I had when I opened my eyes earlier. It was a look of amazement, for these units were truly beautiful. My feet sank into the plush carpet as I admired the furnishings, which were tasteful and expensive. Any elderly person would be more than comfortable here. The bedrooms were spacious with bathrooms large enough to move handicapped vehicles in and out without brushing against the walls. The single unit we were in would accommodate five persons, three in the master bedroom and two in the guest room. I would look at the others after breakfast. On the desk, there was a Visa card for our use while there. Emerson had left it with a note that said, "Don't buy a Mercedes!"

We drove around looking at the sights and shopping. There was a small mall and, of course, a K-Mart. We also found a place to eat and were pleased with the service and quality of the food. There were no other stores on the cape, and it took about twenty minutes to get to town, which bothered me a bit, but it was a small inconvenience, considering the beauty of the place.

Our next stop was to find the hospital. I shuddered when we did; it was worse than I'd imagined. I knew we were in trouble when I received nonchalant and inappropriate answers to *all* my questions. Then I found out the fire department wasn't manned by paramedics twenty-four hours a day, and the fire department was fifteen miles away. The hospital could not afford a doctor to run the emergency room twenty-four hours a day, it didn't carry insurance for malpractice, nor did it have the money for adequate salaries for paramedics. In other words, it didn't have what was required by law in order to open a home for the elderly. I was ACLS certified, which meant I could do life-saving measures, yet their EMT could not. For example, I could start an IV, but the EMT's could not transport the patient in their ambulance with the

IV running. How could we help patients in need of critical care if we couldn't transport them?

I drove to City Hall to see the mayor but was only able to see his assistant. We talked at length. I caught his attention when I told him I was doing the groundwork for placing over three hundred elderly persons in his town. Did the town want the extra revenue that would come in?

I presented my case for a commitment from the town. He was interested but reserved. As we prepared to leave, he did commit himself to taking this problem to the next city council meeting. At least it was a start.

Zoning was no problem, but fire protection was. There was no fire station on the cape, nor did the town have a volunteer fire department. I called the mayor's assistant and asked him to add fire protection on the cape to his list.

To comply with HRS I knew that some of the contracts would have to come out of Miami, yet I had promised to use local businesses as much as I could.

We stayed several days until I was assured that the buildings could be converted into living quarters for the elderly. I met with contractors and with sheet metal people. The two major projects would be to put a new venting system in each kitchen and to make all the units handicapped accessible. The ramps would have to be built from the upper floor to the ground floor. To reduce the slope, we would need a long ramp. Was there space for these extended ramps? The engineers would have to plan this out.

As we proceeded, I kept wondering where Emerson thought all these elderly would be coming from? Certainly, placing elderly so close to the water would be a major concern of the families. From my conversations with Emerson, I got the impression that we would be recruiting the aged tenants themselves, not reaching out to their relatives. We both wanted alert people who could socialize, yet live alone with minimal assistance. House cleaning and transportation would be included. Good food and service would be a must.

The next day we drove to Miami to visit some nursing homes.

Surprisingly, the administrators were helpful. Residents were paying on average 35% to 40% of their income for private care. This was extraordinarily good. They were encouraging and not at all threatened by the possibility of having our homes located on the cape. One or two of the administrators expressed an interest in working with us.

I took a look at a few ALFs. There would simply be no competition. I would accept both types I and II residents. Type I was the category for residents who needed minimum care, and type II was for those who needed somewhat more care. The people I saw in these homes were type IIs. We would be licensed to admit type I residents, but we would be in a position to keep them there as type IIs if a resident had entered as a type I. Type IIs were those who suffered from a failure in physical or mental health.

By the time the day was over, I had accumulated enough material and information to provide Emerson with a detailed report. My findings showed that it was entirely possible to convert these beautiful condominiums into homes for the elderly.

Mike and I had dinner and prepared to leave the next morning. I was ready to take on this project. It would mean moving again and moving the five people I had with me, but I had a good feeling about the condos themselves. Now if only the town would comply with HRS laws!

As we drove away, I reflected on the property itself. Just to gaze out the window or to stand on the decks looking at the moonlight glistening on the sand was invigorating. I couldn't imagine that this could be another pipedream.

We arrived home that evening, and the next morning I finished my complete report and took it to Emerson. He was pleased and asked me to set the date for the move and to make arrangements for moving my five residents and my own household goods. He was handling the expenses for the move. He gave me money and another credit card to purchase whatever I would need to buy for the residents. We set a date for the first of the next month, which would give me plenty of time to get everything done. I decided to move forward with Emerson's plans because I felt confident that the medical and fire requirements would be met, and, also, I was excited and optimistic about the place. We drove back home, and when we arrived, Sam and Maxcine were pleased for me but also sad. They had been with me for over two years, and I would miss them dearly. Both of them would have to look for jobs now, yet they volunteered to make the trip back down with us and stay for a day or so to help me set up. One of the things I had done while down there was to hire two people to take care of the five residents I would take there. One of the new hires would work days and the other one, nights, and they were flexible enough to help each other. Emerson wanted me to have enough help so that we would be able to open the place.

I did my own packing rather than pay the mover, and we all worked furiously as moving day approached.

Roma would be our problem. She could possibly sit up and enjoy the trip, or she could play dead and have to be strapped to the seat in a supine position with the tube open for feeding. She chose the latter. Her idiosyncrasies were routine to us, but to others who might see this procedure being performed, it would look like a ship of intensive care fools.

The big day finally came. The movers had been to the house several times and knew exactly what had to go; however, when we were about loaded and ready to put Roma in the car, they announced that not everything would fit in the truck. I thought they knew exactly what had to go! We tried to stuff the rest into the van but to no avail. For an additional fee the moving company would send out a small truck for what couldn't fit into the big truck. Sam and Maxcine started out ahead of us in the passenger van after it was loaded with two of the residents. Then we waited for the new truck and made sure all household goods were loaded before we left with the residents. I told the movers we would probably arrive later than they did as we had to stop at mealtime to feed our residents and to make pit stops. They said they would unload as soon as they got there.

Mike and I took the two cats and a dog in our car, along with James, Minnie, and Ilga. I called ahead to let the caretaker know that we were on our way. She would be responsible for accepting the shipment if it got there before we did.

When we arrived, we would move into two condos, one for Mike and me and the other for the five residents. A third unit would be ready for Maxcine and Sam for the time they were there. We caught up with the passenger van several miles down the road. Maxcine and Sam had already stopped several times to pacify Roma and Vera. They had forgotten to take the Milky Ways for Vera, and she complained all along the way. We told the residents we would stop for a picnic, which excited them, but like children they asked,

"How much longer?"

"Where are we going?

"Are we there yet?

"I wish we had stayed at home…I don't like picnics anyway."

We drove for an hour or so before I found a fast food place that had picnic tables and a lot of trees in the back. We parked both vehicles and started to unload James, Ilga, Minnie, and Vera. Vera was babbling and James was yelling, "Some picnic!"

Ilga was quiet but had to go to the bathroom. Vera and Minnie had diapers on. I took Ilga and Vera to the rest room. When it was clear of people, I changed Vera's diaper with her standing up. I guess anything can be done when necessity calls. When finished, we went outside to the benches where I sat them down and asked them what they wanted to eat. I should have known better. They all asked for Milky Ways.

Maxcine fed Roma and cleaned her up. I helped to reposition her and saw to it that she was comfortable. I was going to put Vera in a seat where she could lie down for the rest of the trip. Maybe she would go to sleep. James and Ilga would sit together, and I would position Minnie where her legs would be elevated. She started to choke when her head was down, and no one had ever found the cause. With that in mind we bought the food and relaxed for a while.

With lunch over, we loaded up and then switched vehicles. Mike and I took the van, and Maxcine and Sam drove the car for a change. There was still another four hours to go. If things went well, I figured we would need to make another two pit stops. Mike found a radio station that came in pretty well. The remarkable thing was that it kept getting louder and louder. James and Minnie also kept getting louder and louder, constantly arguing, even though Minnie couldn't speak clearly.

Sam and Maxcine had only Roma and Vera in their car. I wanted to change vehicles again but suffered through the noise instead.

After about an hour or so, we pulled into a rest stop. I needed a potty break, and maybe James would shut up. Ilga kept saying, "This was my last picnic and I didn't need to eat with the ants." In spite of everything I loved this woman. She was so damn cute.

Maxcine asked if we were ready to switch vehicles. I looked at her in disbelief, and then she explained: "Those damn cats of yours are never satisfied. They are worse than the screaming from James and Minnie in your van. The dog is fine. She and Sam got along well. So, can we switch?" I assured her we could and would.

Mike was thrilled. Our passengers had been getting on his nerves, too. Back in the car, we hoped Roma and Vera would go to sleep. When we drove onto US 1, we headed south for the causeway. It seemed that we had made remarkably good time. Then, suddenly, I thought I saw our moving van heading the opposite way. We both turned our heads around and Mike pulled the van over to look. It was our moving truck! We sounded the horn and yelled, but the men didn't hear or see us. How strange!

We decided to go on, and when we arrived at the condos, it was evening, and the moving van wasn't there. That scared me, so I ran inside to see what had happened. The caretaker said the men had unloaded the truck and left. They had said nothing to her. She had no way of knowing the men had not delivered all of the items, including a grand piano. She told us that she never saw three men work so fast to unload.

"They seemed to be in such a hurry."

There wasn't time to try to figure out what had happened. We needed to get the residents' belongings unpacked and get them into bed.

I took the time to call the moving company to see if they knew what was going on with our second load. The person was evasive, even denying that a second truck had been sent. "I watched them load it up," I told the employee. She told me I couldn't have watched them load because it didn't happen. Then I asked her how they expected to be paid if they didn't wait for me. Then she reminded me that the movers had the piano, and if I wanted it back, I would have to pay them. I asked her how they could have my piano when I knew it was on the second load and she denied there was a second load. Was I going nuts, or was she? We were going in circles, so I got off the phone before I exploded. I would have to deal with that problem later.

Settling in went fast. I wasn't worried about unpacking my own things as long as the bed was made up, which it was. The caretaker had made all of the beds. In an hour, we had all the linens, clothing, and belongings put away. The kitchen would take a little longer.

The condos were cream colored with oak cabinets and wallpaper of muted colors in a spray design. Richly finished wood beams crossed the vaulted ceilings, and each condo had a loft over one end of the living room. The rooms were large, perfect for the purpose of having a live-in caretaker in each condo. Also, I would hire a part-time employee when the live-in employee was off work. In short, I had great intentions, but things don't always go the way they are supposed to.

During my first trip there, when I interviewed several persons for work, I was reminded again that it was hard to find good help. Some applicants were lazy, unqualified, or had no concept of personal hygiene. If they could not keep themselves clean, they sure as hell couldn't keep the residents clean. I found out much later that most of my employees came in from Cuba or neighboring Islands. They couldn't speak English, but they worked for less pay than my employees in my home town. I found out that the going rate was $5 a day plus room and board. However, as time would tell, our dietary budget increased each month because they stole food to mail home. In the long run, it ended up costing me a lot of money to hire these workers. Considering what they stole, I felt paid them well, especially so, since the place was new and therefore easy to clean.

The next day while Sam prepared lunch, I went to my unit and tried to get the kitchen in order. I called the moving company again. The representative on the phone denied everything the first one I spoke to did. She did agree that one truck unloaded at the condo, and since there was no one to pay the movers, they took the piano and left. I asked them about all the other things missing, and, of course, she knew nothing about them.

Next I called the police and the county sheriff. They said there was nothing they could do since no crime had been committed. I called a local lawyer who said he would assist me. I had to bring in all the paperwork. I was able to find the discrepancy on the inventory. There were two appliance boxes containing kitchen and miscellaneous items missing that were listed on my personal inventory. Other items included two dining room chairs and two other large boxes and the piano. The movers figured they could sell the piano for the cost of the moving, which was $1500.

The lawyer called the company, but again the company representative denied any wrong doing, even though the missing items were on the company's copy of the manifest, as well as on mine. He threatened them with interstate commerce violation, insurance claims, and with court. I could tell by the look on his face that the representative was not intimidated.

When he got off the phone, he looked at us and said, "Every once in a while, I have to deal with real sons of bitches, but these people take the cake!"

After some thought, he decided that we would just go ahead immediately to court. He asked me to try to remember what was in those boxes, and he would file the papers with the court. I was just sick about all of the items, but more so about my piano. I went home to pick Sam's and Maxcine's brains. They would remember most of the items, especially those in the kitchen boxes. We unpacked and piled everything on the living room floor and then moved items to their proper places. As time went by, I would occasionally reach for something that was not there and would then place it on the list.

Eventually, the lawyers reached an agreement that was not satisfactory to me. They offered me the piano in exchange for $500 for the moving expenses. I would have to pay to get the piano down here.

I had my lawyer ask them for my daughter's wedding album. They denied having it, which told me they just dumped the contents of the smaller truck somewhere. What bastards! I had to let it go and do the best I could.

On the last night my favorite co-workers would be with me, I asked the new employees if one of them could stay with the residents while Mike and I took Sam and Maxcine out to dinner. Twila Mae readily said she would and referred me to several restaurants. The one we chose had fresh seafood expertly prepared. We all enjoyed it. We stopped and picked up a bottle of wine for Sam and Maxcine to enjoy on the deck. Too soon they would be going back to the reality of looking for work.

The next morning, I saw them off and went in to start breakfast. Twila Mae already had everything under control. I had not posted menus as yet, but she was preparing bacon, eggs, and biscuits. The food looked wonderful and the residents were sipping their juice and anxiously awaiting the main course. I went into the kitchen and when I saw what was on the counter, I almost vomited. There was a large block of lard.

I explained to her that I did not use lard for anything, and she would have to find menus that had very little fat in them. She didn't understand. She actually did not know that there was any other way to cook. She was devastated and took everything I said personally. After breakfast, I got out the menus and the food preparation policies, and we went over everything. Finally, she seemed to understand, and I made sure that she would follow the recipes from then on.

I phoned the city employee I had talked to previously to discuss what, if anything, the city was going to do about the paramedic situation. He didn't have any answers for me, and I could tell he was stalling. All I could do was to call Emerson and let him know about the lack of progress. He said he would get back to me in a few days. In the meantime, he asked me not to spend very much money in this town. I was asked to drive to the nearest town if it wasn't too much of an inconvenience. Let the merchants wonder where our money was being spent.

I didn't object. It became a once-a-week outing for me, which I needed. However, in less than a week, I knew this little boycott of ours was having no effect.

I started ordering food from a grocery wholesaler in Miami. The wholesaler recommended a produce company that also delivered to the cape and a shrimp man from Key Largo. Who needed to do business in this town? I could play their game, but I was terrified about the lack of medical care. For emergencies, I signed a contract with Mercy Hospital in Miami, but I understood that the hospital could send a chopper only if one was available.

Emerson was interviewing for a resident physician but was hesitant to hire one for the condos until the numbers of residents increased, and I couldn't increase the numbers until I had a license from HRS and from the city. Why did I begin to think this venture was going to blow up in our faces?

There were only eleven doctors in town, and I retained one to be the resident physician for the residents. He was in the process of trying to calculate just what his job description was worth but usually did what I asked of him. I helped by taking each of the residents in to see him for a history and physical. Even Roma. She had improved and was able to sit up and actually talked a bit with us. However, she still had the G tube in place to make sure she obtained sufficient nourishment. I often questioned the quality of life she had. Her cousin used to visit and socialize but couldn't since I moved her to the Keys. Her entire existence took her from the bed to a chair where she was fed according to my policy and procedure. I prayed for God to take her some other way, rather than have her starve to death.

A few days went by and I hadn't heard from Emerson. It was time to call him. The news was not bad but not good either. He was reluctant to tell me why, but he urged me to start spending a little money in town. There were two pharmacies. One of them already had our business, drugs and medical supplies being a large amount of my budget until the families reimbursed me. I was already paying the doctors and the labs, and my money was reimbursable by Medicare, but now I was to buy some of our food in town, too. I did not support this decision, but I complied with Emerson's instructions.

That evening at dinner, one of my employees, Matilda, called out to me to come to the dining room. I responded quickly, only to see Minnie slumped over. I ran to her and pulled her head up. She was barely breathing. I told Matilda to call the EMTs.

I knew it would be twenty to thirty minutes before the ambulance arrived, so I prepared to keep her breathing. We put her in a bed with her head up and back. I cleared her throat, but there was no obstruction. I tried the Heimlich but nothing came out. She didn't appear to be choking. Her heart rate was slow but regular, and her blood pressure was only a little low. Her skin was clammy and dusky colored. I wanted the ambulance to hurry. I also knew that all the EMTs could do was to take vital signs and transport her to the hospital, which would take another half an hour. I was so thankful for the oxygen tank I had brought with us. It helped a little until they arrived.

I was scared. I had the knowledge and could take steps to help save her life, but the EMTs would have to disconnect any IV or oxygen I started before they could transport Minnie. What a mess!

I heard the ambulance coming down the road and said a little silent prayer. Matilda went to the door, but on her way, she cautioned me not to be surprised at the EMTs who came up the steps. I hadn't the foggiest idea of what she was talking about until I saw the first man come in the door. He was so big he had to turn sideways to enter. The second person was a state trooper. The third person was a lady who must have weighed three hundred pounds. Both of the two oversized EMTs were out of breath from exertion. It would be ten minutes before they could even examine Minnie. I looked helplessly at the trooper. He sort of shrugged. They had left the stretcher downstairs.

I just could not watch this circus another moment. I got Mike and the trooper and the three of us carried Minnie down and placed her on the stretcher. To the trooper I said, "It scares the hell out of me to have elderly people here and inadequate emergency medical service."

"I understand ma'am, but wait until you see what is waiting at the hospital. I have had a lot of people die on the roads because I couldn't get help for them. We've all tried to get better care, but the city doesn't want to make changes," he said.

The overweight EMTs would have died of exhaustion if they had had to do CPR. Somehow they picked up the stretcher and placed Minnie in the ambulance. I hugged her to reassure her that she was going to be okay. Deep down I knew she wasn't because I hadn't the slightest idea of what was wrong with her. It could have been a stroke, but I didn't see the classic signs. The trooper assured me that he would make sure she arrived at the hospital alive. Mike and I followed the ambulance as the trooper led the way.

When we arrived at the emergency room, Mike and I were mortified when we overheard one of the nurses say, "I suppose they want us to save her. Look at her; she's ninety-three years old." They laughed. I asked her to please get the doctor and she said, "For what? We do not call the doctors unless there is an emergency."

Rather than argue with her, I went to a phone booth and called the doctor. He arrived in only a few minutes in a fury. I knew that he was not a native of this area because only an import could raise this much hell. He ordered a CAT scan and x-rays. The big-mouthed nurse called him down and said, "Doctor, we do not spend money on ninety year olds in this hospital." He took hold of one end of the stretcher Minnie was on and I the other, and we headed down the hall. I told him to do whatever he had to do to save Minnie. He had a look of appreciation on his face and wrote the orders in a chart as we scurried down the hall.

The first test, a chest x-ray, revealed the unbelievable diagnosis. Minnie had a hiatal hernia that was as large as a football and was situated above and pressing against her left lung. It had turned her stomach upside down. I had to look several times before I knew what it was.

I asked the doctor, "Am I seeing what I think I see?"

"If you think you are seeing a hiatal hernia and an upside-down stomach, you have it right," he said. "Believe me, I thought this was anatomically impossible and would not believe it if someone else told me."

"This didn't happen overnight, did it?"

"No," he said, "this took several years."

"How could routine x-rays, which must have been done when Minnie had a mastectomy, not have shown this?" He just shook his head.

Poor little Minnie held on for a few more days. She always knew when I was there, as she would give me that Mona Lisa smile.

As her condition deteriorated, I had a very difficult time dealing with her impending death. I had never been in a situation like this. Do I bury her? Cremate her? What do I do with the remains? I didn't know what she wanted and knowing became important to me, but now she was unable to respond. I discussed what to do with her doctor. We had a fairly close relationship now and trusted each other. He felt that I should do whatever I was comfortable with. I wasn't comfortable with anything at this point.

I called Social Security to find out if money would be forthcoming for burial. There was a one-time payment of $200, which had been used by her husband. Veteran's Affairs offered nothing but burial in a national cemetery. The closest one was nearly 200 miles away. The VA only opened and closed the grave. Everything else was her expense. There I was, back to square one.

On a chance, I called her previous nursing home to see if someone there had possibly overlooked a relative. No! There was no one. However, a funeral home was listed, which I called. Perhaps a relative would be listed there. Indeed the call did bring me a name, a brother-in-law in Kentucky. I called information, obtained a phone number, and placed a call. He barely remembered Minnie and certainly wanted nothing to do with funeral arrangements. He thanked me after I gave him my name and phone number. I told him I would let him know when she died. The next day I called him.

Social Security pays benefits a month late. For example, a check issued April 3rd is for the month of March. If Minnie died in March, even if she died on the last day of March, her check dated April 3rd would have to be returned. This was one more example of abuse and fraud against the elderly. In this way Social Security gained billions of dollars illegally. How was this abuse justified? I was angry not only for Minnie, I was angry for myself. I would have to pay for her burial out of my own pocket. The Pauper Law did not apply to her since she had Social Security income.

I went to the only funeral home in town and made the arrangement to have her cremated as I didn't know what else to do. I would dispose of the ashes. They quoted me an inflated $600 price but finally accepted

$250, which was much closer to the norm. The April S.S. check covering March had to be returned. She died on March 31.

I called her brother-in-law to tell him of the death. He then told me to send her body to Kentucky and he would have her buried there. I called the funeral home. It was too late. The body had already been sent to Miami for cremation. One more phone call to the brother-in-law. He was upset! I couldn't believe this crap. Why all of this sudden interest in Minnie's remains? I have said this over and over again: relatives crawl out of the woodwork when they think there is money involved. I don't think I mentioned to him the fact that she was penniless. As a last resort, he asked me to please send the ashes to him. When I asked him how he would like to pay for the shipment, he said, "Why me? I am on a pension and can't afford to pay." I agreed to pay the postage and hung up.

After shipping Minnie off to her brother-in-law, I continued to work on getting everything done at the condos for licensure. The people I had hired out of Miami worked fast, and their work passed inspection. Emerson had asked me to attend the next city council meeting. I sat through the entire meeting and when nothing was said about starting an ambulance service, I brought it up. I asked if something was going to be done. The reply was, "We will discuss it at the next meeting."

I was nervous. It was not my money, but it seemed to me that Emerson was putting a lot of money into something I did not believe was going to happen. I went home and called him to report my findings. He was convinced it was just a ploy since they weren't used to working with a woman. He would come down for the next meeting, and see what he could do. I knew in my heart that Emerson was losing his butt on the condos, but surely he could convey our needs to the town fathers. If only I knew then what I would eventually find out.

Nevertheless, I continued writing up the policies and procedures, while the workers put the vent systems in the kitchens, the fire and smoke detectors in rooms where needed, and the alarm system for the nonexistent fire department.

The county, the HRS inspectors, and I together decided to use only one kitchen for all of our cooking. The other three could be used for snacks, but I had to disconnect the stoves and use microwaves only. Doing this would save a lot of money.

The handicapped ramps became as difficult to build as I had anticipated. When they were finished they would be over a hundred feet long.

When the brochures advertising my condo home for the elderly were ready, I started my marketing all over the area. Surprisingly, people were receptive to our facility and me. There wasn't another in all of the Keys. I told everyone I would notify them of the open house, which would be held prior to the formal opening.

When Emerson arrived, he was surprised to see so much progress. I would be able to call for an HRS inspection in about a week. He was pleased. He went to the council meeting the next night without me.

Emerson was not a happy camper the next morning when he came to breakfast, but I politely waited for him to talk. He said very little except to start buying everything I could from the local merchants and go ahead and let the contractors finish their jobs.

Our required manuals and all of the enormous paperwork were done. I mailed copies to HRS for their pre-approval so I could make corrections before the final inspection. The condos also had to be inspected by the state and county fire marshals and the county health inspector. I called them to arrange for appointments.

Despite all the work I had to do, I managed to spend some time with our residents.

All seemed to be doing fairly well except for Roma. The doctor actually came out to see her every day or so.

After breakfast one morning, I asked the employees where I could find some good barbecue. Matilda immediately told me about a place that had the best. I wrote down directions and decided I would buy some for dinner that evening.

Later, while I sat outside, Twila Mae, a local, came out and sat down with me. She whispered to me that I couldn't go there for the barbecue. I asked her why, and she told me white folks didn't go to that part of town. This woman was dead serious and insisted that I wouldn't be safe there. I was surprised to find this attitude. After all, this was the 80s! Me? I didn't care what color anyone was. I wasn't afraid to go into any part of town. I decided I was going to have barbeque, regardless!

When Twila Mae left, I asked Matilda, another local, for more specifics. She laughed but was unwilling to talk. I asked, "Is it safe for us to go or not?" She said it was and smiled again. It took Mike and me a half hour to drive there, and we liked the place and the people. They were kind to serve us French fries without charge while we waited for our order. As we drove back, the aromas tantalized us. James and Ilga picked up the smell as soon as we opened the door. Matilda had the table set, and James, Ilga, and Vera were ready to eat.

While we ate, Matilda proceeded to explain the matter of the bad part of town. Twila Mae was no longer on duty and had gone home. Matilda was about to bust a gut the entire time she was talking and finally had to quit so she could let out some loud chuckles. She laughed so hard that everyone at the table had to laugh, too. It seemed that Twila Mae's husband told her about the bad part of town and that she must never go to that side of the tracks for any reason. He would take the dry cleaning when it needed to go. Finally, Matilda blurted out, "Jimmy, Twila Mae's husband, has a black woman with four children including a set of twins there that he doesn't want her to find out about."

Mike and I laughed until we were hysterical, and James and Ilga were going along for the ride. When we calmed down, we talked about how awful it was for the husband to pull the wool over Twila Mae's eyes. How could he keep all of this a secret? We felt that she must be terribly naïve, and since she never went for barbecue, we guessed she would never find out.

Despite all the work I had to do, I managed to spend some time with our residents. All seemed to be doing fairly well except for Roma, whom I checked on frequently. The doctor actually came out to see her every day or so. Her condition was terminal, and soon there would be only three residents. One day I called her doctor to ask him to come see her again. I had promised him a condo for a weekend and apparently this was the weekend he wanted it. This was fine with me, but I did not want to disturb him while he was here. The only thing I would ask of him was to legally pronounce Roma dead when she actually did die so that I could send her remains directly to a funeral home. There was one in Key Largo that would come for the remains and send them to her cousin for burial.

The doctor and his family arrived Friday afternoon. He immediately examined Roma and agreed that she was near the end. Roma died about three hours later and her remains were taken away within the hour. The residents did not know what happened and I said little about it. Death comes so frequently when dealing with the elderly that these preparations seemed more and more routine with each passing.

The next day Twila Mae said that all the townspeople were flapping their mouths about people dying on the Cape without first being sent to the hospital. If nothing else, we sure had the townsfolk's curiosity aroused. Mainly because of the town's mindset, I felt that we would never be able to open our residence, but Emerson was convinced that his money could buy anything. Time would tell.

HRS came Friday. Since I had lost two, I now had three residents, which were legal. Actually, I could have had three of the elderly in each unit without a license, but I could not advertise without that license. I was anxious to get the approval process over with. The state and county fire marshals would come out on the same day. I had not yet heard from the health department.

Ever since we had been at the condos, I noticed some fairly strange, consistent goings on in the town. I was usually so busy that I couldn't take the time to look twice, but the strange behavior was always in the back of my mind. Mike noticed it, too, and he asked me about it. He often went fishing and several times asked me if I knew what was going on when those great big trucks backed down to the water. We both observed that a state trooper car parked on the side of the road near the water when the big trucks were there. They always came on Wednesday nights and Sunday mornings. Because I had no idea of what was going on, I asked Matilda one morning. She averted her eyes and avoided answering me directly. Knowing what the trucks were doing wasn't really important to me, so I let it go. It wasn't particularly important to me, either. However, as I thought more about it, it struck me as curious that Matilda and Twila Mae always seemed to be busy on Wednesday and Sunday mornings and therefore couldn't work on those days.

One day on the way to shop in Key Largo, I thought how much I liked The Cape. I loved the laid-back lifestyle, especially the casual dress, which was shorts, pants, and bright blouses and shirts, Panama straw hats, and flip-flops or leather sandals. At an outdoor restaurant I stopped to grab a sandwich. A lady, her skin so tanned it looked like bronze, started chatting with me. Ginger was a nice lady, who indeed had lived there all of her life. I told her who I was and what I was doing on The Cape. She looked surprised and then asked me if I worked for Emerson. I told her I did.

"Carolyn, do you know anything at all about the circumstances of how Emerson built those condos?" she asked.

"No, he hired me to turn the condos into a retirement home, and I have almost completed my task."

She chuckled. I asked her if there was something I should know.

"Well, I don't think you will be able to open."

"Why?" I asked.

"Because the town doesn't like Emerson very well." She said. At this point I could have chalked up what she was telling me to gossip and leave, or I could ask more questions. I wanted to leave, but I wanted to finally know what was going on.

"If there is anything that will affect me, I would like to know about it," I said.

"Do you plan to stay there if they won't let you open?" I thought about it but then had to say there wouldn't be any reason to stay if there wouldn't be a home. I shook my head.

She simply said, "He left this town owing a lot of money to the townspeople. You are the third one who has been here to open up a home."

Before I could respond she said, "And I understand you have everything ready except for the health department. None of the others got past the contractors. Carolyn, the health department will let you bring the condos up to code and then not let you open because of the septic tanks."

"What's wrong with the septic tanks?" I asked her.

"Nothing," she replied, "but they will come up with something." I was furious with Emerson and also with myself for not checking him out more thoroughly. How could he be so dishonest with me? I sat there in dismay but then remembered what I was going to ask her. "Tell me, what goes on in town on Wednesday nights and Sunday mornings?"

"They have church," she said.

"I know they have church, but not every body goes to church."

She laughed and said, "Yes, half of them go on Wednesday night while the other half run drugs. On Sunday morning, the half that went to church on Wednesday runs drugs on Sunday mornings." We both shrugged and laughed. Who would have thought that?

I shook Ginger's hand, thanked her for the information, and told her how delightful it was to have met her.

When I arrived home, I told Mike about my conversation with Ginger. He thought I should call Emerson right then and confront him, but I had to give Emerson the benefit of the doubt. After all, a total stranger had given me this information.

I helped Twila Mae put the finishing touches on dinner. She had been quiet while I was talking to Mike, but I had decided not to ask her any more questions. I brought Vera to the table and called James and Ilga. James came out of the bathroom, but Ilga did not come out of her room. I looked around, but she was not there. I asked Twila Mae if she had seen Ilga recently.

She said, "She and James came in together, and I thought she went in to lie down."

James was in one of his belligerent moods. He denied even knowing an Ilga. They had been trusted to walk on the beach, and, up to now, they had always made it home. This in itself was surprising, since most of the units looked so much alike. I had often wondered how James knew which one was his.

I looked for Ilga, covering each unit while Mike drove the perimeter road, but Ilga was nowhere to be found. Twila Mae fed the other two residents and continued to question James.

As I walked in I heard him say, "Do you mean the old lady on the sand?"

"Yes, do you remember where she went?"

"Yeah, she went to the store." Oh, if only I could laugh…

There was a convenience store several miles down the road. We headed in that direction. I saw an older couple standing on their porch. Mike stopped the car, and I asked them if they had seen a tall, elderly woman.

"Yes. She went by awhile ago." They had no reason to stop her. She looked perfectly normal.

When we got to the store, I went in and inquired about her.

The woman said, "Yep, she was here, but we called the sheriff."

"Why did you do that? You could have called me."

"We figured you couldn't take care of the ones you have and didn't deserve to get her back. We hear you got forty or fifty of them hid out over there." I was furious, but I couldn't say anything except to correct her on the number there.

The man then popped up to say, "How about them that died? There was a mess of them."

We returned to the car and drove to the jail. Yep, she was there all right. I started to explain about Ilga, but policeman in charge didn't want to hear about it.

"You got enough problems as it is," he said, as he released Ilga to me. I was so grateful to just get a pleasant response from him. I thanked him and started to leave when he said, "She sure has a rap sheet, doesn't she?" We laughed. Yes, she sure did. She still had her ID bracelet on.

Friday morning I was ready for HRS when four representatives arrived around 10:00 a.m. . After the introductions, we gave them coffee and Danishes and then split up. The dietitian wanted to be alone and would talk to me later. She asked if it would be okay to ask Twila Mae questions.

"Of course," I said.

Two of them picked up the policies and procedures manual and found a corner to sit in to read. The fire inspector asked me to accompany him on a first round; then he would go over the fire policies and procedures portion of the manual.

He found nothing wrong, but did question who engineered the handicap ramps. They had done an excellent job, according to him. There was a major problem with not being able to hook up directly with a fire department, but I would be able to open since I had completed the optional, alternative items.

The city and the county still had not provided paramedics or a fire station. Perhaps the lady at the sandwich shop really did know that what she told me about the city was true. We ambled back to the condo after completing our tour. The fire inspector was stunned at the beauty of the place. He lived not far from there and put in his request to reserve a room. The weather cooperated, with only a hint of rain. A nice breeze was whipping away the fog that had set in earlier.

The others were deep in thought. The dietitian had had a few questions, but Twila Mae had safely answered most of them. I gave the fire protection policies and procedures manual to the fire inspector, who took some water, found a spot that was comfortable, and prepared to read.

One of the ladies observed Twila Mae do her baths and morning care. The lady questioned Vera's ambulating ability but soon saw why we kept her in a reclining chair most of the time. She was not restricted but believed that she was. Apparently this was acceptable.

James and Ilga were on their best behavior. An eyebrow went up with them sleeping in the same room, but no one said anything about it. I'm sure they had already read the permission papers in their files.

All in all the inspection went fine, even with the few corrections that had to be made. I asked for thirty days to correct the deficiencies, and they agreed. This meant they would be back in thirty days or so to make sure everything was done. They gave me permission to open as soon as I received the occupational license, which would be issued as soon as the city and county had finished their inspections.

I called Emerson to tell him the good news. He was happy but a little reserved. When I told him that all we needed was inspection by the city fire inspectors and the County Health Department, he was quiet.

The city fire inspector showed up that afternoon. I think he knew that if the home had passed the state inspection, the city had no choice but to approve, also. There remained the problem of having adequate fire protection from the city, but that was his problem rather than mine. I had spent a lot of money on the handicap ramp and all of the extras just so that the condos would pass inspection. I could have built a fire station for what I had spent and originally offered that amount of money to the city for that purpose.

He gave me a clearance to open pending inspection by the County Health Department.

Again I called Emerson to let him know that the fire inspector cleared us. I again asked him if he could think of any reason why the County Health Department would not clear us. He said the Condos were built according to the codes, and there should not be anything more required than what he had already complied with. I had personally seen to everything that was required by HRS, which usually worked together with city and county regulations.

There was a chance inspectors would be there that day. It would be awfully nice to get the last inspection over with. Improvement costs had been well over $100,000, some spent in town but most in Miami, not to mention my salary, our monthly expenses and all my effort. There couldn't be anything else major to stop us, could there? Ginger's words still haunted me…I prayed she was wrong.

The County Health Department came out the next morning. They checked the policies and procedures in the kitchen to be sure trash containers were closed and the personnel files to be sure everyone was food certified, although the food handlers had to go to Miami to take the class. Apparently, everything was okay. They wrote out a certificate and gave me one to hang on the wall. Another man arrived just as I was asking the first one if I could go get my occupational license now. The second man, who evidently represented the City, interrupted by asking me if I had done anything to the septic tanks. I told him I hadn't. He said that, according to the original building plans, they were acceptable for five residents. Before I could say anything else, he started writing on a clipboard and said to me that they would not give me a license. I felt my blood begin to boil, but I remained calm. "Sir, please explain why."

He proceeded to say that the septic tanks were not large enough for the elderly.

I asked, "What do you mean by *the elderly*? Are they different from the young? Please make yourself clear." He lay down the paper he had been writing on and started for the door. I asked him to come back. "This doesn't tell me anything. I need to know what you mean."

"Ma'am, I do not have to give an explanation. Just call your boss and tell him to pay his bills the next time he comes to town."

Matilda had come in to relieve Twila Mae. She motioned for me to shut up. I did because I was in shock. I'm not sure I understood what had just happened.

The first man shook his head and walked out.

I was sure that the man representing the City could not get away with his objections, but quite frankly I had no idea about where to get help at this point. Surely, I wasn't thinking straight. I had a cup of coffee and called Emerson. He was so quiet I wondered if he was still on the line. I waited a few moments and then said, "Emerson, what do you want me to do. I could start bringing in residents tomorrow." He asked me to wait and said that he would be down the next day.

When I hung up, Matilda said, "I wanted to say you would have trouble, but I thought that maybe things had changed for the better."

"What things?" I asked.

"Carolyn, Emerson has a bad reputation in this town. The townspeople have vowed to get even and now they are doing it. I don't know that he still owes them money, but he didn't pay his bills when he built these places and he stepped on a lot of people's toes who don't forget easily. We're surprised that anyone did anything for you, but you paid them and they needed money. These fishermen are starving. Me and Twila Mae took a chance with you, but you always paid us."

"What do I do now?"

"Just wait and see what Emerson tells you tomorrow."

I went for a walk on the beach and waited for Mike. He was fishing.

When he came home, I suggested we go for a ride out of town for dinner. We went, and during dinner I told him about the events of the day. I knew in my heart that we would be moving back up north and I would have to move those three residents again.

When Emerson arrived the next morning, we went to his condo to talk. I told him about passing all inspections except for the septic tank one, and he knew that I was upset.

"Let me contact some people I know as a last resort," he said.

I had no choice but to agree. He voiced his pleasure in my work. He complimented me, told me that he had sent two other persons down here earlier who didn't even know where to start making home for the elderly out of the Condos. I wondered whether they didn't know where to start or if they simply received the same treatment I had just received. Emerson left for town.

Maxcine, Twila Mae, and I prepared lunch and just sat around. None of us had the energy to do anything, and I told the women to just take it easy.

"One of you can go home if you want to," I said.

They didn't. They had a lot invested in this project and thought they had found their future here working for me. Hell, I thought, what about me? I thought I had my future here, too.

Emerson was back in the early afternoon. When he came through the door, he didn't look well. He asked Mike and me to come to his unit. We went together.

His face was gloomy and he was definitely despondent.

"Carolyn, I am going to have to call in some markers and that will take some time. Are you with me?"

"Yes. I am only concerned that you might not be able to carry this place with no more income coming in. I can still legally put three in each unit with one caregiver, and there isn't a damn thing they can do about, but what if I do move more people in, and then we have to close down?"

Emerson said, "I would rather wait and see what is going to happen before we bring any more in."

"That's fine with me," I said. "I will just keep things the way they are until I hear from you."

"Okay. You just hold the fort down here."

So, I did just that. It was pleasant not to have anything on my priority list. Now I had the opportunity to do some things with James and Ilga. I asked Twila Mae if there had been any mail for James.

She said, "No. Does his daughter not care about him at all?"

"The only thing she cares about is his money and keeping that money away from his wife," I said.

"Wife? I didn't know he had a wife. I thought he had only Ilga."

"Twila Mae," I said, "Those two don't have one brain cell between the two of them, but they do share some kind of love or bond that seems to keep them together. Then, when they are apart, they quickly forget about each other. Their relationship is strange. He does have a wife who is probably looking for him right now. When his daughter acquired guardianship, I had to abide by her wishes, which were clearly spelled out. His wife was not to see him. I have fought off the militia trying to keep him away from Ilga, the daughter and the wife, but I am about to forget anything that does not benefit James."

"My God," she said, "I had no idea what you have been through with that poor man."

That night I took James, Ilga, and Matilda out for barbecue. Ginger was thrilled to see us, and since she wasn't busy, I asked her to join us. Ginger offered to help any way she could to get the city fathers off my butt. I had the feeling that she knew more than she was letting on. Aha! A sudden revelation came to me. If Twila Mae's husband had a woman on the dark side of town, then maybe some of the influential townsfolk did, too.

James, Ilga, and Matilda enjoyed their dinner. They actually seemed lucid. I think the ride in the car did more for them than anything. Tomorrow, I decided, I would take Twila Mae out to lunch, but not on the dark side of town.

The next morning Emerson called. The tone in his voice was not reassuring. He told me City Hall had him by the balls. Apparently when he filed the original building plans, the blue prints indicated an allotted space per septic tank. The tanks had been built for only four persons per unit, and they could not be changed.

I asked him, "Couldn't we open with four per unit?" He told me that his backers and investors would not approve that.

"Emerson, a bird in the hand is better than none." Now our frustration was beginning to erode our relationship. "Well, how does this affect me? And what should I do?" I asked.

"The truth is," he said, "I just don't know at this point."

Unfortunately, I did know what to do. I called my mother and asked her to see if she could rent two apartments together back home for us and to start looking for someone to work for me. Would she please call Sam and Maxcine to see if they'd come back to work for me. I contacted a mover to give me an estimate, and I started collecting boxes. I also gave Twila Mae and Matilda notice.

The next morning I received the phone call I was expecting from Emerson with all of the apologies I could handle. I would receive a severance check and a thousand dollars to cover my move. He was also paying Matilda and Twila Mae good severance checks. I told him I would take what was mine and leave the rest for him. He insisted I take everything I had brought up regardless of who had paid for what.

"Just leave the units as they were," he said. I was numb and not able to think on the drive back up the coast.

Chapter Eighteen
The Incarceration

The two apartments Mother found were waiting for us when we arrived back home, one upstairs for Mike and me and one downstairs for James and Ilga. I had made arrangements to place Vera with a friend since my grandmother would be joining me again. Her money was running out at the nursing home where she had been living, and my mother wanted to hang on to what was left. Oh well! Once again I became the patsy!

Because Maxine and Sam had taken other jobs, I phoned three ladies who were looking for work to come over that same day for interviews. I made a quick decision on one named Mary, and she started working immediately by assisting me in unpacking and putting away everyone's boxes of belongings, which had been carefully marked.

With Mike helping us, we had everything set up before the day was over, and then my mother brought my grandmother over. Mimmy was not a happy camper. She wanted to be upstairs, but we could never get her up those steps. She was not happy about staying downstairs.

When I was sure the residents were set for the night, I made an attempt to put some of the upstairs together. Mike set up the beds and opened boxes of necessities. I was actually hesitant to open too many boxes since this living arrangement was temporary. By now I was weary and completely disillusioned about owning and running assisted living facilities and trying to bring quality into the lives of residents. I wanted out of this business as soon as possible.

A loud knock on the door woke me the next morning. Mike wasn't in bed so I assumed he had gone somewhere and locked himself out (a bad habit of his). I grabbed a robe and stumbled to the door. There were two police officers standing there. I was sure something had happened to Mike. Immediately, my heart started pumping hard, I felt sick at my stomach, and I broke out in a cold sweat.

"What has happened to my husband?"

"No ma'am, nothing has happened to anyone. We are here to talk to you."

Relieved but apprehensive, I asked what they wanted to talk to me about. Instead of answering, they asked me to sit down. I had to pee and my mouth was not very pleasant tasting, so I asked if they would excuse me for a moment and headed to the bathroom. One of the officers was female, and she dashed in front of me and looked in the bathroom before allowing me to go in. What the hell was going on?

After coming out of the bathroom, I asked what they were here for. I wasn't looking forward to hearing the reason. As a matter of fact, I felt as if I were going to pass out and had to quickly sit down. The male officer asked me if I were okay.

"No! Would you please tell me what's going on?"

Before he could answer, there was another knock. The door opened and another female officer stood in the doorway and motioned for the male to go outside.

I heard her say, "There are three of them down there. Are we going to take them all in?" He shrugged his shoulders and radioed for directions. I could tell what the answer was because the female officer left, stating she was going downstairs to pack the elderly people's clothing. Why were they taking them in? And what did they want with me? Apparently Mike wasn't their target. I was!

When one of the officers came back in, I said, "You must tell me why you are here. That is the law."

The female officer said, "Ma'am, just let us ask the questions."

They did. For over two hours, they fired questions at me, questions like, "Do you know a person by the name of Anderson? How many people did you bury in the yard at your last house? Did you drown all of them in your pool? What about a Mr. Oslo? Do you know him?" Of course, I couldn't answer any of these questions. I was bewildered, becoming exhausted, and my nerves were frayed. I began to think that someone had framed me. Finally, I said I wanted to call my lawyer. They ignored me. When Mike came in and realized what was happening, he picked up the phone to call the lawyer, but the male officer told him to put it down.

"I believe this is my phone and unless you plan to arrest me, I am going to use it," he said. I motioned to Mike to leave. He got the message and went to find a phone booth.

At first I had this crazy idea that if we cooperated, they would just leave. Fat chance. They weren't leaving any time soon, no matter what we did.

"What do you want with me, and do you intend to arrest me?" I asked.

At that point the male officer read me my rights and said I was being placed under arrest. He still did not tell me why.

Panic struck. I sat there in tears feeling absolutely helpless, clueless, and growing sicker by the minute. I was falling apart inside. Where was Mike? What was keeping him? I reached for my purse and opened it to get a Valium. The female officer grabbed my hand so hard that later I had bruises. I explained to her that I had an, as yet, unidentified health problem, and the doctor prescribed Valium in times of crisis.

"Which would you rather do, take me in or take me to the emergency room? If you don't pull your hand away, you'll end up taking me to the hospital." She looked at the other officer, who nodded, and she backed off. She glared at me.

Mike came storming in after making the calls, his face red with anger. "You have no right to treat my wife this way," he yelled. "My attorney is on his way, and according to him, your job is to take her in, not question her like a common criminal. Now get the hell out of my house!"

I felt very faint. Regardless of what the law was, they had guns, and I didn't see any attorney yet. In a loud voice the male policeman said, "You hold on a minute, mister. You are not implicated at this time; but you keep this up, and we'll haul your ass in for disorderly conduct." Mike looked at the officer, then at me, and, thankfully, shut up.

I could feel the Valium taking affect. Maybe now I could comprehend some of what was going on. Apparently the female officer downstairs had left with James, Ilga, and my grandmother. I found out much later that my grandmother had given the police officer such a bad time that she had to call for assistance. Mimmy literally kicked her as hard as she could and called her a smart-assed pig. I knew what a bear she could be, and I guess she was really pissed off to be moved two times in one day.

I sat in silence while they kept asking me questions about this and that person…names I had never heard of…and events I knew nothing about. I just sat there and shook my head in answer to their questions. After another hour they allowed me to get dressed so they could take me in.

I was put in the police car, but the officer decided that I did not need to be handcuffed. How generous of him! When he started the car and we were traveling down the road he said, "Ma'am, I will tell you why I have to arrest you now." I said nothing. What could I say after two and a half hours of grilling? He was now finally going to tell me why he had put me through hours of questioning? It seemed like he was opening up because the bitchy female officer wasn't around. He had seemed greatly intimidated by her. I didn't blame him.

He was listening for a response but got nothing. "Ma'am, I will ask you one more time. Do you recognize the name Ann Marley?"

Again I said, "No, I have never heard of the name."

"Well, do you know the name Richardson?"

Once again I said, "No."

"Can you associate any of these names to Kentucky?"

Bingo! A bell rang. "I have known only one person from Kentucky, and I really only knew his name, but it wasn't Richardson, it was Cunningham," I said.

He pulled off the road and looked at the computer print out once again and asked me who he was. I answered that he was a long, lost relative of a resident I had taken care of in the Keys, but she had died. I found out about him while trying to locate somebody to bury the poor soul.

"Did this man assume any responsibility for her?

"Yes. He ordered me to pay for her cremation and have her ashes shipped to Kentucky."

"Did you ship them?" he asked.

"Yes. I paid for cremation, the shipping, and arranged for the funeral home in Key Largo to ship the ashes." I looked at him through the rearview mirror. He had a funny look on his face but said nothing more. A few minutes later he asked me the names of the three residents they had taken in. I told him. He then asked me if James had a wife.

I said, "Yes." Whatever he put together, he didn't share it with me. The discussion stopped there. Just before we reached the jail, he said, "Now I will tell you why I had to arrest you. You had an outstanding warrant for a water ban fine that has never been paid…"

"A WATER BAN FINE! ARE YOU OUT OF YOUR MIND? HOW DARE YOU SUBJECT ME TO SUCH…?"

"Now you calm down, Mrs. Connelly, and let me finish. There's more. Apparently James's wife filed a complaint that you had murdered him and buried him in the backyard of your last home. We know you didn't, because we dug up the entire yard. At the same time, a call came in from Kentucky stating that the relative never received the ashes you were supposed to have sent. The only problem was that all the names were wrong, and I apologize for that."

"Sir! It will take more than an apology to compensate for what you have done to me today. I'll have your job for this!" He ignored me and said nothing.

They booked me and threw me in a cell full of the scariest looking criminals imaginable. "Hey, Momma, whaddaya doin' here? Pretty ol' nana like you doin' time? Wassa matta', you ain't scared now? Com'ere, I'll protect you." I backed up from each one but soon found myself surrounded and wetting myself.

"GUARD! GUARD! HELP ME.GET ME OUT OF HERE!!!" I yelled. The cell mates laughed at me but backed up just the same.

"All right, ladies, leave the poor girl alone and get back to your own bunks," said the guard on duty. He must have been watching, because he responded immediately. He probably got a kick out of seeing me squirm. Thankfully, however, he did move me out of the cell and into an empty one for my own protection.

It took several hours, though it seemed like several days, for Mike to get the bail money and process the paperwork. I was never so glad to see him as when the guard opened that cell door. I fell into his arms weeping uncontrollably. He held me close, guiding my every step to the car. We didn't say a thing to each other, we couldn't. The emotions were too extreme, and the situation was too horrible for words.

I couldn't go home. The humiliation and embarrassment were overwhelming. Mike drove to my mother's house where my grandmother had been taken.

I was there less than an hour when I had to go to the emergency room. There the doctor thought I might have Addison's disease. With this disease, the body sometimes requires more adrenaline than can be produced, and adrenal crisis results. My cortizol level was down to 4, a seriously low level. I needed cortisone immediately. This alone confirmed the diagnosis of acute adrenal insufficiency, but time would tell if it was Addison's. I was cold, clammy, unable to speak or move, unresponsive, and disoriented. I would require immediate treatment and several months of rest.

However, after only a couple of weeks of recuperation, I grew restless and began searching for a house. Everyone kept telling me to rest, but I would not feel peaceful until we were settled.

A friend was watching Ilga, and apparently James was staying with his granddaughter. I was still responsible for the residents and needed a place to put them. The apartment arrangement wasn't working out.

Tired of hearing me bitch and moan, Mike took up the search for a house and found a lovely one in a good part of town. He brought me to see it, and we wasted no time in signing a lease that started immediately. When we went back to my mother's house, I called our current apartment manager. Amazingly, he agreed to cancel our leases and to return the deposit and unused rent money. He seemed rather eager to get rid of us. I guess something good had come from the police scare.

The next call was to a moving company. Again we struck gold. The moving truck would be able to come out that very morning. Luckily, I had not unpacked many of my belongings. Shortly thereafter, Sam, Maxcine, Kris, and Jim drove up. I was overwhelmed by their concern and love. They worked all day, and by late evening everything for the kitchen in the new house was put away, the beds were set up, my grandmother was moved in, and Mike had gone after Ilga.

Sam and Maxcine brought in take-out for dinner. We stopped to eat and to tell them the whole story of what had happened. They knew I had been taken to jail but didn't know why. I was so full of anger at the families and at the police department that, as the story unfolded, my body began the all-to-familiar climb to trouble. Recognizing the danger signs that they'd seen before—diaphoresis, cold limbs, lethargy—Sam and Maxcine got up to leave so I could rest. They said they could come back to work part-time. I hugged them both tight, thanking God for my good fortune.

Now that we were settled in, it was time to deal with Barnaby. I had given him the money to pay for the water ban fine, and obviously he didn't pay it. I called the Bar Association. They told me how to file the complaint and to be sure to include a copy of the receipt of my payment to Barnaby for the fine.

Rest and relaxation were impossible until this was taken care of. I pulled out the typewriter, wrote, and sent the complaint out in the morning mail. I was full of hatred for the emotional turmoil Barnaby had put me through. I hoped he would be hung by his toe nails. Justice at last! He lost his license to practice law for a year, and was fined $5,000. However, the most pleasing thing to happen was the write up in the press. Apparently, I was not his only victim. A lot of people had filed complaints against him.

I received a call from James's daughter. She acted as if she knew nothing about the police matter. For awhile she simply chit-chated. When she asked to talk to her dad, I told her I presumed he was at his granddaughter's house. Of course she knew this already, but she really turned on the acting skills. She said she was sorry and that she would see that her dad was brought right back. I'd seen this act before when she was caught in a lie. All she wanted was to be rid of the responsibility of caring for James. That is why she had not been answering her phone and now pretending she didn't know where he was.

I told her that the only way I would take him back would be for a monthly rent of $2500 and a written, notarized statement that Ann was dead. If she would not pay this rent, then I would keep James only if I had a restraining order to keep her away from me and James. She said she would call Barnaby right away. I laughed myself silly and told her she had better find another attorney fast. After hearing what Barnaby had done, she said she would. She didn't question the rental price and agreed to pay up front before James was brought in. I never dreamed she would even consider my demands, or I would have just told her I wouldn't take James at all. Oh well, I was already caring for one person. I might as well care for two.

James and his granddaughter arrived the next morning, check in hand.

When Ilga saw James, she grinned for a moment or so.

James greeted me familiarly and asked, "Does that man still live here?"

I wasn't sure if he was talking about Sam or Mike, but he didn't seem to be too interested in getting an answer anyway. I took him to the room that he shared with Ilga and put away the belongings that the cop had packed. I still became angry when I thought about those policemen's methods.

After that things settled down to a routine, but I was still terribly sick. It was going to take a long time to pull myself out of this one.

Several months later Ilga began eating less and less. She was thin, and her belly was sinking between her hipbones. I took her to a doctor, but he couldn't find anything wrong with her. I questioned him about inserting a gastronomy tube, but he was reluctant to discuss this possibility. We fed her all the foods I knew she liked, and even took her to her favorite restaurants. Nothing helped. In Ilga's weakened state of mind, she was ready to go home. We were just not ready for her to go. I guess she was the one we were the closest to and the one we loved so much because she had found her way into our hearts. In the last few months of her life, she had run away and we had searched for her daily. She died in the hospital. All of us suffered the loss except James. He never realized she was gone.

Chapter Nineteen
The Investigation

After Ilga died, only James and my grandmother were left. James was quiet most of the time, but occasionally he went on one of his rampages. He could trigger fast when something was bothering him.

I had learned years before that with residents like James, any kind of physical barrier, such as a chair in the way, could result in a crisis. For some reason it might also block mental function. In James's case, if he failed to see an object in his way or was unable to find something when he wanted it, he quickly went off the deep end. Lately, James seemed to be off much more than on. I tried to pacify him, but he was past the point of reason. We just had to wait for him to calm down.

In addition, Mimmy had turned against me again. I treated her with all the love and dignity I could muster, but it seemed that every time I opened my mouth, she went on a tirade. After finding several cigarette burns on the carpet, I had to tell her that she could only smoke at the dining room or kitchen table. She would carry her cigarettes in her mouth until the ashes were as long as the cigarette, and then they would fall off on the floor or on her clothes.

I wasn't concerned about the carpet, although that had to be considered. I was more afraid of a fire or of her being burned. I never noticed all of the small scars on her from burns until I started bathing her.

One morning I was busy making beds and cleaning the rooms while James and Mimmy ate their breakfast, when I heard her yelling for me. When I reached the dining room, Mimmy was screaming, demanding a piece of toast.

"This is the damnedest place I have ever been in. I can't get a thing I want. Now you get me a piece of toast before I call your mother."

Okay, I thought. What was the big deal? James became irate and actually said her name, swearing at her because she was a woman. This was a new one from him. I had to laugh. He never called anyone by name except me.

After she calmed down, I went back to finish cleaning the bedroom when I heard her at it again.

"Gimme some more coffee," she yelled. I'd swear her cup was full when I left the table. I poured coffee for both James and Mimmy, and then fixed a cup for myself and sat down.

James shoved his plate at me and screamed, "I don't believe I ordered any eggs this morning. I wanted some pancakes." I explained that pancakes were on the menu for tomorrow.

He stood up, shaking his fist at me, and yelled, "I come here every morning and order my breakfast and if you can't fix me what I want, I will go somewhere else." At that point I told him to go. He did! He stalked out the back door to the garden and patio.

In only a few minutes he came back in and said, "Carolyn, you need to water the flowers."

Mimmy finished her breakfast, totally oblivious to James's outburst. I sat with her while I finished my coffee. Both of us were silent.

When she was sure there was no more food, she said, "Carolyn, I raised you and loved you all my life and you treat me awful." She was starting to cry. The tears wouldn't work this time. There had been too many of these episodes. I had had it.

"What have I done this time, Mimmy?" I asked her.

"Well, your mother wouldn't treat me this way." She lit a cigarette and pulled away from the table in her wheelchair.

"Mimmy, I told you that this was one of the places you could smoke. Did you forget?"

"Naw, I didn't forget." As she turned, she threw the lit cigarette onto the floor and wheeled off to the bathroom. My patience and my ability to tolerate irrational behavior were fading fast. The verbal barbs and mental abuse were taking their toll. Right now all I wanted to do was go outside in the garden and play with the snakes. I did. James and Mimmy could fight it out with each other as far as I was concerned. I couldn't take any more of their abuse today. I sat outside for a few minutes before I heard Mimmy at it again and my mother's voice.

When I went inside, Mother was hugging Mimmy and saying, "It's OK, I will take care of you and love you." I felt betrayed. How dare Mother to take Mimmy's side of the story? I was the one doing all I could to give Mimmy a good life, but Mother was the one Mimmy favored.

I said nothing. I found Mimmy's luggage and packed her clothes. I rounded up everything including her cigarettes and placed them in the car.

When I came back in, Mimmy said, "Why, I had more cigarettes than that. She stole some of them."

Was she talking about me or Maxcine? I would never know, for I just walked away. The next door neighbor was out weeding, and he had heard everything. He told me to go inside and he would help get Mimmy in the car.

My grandmother had turned on me several years before, and I never knew why. This time I vowed never to have anything to do with her again.

If I thought the worst of the day was over with, I had another thing coming. Soon after they left, the doorbell rang. Two men in suits stood on the stoop. Their expressions spelled trouble. They identified themselves as from the state's attorney's office and showed proper identification.

"Are you Carolyn Connelly?" they asked, and I nodded. We need to ask you a few questions. May we come in?"

I wanted to scream, Hell no! But thought better of it.

"Are you here to arrest me?" I asked them.

They answered, "No."

"Are you here to arrest me on the basis of any answer I might give you to any of your questions?"

They looked at each other and said, "Ma'am, we're here to ask you some questions. If you do not want to do this, we will be back with a warrant." Considering my choices, I let them in.

They asked me why I was so carefully screening them. I explained that my attorney taught me to screen questioners carefully, since I had been illegally questioned by three police officers. They suddenly understood.

At first, the questions were strange. I did recognize names and places but couldn't figure out their purpose in asking about them. I must have looked terribly puzzled because one of them looked around and saw a newspaper on the counter, which I hadn't read.

"May I?" he asked.

"Of course," I said.

He handed me a section of the paper, and there was a picture of one of my friends named Margie, who was and ALF owner. There was also an article accompanying the picture. Apparently, Margie had blown the whistle on one of the legal guardians who had asked her for a kickback, and he was under criminal investigation. More than a few legal guardians were involved in these kickbacks, ALF and nursing home owners usually kept quiet about them, even if they refused to take part because they needed legal guardians to handle their residents' finances, mainly rent.

This is how kickbacks worked. When crooked legal guardians placed their elderly charges in the care of ALFs or nursing homes, they would offer to pay more rent than was required. If the rent was $1200 per month, they and the ALF or nursing home owners would agree to increase the amount paid by perhaps $300 and then split it with the ALF owner. This was called a "finder's fee". If the legal guardians' attorneys were in on the deal, the kickback amount would be split three ways.

Legal guardians had to be overseen by attorneys. Each attorney who did this kind of work usually had about ten legal guardians as clients.

Then each attorney had to report to a judge each month as to the payments legal guardians made to the ALFs or nursing homes per each elderly charge.

Unfortunately, "finders' fees" were common on the geriatric scene. The practice of taking kickbacks was so widespread, in fact, that owners of homes for the elderly, legal guardians, and especially attorneys became filthy rich from the practice.

I had known for a long time that Margie was playing the kickback game with this particular guardian. She would charge guardians extra, and then give some of it back to him in cash. Why in the world would she blow the whistle on an illegal practice when she was as guilty as he was? I suspected that he had decided to stop the practice, at least with Margie.

As I read the article, I found a small but glaring discrepancy in her story. She said the guardian threatened her by slapping his right hip where he carried his gun. I knew this guardian and knew he was licensed to carry a gun; however, he used a shoulder holster. I kept this observation to myself, still wondering what in hell Margie was up to.

When I finished reading I asked the men how I could help them, and they started an inquiry. I answered their questions truthfully and to the best of my ability. They seemed pleased but told me I would be subpoenaed for questioning by the state's attorney. After they left, I tried to understand why Margie would blow the whistle on the hand that fed her. It just didn't make sense.

I had met Margie as a business acquaintance and had known her for a number of years. She had some peculiar habits such as acting like there was something to hide when there wasn't, but I liked her in spite of her idiosyncrasies. Occasionally, she called me to perform nursing procedures with payment to be on the first of the following month. I finally had to cease helping her because the first of the month never came.

Her ALF, especially the patients' area, was expensively furnished. Several of her friends questioned where she got the money she always seemed to have. We all knew how much money everyone else made in the industry, and her income far exceeded the amount of money her three residents could possibly pay.

I also knew she owned several apartments, but she had always been evasive about where they were or to whom she was renting. Now I knew why. She had been warehousing patients in them and would bring them to her ALF when a resident left. So what was her game? According to the article, she had already admitted to having elderly renters at the apartments. She had to be crazy. With HRS involved and the state attorney investigation, I sure as hell wouldn't have brought attention to myself if I had been her. Something drastic must have happened to force her to do it. I decided to call her, but it turned out to be the wrong thing to do. She was as cold as a fish and did not want to talk to me. I didn't pursue the conversation. She knew I was aware of her illegal practices and was probably afraid to speak to me.

News of this scandal rocked the bay area. Radio and TV stations, the newspaper, and even the city council seized every opportunity to lash out at this elder abuse. With every report I became more apprehensive because I was uncertain about what my role in the scandal would be. I did know many ALF owners because I had written a book about how to open an ALF and had helped several people open and operate them. Also, HRS inspectors considered me to be on the inside and would believe I would know who was taking kickbacks because I knew how the elderly care system worked. Still, I didn't want to rat on Margie but would tell the truth under oath.

In a few days, I was served a subpoena. I was to appear on Friday, which was only three days away. I called the attorney who had bailed me out of jail. He was pleased that I had the intelligence to call a lawyer instead of being intimidated and probably verbally abused by the state's attorney. He explained that he was on a mission and would not stop until he got what he wanted.

My attorney and I went as ordered. The closer we got to his office, the more frightened I became. The state's attorney was huge, both politically and physically, and I felt intimidated by his gruff, demanding voice. He introduced himself and apparently knew the attorney who was with me. I had been instructed to stop if I didn't know how to answer a question and ask my attorney how to proceed. I did well until the state's attorney asked me why I was so frightened by his investigators when they came to my home. He wanted to know what I was hiding, and why I hesitated to let them into my house. I didn't have to answer that one. My attorney told him I was a little gun shy. Of course he wanted to know why, so I told him about my prior dealings with the friendly police department. His anger built up with every word. He wrote notes furiously and his eyes flashed in anger. He looked as though he wanted to kill someone.

When he asked me questions about Margie, I answered them to the best of my ability. He asked me why she would lie about something taking kickbacks, and I told him I honestly could not figure out her intent, but I felt that she was lying because of the gun and holster description. Because I knew the guardian, I was peppered with questions about my dealings with him. The state's attorney was thankfully satisfied with my answers and moved on.

Finally, he made it clear that he was after an overseer who had apparently skipped to the islands. Overseers are attorneys appointed to make periodic reports to the courts about their guardian clients. This lawyer was the overseer of several legal guardians who were now under investigation.

While I was sitting there, I remembered a mysterious trip Margie had taken to an island several months before. Could her trip be related to the matter at hand? I asked if I might speak to my attorney privately. We went to the hall. I asked him if I should volunteer this information. He thought about it and decided that it would be better if he himself told him. That was fine with me.

The state's attorney raised his eyebrows at this news and angrily asked me if I remembered the name of the island. I said I only remembered it was one of the Cayman Islands.

He looked at my attorney and said, "I started to investigate one incident, and now I have three more to attend to." He dismissed me and thanked me for the information but wanted to talk to my attorney, so I left.

A few days later, I received a letter from the state's attorney's office once again thanking me and saying that the police department was short two police officers. Why not short three? I wondered.

The police and the men in suits left me alone after that. The scandal kept drawing attention until several lawyers, legal guardians, and owners went to jail. Margie received immunity for her allegations and left town, never to be heard from again. No one ever found out for sure what her motives were. It didn't really matter because the practice was stopped or went further underground, and the business is better off because of her actions. Thankfully, I remained unscathed, even though I knew about the kickbacks and could have been considered an accomplice. At least this battle was won, but the war against elder abuse still waged on, both in my own home, and in the industry itself.

Chapter Twenty
Exodus

Because many months had passed since I had heard from the social worker at the hospital, I was surprised to hear her voice when the phone rang one morning.

"Hey, Carolyn. It's been ages."

"I know it has. How are you?"

"I'm fine but have thought of you often. I honestly thought you had gone out of business. Did I hear correctly that you moved to the Keys to open up a place, and then suddenly came back? What the heck happened?"

"Mandy, you wouldn't believe my story. Let's get together for coffee sometime…sometime when you have LOTS of time…it'll take awhile. Suffice it to say that it was hell in paradise, and we had to come home." Mandy laughed, knowing that if it involved me, the story had to be a doosey.

"I'm sorry, Carolyn, it must have been horrible. Do you still have residents with you?"

"Yes, I have one. His name is James, and he's pretty much worn out his welcome. After Ilga's death—did you know?" She did, so I continued, "He was just impossible to live with. He has the nastiest disposition, never a kind word for anybody and always bitching about something. I have actually been afraid of him at times. He has black, beady eyes that make him appear possessed when he's mad." Anyway, I've been trying to get hold of his family to take him home. I am so tired of taking care of the elderly, Mandy. It's taken too much out of me."

"I'm sorry to hear that. In fact, that's one of the reasons I called."

"Don't you dare!"

"Come on, Carolyn, you can't give up yet. We still need you!"

"Definitely not. I want out of this business. That's my final answer."

"But this is a special case. She has no one to handle her affairs or her finances. Won't you please reconsider? I am desperate, and she needs someone to care for her who has compassion. No, I am not trying to flatter you. I just know it will take a special person to meet her needs." She told me how lonely, sweet, and poor the lady was. My heart started melting again. Ever a sucker for the desperate and needy, I asked Mandy if I could go meet the lady before we discussed it any further. I hadn't made definite plans yet for my future, and the money would come in handy. The need for money could always get in the way of my good sense. You would think that the memories of the last few months would have burned an emphatic NO! in my brain.

I visited the lady the next day. She was somewhat withdrawn and looked the other way when I walked in. I spoke to her and called her by her name, Jane.

She turned her head towards me and said, "Hello. Who are you?"

I told her my name and asked her how she was.

As fast as she could get the words out, she said, "Are you the person who is going to take care of me?"

"Well, Jane, I did come to visit you to see if I could provide the kind of care you need. What kinds of things can you do for yourself?"

I had a feeling that what I saw was not what I was going to get. She was young, only 65, and very pretty, with beautiful hair and complexion but disabled by left side paralysis.

"I can't do much because they haven't worked with me. They let me lay in this bed until I can't walk anymore," she said.

"Who are *they*, Jane?"

"Oh, the nurses and everybody else," she said.

"Are you sure they didn't try? Perhaps you are the one who wouldn't work with them to strengthen your muscles," I suggested.

"Where are you from?" she asked sweetly, quickly changing the subject. It was just as well, for the nurses had already told me how uncooperative she was.

"Tennessee."

"What part?"

"Knoxville."

She tried, unsuccessfully, to sit up. "I'm from Knoxville too! The Kingston Pike area."

Boy, did she have her facts right. It was as though she had been waiting for someone to listen to her so that she could gloat. Anyone from Knoxville knew Kingston Pike meant old money. It had at one time been considered the place to live if you were somebody but had since become old and rundown. Some areas had been rezoned for commercial use. Many people who had grown up there left for the suburbs. Despite this transformation, Kingston Pike was still unique and majestic.

We chit-chatted for awhile about her health and finances. Apparently, she was an out-of-control diabetic who had bottomed out in a nursing home and was sent to the hospital. She did not want to go back. Her finances would just barely cover the rent, and I had a feeling she was going to need a lot of attention. She told me she had a friend in town but that she had no relatives alive. A little picture of a sailor was on her night stand. I asked her who he was. She replied, "That is my husband. He died while in the Navy."

When I was ready to leave, I told her I would talk to the social worker about someone to handle her finances.

Then Jane said, "Tell her to contact Marcie. She will do it."

I asked her who Marcie was, and she said that Marcie was an old friend.

"Don't worry, Jane, I'll call Marcie and we'll get you settled in somewhere," I leaned down to give her a kiss on the cheek, knowing my mind was already made up.

Marcie agreed to help us out, so I agreed to take Jane. Regrets were sure to surface in the future, but if this sweet lady was easy to take care of, her rent would supplement our budget until I found a job. I figured that her rent would be worth the trouble of caring for her.

Before long, Jane responded positively to our quality of TLC. She was a controlled diabetic, had no bed sores, neither gained nor lost weight, and was cheerful except when she and I fought. This wasn't often, but our disagreements could become ferocious.

Usually, she would set me off by playing mind games with all the people who helped with her care. She was the greatest manipulator I had ever encountered. For example, I was careful about her diet. However, when I was away, she loved to tell her caregiver that I allowed her to have pecan pie once a month and that it was time to have a slice. She would even give them money to buy one. After eating a large slice, she would tell the caregivers that they could take the rest home but to put the pie in the car and not let me see it because I would swear to them that it wasn't the day she was allowed extras.

In order to protect both of us, I did not allow anyone to check her blood sugar and administer her insulin. I would hire a nurse to come in to perform these duties when I was unavailable.

Several months after Jane came to live with us, Mike and I decided to get away for a weekend. I paid an R.N. $150 a day to take care of her and keep an eye on James. When we got back, the nurse held out her hand for her pay and ran to the nearest exit without telling us goodbye. I asked Jane why the nurse would leave so abruptly. Of course, she had no idea. I waited a couple of days before calling her to see if she would tell me her story. The first words out of her mouth were, "Don't ever ask me to watch that woman again!"

I said, "I know she can be manipulative, but what did she do that was so bad?"

"Well, you could have told me she stayed awake all night. I didn't get any sleep."

I was dumbfounded. "Jane has always slept at night. I don't believe I have ever been up at night with her. I can't imagine this happening."

"Not having any sleep for three nights and then spending all day waiting on her hand and foot was just too much. If it weren't for your neighbor next door who helped me pick her up, she would have stayed on the floor. Has she ever thrown herself out of bed before?"

"Yes, she did this during the day the first few months we had her, but after I picked her up a few times and placed her back into the bed; I had to get firm with her. I simply told her that if she insisted on falling out of bed, she could lie there until I called an ambulance to haul her to a nursing home."

"What did she do then?" she asked.

"She stopped and hasn't done it until now."

"You know what? I have taken care of a lot of people just as you have, but this woman is damn mean and nasty. I'll watch James any time. He was good," she said.

What a switch, I thought.

Jane was in easy hearing distance of my telephone conversation. I didn't know how I would deal with her and, quite frankly, I was so angry with her that I didn't want to see her. Unfortunately, Mike was already giving her hell over her behavior. I called to him to come away from her.

I felt protective over Jane and really loved her, even though sometimes she deliberately tried to annoy me. She was part of our family now in spite of her shortcomings. I kept her for many reasons, but one was selfish. I wanted to write, and as long as Jane and James lived with me, I had to stay home and couldn't go looking for a job. We had to set up ground rules to be able to survive Jane's annoying habits such as calling me every ten to fifteen minutes for no good reason, blaming the dog for stealing her banana, or, worst of all, making up little stories or little white lies.

As for James, he was like a time bomb waiting to go off. There was still no response from his family after two months of trying to contact them. Finally, I phoned the company where his granddaughter worked and was transferred to her exchange. When she answered, I told her who I was. Quickly her voice changed. "Oh, I'm sorry, but you were put through to the wrong desk. I will switch you."

I knew it was the granddaughter who answered the phone because I had spoken to her before and was astounded she so blatantly lied. That was it. It was time for action. I sent a letter to the daughter, requesting that she pick up her father from my home within thirty days or I would place him with HRS. Surely, she didn't want this to happen because that agency would find out about the money she had previously confiscated from James.

I waited thirty days and heard nothing. HRS came within two days to visit with James and to talk to me. Apparently, the HRS had been searching for him because Ann, his wife, had not given up looking for him after the last stunt she pulled of trying to get his money. I opened the legal guardian papers and showed the HRS's representative the notarized papers prohibiting me from letting her see him. I also showed them the restraining order.

This was all legal as long as I had him in my home, but I had requested that he be placed elsewhere and that was what they were there for. We packed his belongings, and they took him away. I never heard from his daughter, and I never knew what happened to James. He had some good years with me, but I'm sure he would not remember any of them, and toward the end he had become extremely difficult to care for

I watched the car drive away and with it my career as an ALF director. Even though we still had Jane, I had come to think of her as a relative rather than a resident, so I was officially out of the business—for good this time! Suddenly, I was more tired than I had ever been in my life. It took all the strength I had just to walk back into the house. Little did I know that this weakness was a sign of new bad health problems. Because I hadn't rested as prescribed, I'd gone into adrenal crisis. One adrenal gland had totally atrophied, causing severe fatigue, constant perspiration, and an energy level so low that I couldn't function. I had to go to bed for hours. When I was able to get up, I sat in a recliner unable to do anything else.

Jane had to be admitted to a nursing home and stayed there for months while I recuperated because I couldn't take care of her. It was the only one with a vacancy on such short notice. While there she suffered unimaginable horrors. All of her clothing and an heirloom afghan were stolen. If not for constant visits from my family and friends, she would have lain in her own filth for days on end. Her arm and shoulder were broken, supposedly in a fall, but in reality from a bungled transfer by a staff member.

As the weeks passed, she deteriorated to a frightening level. She acquired MRSA, Metheline Resistant Staphylococcus Aurous. MRSA is almost impossible to cure in a healthy elderly person. Jane was far from healthy. Her skin was ghostly pale and peeling away from her lips, and she smelled sickeningly sweet, like a field of honey hives. When I asked Mike how her body looked, he said he was always afraid to get close to her or turn her over. He was afraid of what he might find.

The final horror began with severe abdominal pains that wracked her frail body with violent convulsions. She was admitted to the hospital for abdominal surgery, and she never returned to my home. She had an aneurysm on the wall of the abdominal aorta. Removing the bubble is a difficult but common procedure, but complications arose immediately. She died on the operating table.

The doctors gave no explanation for her death; in fact, they didn't seem to care. I cared a great deal and felt overwhelmed by the tide of emotions her death caused in me. To this day, guilt remains with me over Jane's fate. I loved her so much that it broke my heart to think of the misery of her final months on earth. She was the last resident I cared for and the one who taught me the most about aging. We shared laughter and tears, and the time we spent together was rich and full. Even though she had given others and me a lot of grief because of her bizarre behavior from time to time, nevertheless, she had endeared herself to me and my family by her caring nature and good humor, which were dominant in her personality.

When Jane first come to live with me, she asked me to arrange a "full funeral for all of her friends so that they could say goodbye to her. When the time came, however, we had no money, she had no money left, and she had no friends. Even Marcie had deserted her. She would be buried in a simple pine box.

It was the most depressing funeral of all that I had attended. Mike and I, the priest, and a few unfamiliar faces were there, and, of course, Jane in a plain pine box. What a far cry this was from the "full funeral for friends" that she had requested.

The priest droned on and on, reciting the same eulogy he'd used for hundreds of elderly women with no families to speak of and nothing to call their own. We'd heard it too many times during the last twenty-five years, but this one was particularly disturbing. She wasn't just anyone; she was family.

"Yea, though I walk through the valley of the shadow of death, I will fear no evil..."

My tears fell unheeded as guilt engulfed me. If only I had not allowed her to stay in those horrible conditions at the nursing home. I knew in my heart I should have brought her back to my home, despite my illness. I kept telling myself I had no choice because I couldn't have taken care of her myself, but my mind wouldn't give me peace. What she endured in the last few months of her life would haunt me forever.

Finally, the service neared its end. The soothing familiarity of the last lines of the 23rd Psalm provided me with some sense of comfort:

"...Surely goodness and mercy shall follow me all the days of my life,

and I will dwell in the house of the Lord forever."

However, when the funeral was over, any sense of comfort was shattered when a lady came up to me, put her hand on my arm, and said, "You must be Carolyn."

"Yes, and who are you?" I said.

"I am Sarah, Jane's sister."

I was so completely astonished that I withdrew my arm and walked away from her, thinking, how dare she? She had never tried to contact her sister in all the months Jane had lived with us. I knew she existed because Jane occasionally had spoken of her, but she never returned our calls or answered our letters. The two sisters were so estranged that we didn't even try to contact Sarah about Jane's funeral. I never knew how she found out about it.

I rushed away without even thanking the priest. I rushed away from the dismal funeral, away from the finality and aloneness of death, away from my past as caregiver, away from my anger and my sorrow. I ran out into the sunshine and felt the balm of the salt breeze on my perspiring face. I walked to the waiting car, and there sat Mike in the driver's seat, waiting for me, as always. We went home.

Epilogue

About a month after Jane died, I spent one night in a nursing home for cardiac rehabilitation. It was one of the better homes, and I was supposed to be there for three weeks. It didn't take long for me to know I wouldn't last that long.

Sometime in that first night I heard a pleading female voice down the hall. It woke me from a deep sleep.

"Please, somebody, please help me. I just want to be your friend and visit for awhile. Please share your room with me and let me talk to you for a few minutes." The voice became shrill and echoed down the nursing home hall. Though I felt concern for the person owning that voice, I began to wonder how anybody was supposed to recuperate in such a place.

"Please let me be your friend. Can I come in? Stop it! Don't make me leave. Please share your room with me and let me stay for a few minutes."

Now I heard her begin to cry. How pathetically lonely she must be! The voice was coming closer.

"I just want to be your friend."

Then I heard another voice. This one was male, and he screamed as if in terrible pain. "Oh, God! Ohhhh, Godddd!"

"I want to be your friend." The woman was whimpering now.

"Ouch! Don't hurt me. Quit shoving me…"

The words stopped; I heard only wailing now. Her wheelchair wheels squeaked on the tile floors as she feverishly wheeled from room to room.

"Ohhhh. Oh God, heeellpp mmeee!" the man screamed and then choked on his own voice. The loudest and longest cough I have ever heard drowned out the screams. I was sure he would choke to death. Finally, he caught his breath and started a low, sorrowful moan.

At least he's alive, I thought in relief. I couldn't have saved him anyway. I thought I must remember to bring this neglect to the attention of the director of nursing in the morning—the man really needs help.

The woman behind the wheedling voice wheeled herself frantically now and in the direction of my room. Her voice was now louder and more demanding.

"Please God! Find me a friend. I can't live like this anymore."

I noticed my door was open, and I said my own prayer: "Please, God, don't let her come in here. I am not strong enough to deny her friendship." I wondered which one of us God would listen to.

The man began a series of wracking coughs. I could imagine how much it hurt—where was the staff?

"I can't live like this any longer." The woman began to scream again, and finally, I heard someone yell at her and take her back to her room.

"Don't yell at her!" I yelled, even though no one could hear me. "She needs friendship, companionship—just someone to talk to." Then I thought, give it up Carolyn; it's not your concern anymore. I begged God to listen to me—to listen to them and to help all of us because it was obvious no one else was going to help.

The sounds of the night continued to pierce through my door as if it didn't exist. Moaning, crying, screaming, coughing, incoherent strings of words—they were disturbing, frightening, pathetic sounds that went on and on until the light of day when finally the morning shift came on and paid attention to the residents and their needs. I had never heard such sounds during the five years I was in the nursing home industry. After I stopped working in nursing homes and became an owner of

ALFs, I seldom visited nursing homes at night. Thankfully, my ALFs never sounded like this one.

As the sounds continued to invade my privacy, thoughts of the monumental problems the elderly face and the insignificant role I had played while trying to improve their lot haunted me.

The night shift certainly neglected the patients because seldom did a staff member come to check on commotion. I suspect they spent more time gossiping and eating than they did taking care of the residents. Earlier, I had noticed there were few, if any, amenities such as newspapers, magazines, or books available to residents and, apparently, no way to acquire them. In addition, the food had little nutritional value and was tasteless. I'd be damned before I'd stay there one more day, so I called my husband to come and take me out of there.

While waiting for him, I mused that there had been virtually no changes in the nursing industry since I had left it over twenty years before. As an ALF owner I did all I could to better the lives of the elderly, to improve their sad conditions, and to fight the system to achieve those goals every step of the way—to what end?

I rolled over into a fetal position, facing the wall, and cried and cried and cried. I cried for myself. I cried for the lady in the hall and the coughing man. I cried for the aging, pleading voices calling out for help in vain because nobody was "home" to care.

All my pent up emotions came flooding out, all the frustration, guilt, anger, the sense of helplessness. I was finally confronting the futility of all I'd tried to accomplish.

Finally, the tears stopped. I felt empty and desiccated, like a piece of chaff. I wiped my eyes, arose from bed, dressed, gathered my things, and sat in my chair to wait.

About the Author

Carolyn Connelly is a retired Registered Nurse. She graduated from the University of Nevada, School of Nursing in 1972, and specialized in geriatric nursing for over twenty-five years. Her first employment was as a Director of Nursing in a large nursing home, later as a Home Health Nurse working in four states and in U.S. territories in the Caribbean. Carolyn progressed to become the director of several nursing homes, and then ultimately to owning and operating her own upscale adult living facilities for the elderly.

This varied, full-spectrum immersion in nursing over the years led to Carolyn's unique perspective on the living conditions of the elderly.

This is Carolyn's third book, and more are on the way.

"In the beginning, there was a man, a woman, a house full of kids, two dogs, a bird that whistled *Yankee Doodle Dandy,* and cats—I never knew how many because the kids hid them—and an empty bank account.." Nothing has changed.